The
TRADER

Published in the UK in 2021 by Malahide Press

Hardback Colour ISBN 978-1-7399286-2-9
Hardback Black & White ISBN 978-1-7399286-3-6
Paperback Colour ISBN 978-1-7399286-0-5
Paperback Black & White ISBN 978-1-7399286-4-3
eBook ISBN 978-1-7399286-1-2

Cover design and typeset by SpiffingCovers

The
TRADER

The real life story of a Colonial boy who became an
international trader, arms merchant and intelligence agent

BILL PELLEW-HARVEY

This book is dedicated to all my children whom I love so dearly - Adrian my firstborn who died so young, my children Warren, Alix, Jordan and Grace who live in America and last but not least my daughters Justine and Katy who are still teenagers as I write this book, their godparents and trustees Maria and Michael Denning, and in memory of my brother Stephen, and my late wife Irina.

The Pellew family crest

"Our greatest glory is not in never falling but in rising each time we fall"

CONFUCIUS

Contents

Introduction

This is not a work of fiction - every event described actually happened. How do you introduce a life?

Why should my life be of any interest to others?

My life has been a combination of both luck and ego!

Luck because I happen to have lived my youth in Kenya with all the life style advantages of the privileged European settler class while Britain still retained the remnants of an Empire albeit Harold Macmillan's "winds of change" were starting to blow and the status of British Colonies were approaching their sunset.

Luck because I was witness to and participated in some of the most extraordinary military adventures of the latter part of the twentieth century.

Luck because in business I sometimes happened to be in the right place at the right time.

A large enough ego to provide the confidence to undertake some of the financial and physical risks involved because in each of us is the urge to leave our own little imprint on the footsteps of history.

This book is the story of my life "warts and all".

I have made no attempt to hide or gloss over my behaviour which on occasions perhaps left a lot to be desired and by some will be considered either immoral or unethical.

However I am proud that I was able to assist the Allied causes in Afghanistan during the Russian occupation and later in Iraq.

I was subsequently hounded by the media in regard to my activities in Iraq but always refused any media contact so this memoire presents an opportunity to set the record straight.

In order to ensure an element of privacy for those whose lives crossed mine I prefer to write in the third person and on some occasions to change names in order to protect the identities of certain individuals.

I was not always an ideal husband or parent but I hope that after they have finished reading this book my children will have a greater understanding and perhaps tolerance of their father!

CHAPTER 1

Kenya 1955

The boy was up by dawn and minutes later slipped out of the house. He was dressed in khaki shorts and shod in strong hunting boots. A large leather belt holding 25 rounds of ammunition and a hunting knife encircled his waist. He carried a small calibre bolt operated .22 BSA rifle with V sights. It was a very light weight weapon but quite deadly in the hands of a good shot. His two dogs, waiting patiently outside the house, joined him with little jumps of excitement and the trio moved off at a brisk pace.

The house, along with its four neighbours, was built atop a high knoll overlooking the Thika river. The houses formed a natural cul-de-sac and at the rear were surrounded by row upon row of well kept coffee bushes. A huge avocado tree at the side of the house provided ample shade for parked cars in addition to yielding a huge annual crop of fruit. During avocado season the dogs, who loved the fruit, grew fat and their coats glistened.

The boy took a steep track leading downhill towards the Thika river. The air was still cool and fresh, thanks to the high altitude of the Kenya highlands, but soon after sunrise the African heat would arrive with astonishing speed, lest you forget, that Kenya sits astride the Equator.

It was July, the start of the boy's summer holiday and dry. The rainy season of April and May was long finished and it would be many weeks before the first signs of the short rains. The track was strewn with large grey stones and little puffs of dust marked each silent footfall. The dogs padded softly behind, with an air of contained excitement, keeping well to heel. The river valley below was heavily forested and thick undergrowth lined the bank blocking any view of water. However the river made its presence felt by the continuous sound of rushing water over large rocks as it swept towards the falls a few hundred yards downstream.

The native insurrection by the Kikuyu tribe known as the "Mau Mau" rebellion was now in its third year following a state of emergency declared by the British Government in November 1952. The Kenya Regiment, the Kings African rifles assisted by British troops and police activities had

3

succeeded in reducing considerably the activities of the larger Mau Mau gangs who were being driven ever deeper into the forest of the Aberdare mountain range, but gangs, many of them small sleeper units, were still known to be active and attacks, often deadly, on lone Europeans and loyalist natives were not uncommon. The gangs were known to hide out in the Thika river area so the boy was particularly alert.

The little group arrived at the bottom of the valley, crossed a dusty road and headed down a path into the undergrowth. The trees provided ample shelter from the increasing sunlight and perfect camouflage for both human and dogs. The boy halted at the edge of the trees and studied the opposite river bank carefully for signs of movement. When he was happy there was none he emerged onto a small open patch of grass then carefully evaluated the water level and currents to be sure that a safe passage to the opposite bank was feasible. Satisfied he entered the water which was waist high and proceeded to cross holding his rifle above his head. The dogs swam ahead, climbed up the far bank, shook themselves and sat down to await their master's arrival. The trees were very still and no forest sounds could be heard or movement detected above the rush of the water. They set off down a small trail running almost parallel to the water and halted in a small clump of trees facing a large open space, which had once been cultivated but was now overgrown with weeds.

He spent some minutes carefully scanning the tree line on the opposite side of the clearing and although he could see no sign of movement decided to re enter the forest and to continue moving gently parallel to the river bank. The dogs remained at his heels. An hour or so later found him several miles upstream in unfamiliar territory. The river ran faster over large granite coloured boulders and the banks had become steeper hemmed in by outcrops of rock and gnarled tree roots which made progress difficult. A halt was overdue so the boy and dogs sat and rested in the shade of a small natural cave set back from the river bank.

Suddenly, above the sound of water, human voices could be heard from the direction of the opposite bank. Two figures, totally naked, appeared from the undergrowth and squatted on a large flat boulder that jutted out into the water. They appeared confident that they were alone.

The boy studied them carefully. Their appearance attracted his attention and stirred recollection of the Mau Mau corpses his father had shown him some months earlier laid in a line outside a police station.

Who were these two men and what were they doing in this isolated place?

The pair were of indeterminate age but looked lithe and fit with long unkempt curly hair. They shuffled gently from foot to foot with small quick animal like movements and appeared uneasy, casting continuous furtive glances up and down the river. Their only accompanying attire appeared to be ragged shorts and dark heavy blankets each of which had been placed carefully on the rock.

However the boy's attention was drawn to the two long pangas resting casually by their sides and even more alarming what appeared to be some type of rifle nestling on one blanket.

Rex, the larger of the two dogs, could contain himself no longer and let out a series of loud clipped barks. The men instantly froze in their squatting positions, their black skins blending into the rocks and stared in the direction of the sound.

Suddenly one of the men reached over for the rifle.

The boy already had his rifle trained on the men and without hesitation fired a single shot directly at the forehead of the man hoisting the rifle. No sound of impact could be heard above the noise of the water but the man toppled forward into the river still clutching the rifle.

The boy quickly chambered another round all the while keeping his rifle trained on the remaining figure in order to place a second shot to the head. However the other man was already on his feet and bounded into the undergrowth leaving behind the blankets and pangas as the only sign of their presence. The boy remained in place and refocused his full attention to the swirling waters. There was no sign of the body in the water which must have sunk or more likely had already been swept downstream by the strong currents. The boy stood up and followed by the dogs moved carefully out of their shelter into the bright sunlight moving as rapidly as possible downriver until he was able to slip back into the forest. He followed his original route back to the river crossing trying to make as little noise as possible in order to avoid attracting attention to his passage and at the same time to remain alert for any possible danger.

His adrenalin level gradually subsided but was quickly replaced by a new worry. What should he do now? He started to relive those long moments upstream. Was it self defence or had he killed an innocent man?

No - the man could not possibly be innocent! It was strictly illegal for unauthorized natives to possess firearms and under the emergency regulations the death penalty could be, and often was, applied to those Africans who broke the gun laws. Should he have attempted to "arrest" the two men and only fired a warning shot? No - there had been no time and in any event he had seen the man raise his rifle no doubt in preparation to shoot.

Satisfied with this conclusion the boy then addressed the next question which came to mind.

Would he or would he not report the shooting to the police or his parents and if so what would follow? Questions would be asked as to why he was alone in such an isolated place and how could he be sure that it really was a rifle that was being raised? Reports might appear in the local newspapers and could thus expose his family and in particular his father, who employed locally several hundred Africans, to danger.

By the time he had arrived back at his original river crossing his mind was made up; he would say nothing. Should a corpse be found far downstream it could well be unrecognizable as its likelihood of surviving intact after a drop of more a hundred feet over the Thika falls was remote.

Furthermore the river banks downstream of the falls were heavily forested and contained much wild life who would not be averse to a free meal! Even if the body was by chance recovered it would likely be treated as just another casualty of the emergency.

The boy arrived home without further incident before noon, cleaned his rifle and locked it into the gun safe in the house which was compulsory under emergency regulations. He then changed into clean dry clothes and joined his parents and sister for lunch.

Later that afternoon he and his sister walked to the nearby Thika Club to join their friends for tennis and were promptly collected by their father in time for dinner as it was considered unsafe for Europeans to walk after dusk even for short distances.

After dinner the boy took his bath. He stripped and while the water was running studied himself in front of the full length mirror.

He had grown fast in the previous months and his boyhood puppy fat had been replaced by muscle. His penis, which had recently lengthened and thickened, was now surrounded by a small tangle of dark hair.

His hand moved down and he slowly stroked his member which stirred to life and was soon erect. Suddenly he felt a deep well of pleasure which heralded his first ever orgasm.

A smile crossed his face as he reviewed the day's events which he felt sure marked his passage from boyhood to manhood.

Bill with rifle and dog at Thika 1955

CHAPTER 2

Kenya – Early Days

The boy's name was William Pellew-Harvey, invariably shortened to Bill and later in life he was often to be called Mr Bill! Born in December 1941 in North Walsham, Norfolk he had a typical English middle class early boyhood and attended Taverham Hall preparatory school.

His paternal grandparents were both Cornish - born in the village of Chacewater near Truro.

Grandfather William was an Engineer and Assayer who moved to Canada in 1892 where he made his fortune following his appointment as Chief Assayer of British Columbia and his subsequent appointment as Dominion Assayer of the whole of Canada in 1901.

His duties involved oversight of much of the gold mined during the Yukon gold rush of 1896. He left Canada for London in 1901 having acquired diamond mining stakes in Kimberly, South Africa followed around 1904 by the acquisition of gold stakes in the Urals in Russia.

He also represented the Rio Tinto Company in Russia and maintained offices in St Petersburg during this period but was forced to move his operations back to England upon the outbreak of the Bolshevik Revolution in 1918.

His maternal grandparents were of old English and Scots heritage.

Grandfather Bernard Hallowes - a priest of the Church of England - hailed from Derbyshire while his grandmother was from a leading Dundee family called Thoms and heredity chieftains of the MacThomas clan. The current and 19th chief MacThomas of Finegrand is Bill's cousin.

Grandfather William was also a shareholder in Norfolk Canneries when that company was founded in 1931 ,well before the outbreak of the Second World War. Bill's father - Edward - was appointed General Manager of the Cannery; a position he retained until 1951 when he left, following the sale of the business to HP, having opted to look after his fruit farming interests full time.

A major investment in a chicken farm proved a financial disaster resulting in the sale of the fruit farm and the decision to move the the family to Kenya where British settlers were still very welcome.

In the autumn of 1952 accompanying his mother Vyvyan and two of his three sisters Bill sailed to Mombasa on the SS Kenya Castle. His elder sister Ann had remained in London while his father had travelled ahead by air in order to prepare for the family's arrival.

During their voyage the British Government declared a state of emergency in Kenya to combat what became known as the Mau Mau rebellion, an armed insurgency by a radical part of the independence movement led by Jomo Kenyatta that would last almost 8 years and claim the lives of up to 25,000 rebels and countless loyal local people slaughtered by them for being "loyalists" to British rule.

Vyvyan by this time was heavily pregnant with her fifth child Stephen who was to be born in Kenya. The family settled in a house located on Kilifi Creek midway between Mombasa and Malindi.

The only way to cross the creek was by the hand pulled chain ferry. It was a wonderfully novel mode of transport with the head boy blowing on a conch shell and the ferry boys chanting and pulling the chain in unison.

It was difficult to imagine a more extraordinary change of life style from the peaceful English countryside to the wildness of the African coast living in a house with no running water, no electricity and no inside sanitation.

They had no immediate neighbours the nearest being an elderly couple who owned a large coconut plantation.

A year or so later the family moved to a new house located right on the sea.

Their only neighbours were a Mr and Mrs Gedge and their daughter Angela.

They were curious neighbours to say the least - Mrs Gedge rode a bicycle while Mr Gedge drove an ancient model T ford reputedly of 1925 vintage.

Houses on the Kenya coast at that time were built with huge underground rainwater storage tanks, lighting was by Tilly paraffin lamps, refrigerators ran on kerosene and the lavatory was a wonderful contraption called the Choo.

Choos were basically a 60 foot deep pit with a wooden seat on top protected by a small hut. The family's choo had a marvellous view overlooking the sea, and as the beach was almost invariably deserted, the view was rarely interrupted!

Leopards were however somewhat of a problem for the dogs who had to be kept inside as soon as dusk fell otherwise they ran the risk of becoming a tasty dinner for the big cats!

Snakes were also an ever present danger particularly black and green mambas and puff adders.

Whenever Bill was around he was taught by their faithful family retainer Kisungu how to capture or to kill if necessary the more dangerous snakes with a slingshot.

The corpses, much to his mother's annoyance, were then kept in bottles of formalin and displayed on a shelf in his bedroom.

Anti-venom serum was always kept on hand in the refrigerator ready for immediate use in the event of snake bite.

The family gardener was bitten twice by puff adders but survived unhurt thanks to the stock in the fridge.

Despite the somewhat unusual risks to life and limb it was a very pleasant and comfortable existence for the family helped by an abundance of excellent servants.

It was also an idyllic location for the children enabling Bill and his younger sister Tassie to spend most of their holiday time on the beach and in the sea exploring beautiful and unspoilt coral reefs.

The state of emergency and the troubles in the highlands seemed very removed and did not extend to the coast so security was not an issue.

In 1954 the family left Kilifi and moved over 300 miles up country initially to Limuru and then to Thika where Edward had been appointed managing director of Kenya Canners.

Thika is around 27 miles north east of the capital Nairobi in an area that specialises in the growing of fruit, most notably pineapples and coffee trees.

Bill attended the Prince of Wales School in Nairobi as a boarder in Rhodes House. The school was exclusively dedicated to the education of European boys.

Strict separation of children by race was the norm at that time. Europeans attended white only schools while Indians and Africans had their own segregated schools.

There was virtually no racial interaction of any sort between schools and no social intercourse. At the Prince of Wales the only occasions for the Indians to be invited on campus was for hockey games (which they invariably won!). Africans were not invited at all.

Due to the Emergency dormitory buildings were protected by barbed wire, sandbags and British troops in watch towers. Discipline was strict, games including boxing were compulsory and all boys of fourteen or above automatically joined the Combined Cadet Force in order to be ready for induction into the Kenya Regiment at eighteen.

The ongoing Mau Mau insurrection was ever present in the minds of the children and special prayers were offered each term for those boys who "failed to return".

Bill's trips home to Thika on" Sunday leave outs" entailed passing several police stations en route where bodies of dead terrorists could often be seen lined up outside - a constant reminder of the dangers that existed in that area during those times.

Bill tolerated his school days but holidays enabled him to really immerse himself into the art of bush craft, tracking, hunting and the use of big game rifles. He had learned to shoot even before the family moved to Africa and was given his first rifle for his twelfth birthday - the start of a lifelong passion for guns which were to eventually become an important factor in his business life.

His particular favourite was a wonderful vintage 7 mm Mauser - a classic of the First World War - manufactured during the period when Tanganyika was known as German East Africa and his Winchester 30-30.

He was introduced to hunting by the Bowers, cousins of his mother, who leased a 50,000 acre ranch a couple of hundred miles south near Arusha in Tanganyika (modern day Tanzania) at the foot of Mount Kilimanjaro - Africa's highest mountain standing nearly 20,000 feet above sea level.

The ranch abounded in every type of big game and, in those days, poaching was virtually unheard of in the area. Trespassers were warned off and if they returned to poach were shot on sight. Bill was allowed to roam the entire estate on foot accompanied by a local tracker and several dogs.

His first of many skirmishes with wild animals occurred during his first visit when he was charged by a very angry wart hog which had taken refuge in a large burrow while being chased by the dogs.

Bill was determined to climb Kilimanjaro despite being told he was "too young" so in 1955 he and some school friends organised their own expedition.

Rigorous training took place in school and during the holidays prior to the climb date. Funds were very limited so only a guide and two porters were engaged which meant that the boys had to carry their own equipment.

To put his feat into perspective the mountain rises almost 17,000 feet from the plain that it sits on making it the world's tallest freestanding mountain.

Created by three volcanic cones, one of which is still classed as dormant, the mountain takes a climber through five distinct ecological zones going from Bush land to Arctic.

The first westerner to climb the mountain was a German geologist called Hans Meyer in 1889, he called the mountain "Kaiser Wilhelm Spitz" in honour of the Emperor.

The name that had been accepted since at least the 1840's is thought to come from the Swahili word Kilma meaning mountain and the Kichagga word Njaro meaning whiteness - given that it can be snow capped year round that would make sense. On early maps it appears as Kilma Njaro.

Kilimanjaro expedition on the way up - Bill on the right

During the climb, which took three days, the porters refused to climb to the "last hut" at 16,000 feet for the final ascent so only the guide was left to accompany the boys to the summit known as Kaiser William Spitze standing at just under 20,000 feet. The training paid off and all the boys reached Kibo, the highest of the three peaks without suffering too much from the effects of acute altitude sickness. Bill as the youngest member of the team held the record at that time as the youngest climber to reach Kaiser Wilhelm Spitze!

Summer 1957 saw the end of Bill's school days and still only fifteen the wider world beckoned.

His parents meanwhile were due to commence their "long leave" holiday in July and Bill was allowed to join them for the English part of the trip.

The most economical way in those times to fly from Kenya to the UK was to fly with Airwork Hunting Clan who operated the route using a fleet of vintage DC 3 aircraft.

Formed immediately after WW2 they were both independent, privately owned airlines who pooled their resources for the long haul to Nairobi which they called "The Safari Colonial Coach Service".

Pioneers of low cost flying they eventually merged in 1960 to form British United Airways and in 1957 they charged less than two thirds of the price of the BOAC flight!

It is extraordinary in this day and age of jet travel to recall how interesting air travel could be at that time - a real adventure for a young person!

The journey took three days! The trip started with a morning flight from Nairobi to Kampala for lunch followed by an afternoon flight to Wadi Halfa on the Nile in the Sudan. Wadi Halfa old town no longer exists as it was flooded following the construction of the Aswan dam but the "new town" is now located on the shore of Lake Nasser.

Dinner was served in the Nile Hotel followed by an overnight stay on the Nile river steamer adjoining the hotel which was used as the hotel annexe. The next morning after breakfast the flight continued to Bengazi in Libya for lunch thence onwards for an overnight stay in Valetta. The third day commenced with a flight to Nice for lunch and then finally the last leg to London Airport for arrival in the early evening!

Bill had passed his GCEs with reasonable results and had set his sights on becoming a farmer or estate manager so a diploma in agriculture was the next logical step.

He applied to Egerton Agricultural College in Nakuru and was accepted for the 1959 intake provided he completed 12 months training on any one of the farms certified as being suitable by the College.

Meanwhile, with time on his hands, Bill, thanks to his school friend Roy Carr-Hartley, along with several other school friends landed a very interesting job with the Carr-Hartley family on their big game ranch in Rumuruti, around 150 miles north of Thika on the far side of the Aberdare National Park.

The ranch was already famous having been used for the films "Snows of Kilimanjaro" and "Mogambo" a few years earlier and stars Clarke Gable, Ava Gardener and Ernest Hemingway feature in their family photo album.

Tom and Judy Carr-Hartley, Roy's parents ran a tight ship and the boys were immediately put to work as part of the live animal catch team. The family were amongst the very first to master the art of big game capture and the captive breeding of lions and their grandson Mikey Carr-Hartley still runs the ranch offering exclusive safaris.

The capture of wild animals was not for the faint hearted as tranquiliser guns at that time were virtually non-existent and the animals were captured live by hand - usually at night time.

Ex military trucks were used to transport the teams which consisted of a driver, a spotter with a powerful searchlight and the "troops" who were expected to catch the animals, usually gazelles, secure them with ropes and then gently move them into the back of the trucks.

The boys worked in pairs quietly approaching the animal downwind while it hopefully remained stationary being transfixed by the search light. At the last moment the boys charged the animal "rugby tackling" its front and rear legs simultaneously.

Then the hard part started as the boys held on to the animal's wildly thrashing legs as tightly as possible to avoid being kicked or injured until the arrival of the "ropers" who would secure the animals legs with ropes. The animals were then gently loaded into the trucks and transported back to the farm holding pens.

Generally, the animals recovered from the shock of capture very quickly and by the next morning could be seen happily eating fodder in their newly acquired "home".

The capture of rhinos and giraffe was a totally different matter involving day time capture by driving the truck alongside the galloping animal, lassoing its neck using an extended pole and holding it as tightly as possible alongside the truck while the rope teams secured the animals legs with ropes and straps prior to manoeuvring the animal on board assisted by the truck's winch.

Lions were bred in captive pens adjoining the main farm house so the primary task for the boys was to shoot sufficient zebra to keep the lions well fed!

The animals were subsequently moved to newly established wild life parks or shipped to overseas zoos.

Bill returned home for Christmas and started to prepare for the start of his formal agricultural training. He had been accepted as a trainee on a large 8,000 acre Rift Valley Estate near Naivasha, some 100 miles north of Thika, owned by a Major Pardoe.

It was a farm recommended by the College and he started there in the spring of 1958.

As he was not yet 17 he was unable to qualify for a driving license and therefore had to use the estate's horses as his mode of transport. He had no previous experience with horses and in fact had never even mounted a horse so he had to undergo a four week crash course in riding before starting his new job. Major Pardoe provided him with the use of two polo ponies. Both were highly trained to the point that it wasn't long before Bill could shoot from horse back without the horses flinching or moving, a learning curve for all concerned.

The estate actually consisted of two farms with the lower farm at an altitude of 6,500 feet and dedicated to the raising of beef cattle and pigs. The upper arable farm was reached by a high escarpment situated some 1500 feet above the lower farm on the lower slopes of the Aberdare mountain range.

The upper farm dedicated to the growing of wheat, barley and oats had been managed until just before Bill's arrival by Major Pardoe's daughter and her husband who lived with their young children in the upper farmhouse.

The Aberdare forests stretching to altitudes of 12,000 feet were very difficult to penetrate and had become notorious for being the main hide out of the Mau Mau terrorists. The major's daughter spoke fluent Kikuyu in addition to Swahili and it was this unusual ability which was to save the life of her and her children.

One morning while her husband was away on a visit to Nakuru a large heavily armed gang of terrorists, reputedly over 100 strong, converged on the farmhouse threatening to kill the woman and her children. The gang leader was very surprised to discover she had not only been born in Kenya but also spoke his native language which she had learned from her ayah as a child. She was able to persuade him to spare their lives but saw their farmhouse burned to the ground.

It was subsequently decided by the security forces and the family that to rebuild in such an isolated and unprotected location would be too dangerous so had resulted in the farm being run by the Major and his team - his daughter having decided to move the family elsewhere.

Three weeks after Bill's arrival the estate manager suddenly resigned and departed at very short notice. Almost at the same time the Major fell ill and took to his bed. He was never to fully recover and remained a semi invalid.

Much to Bill's surprise the Major told him to "carry on" and that he would train him how to run the estate. He was to report to the Major for instructions daily after breakfast and after lunch. Usually Bill would also be invited to join him for dinner - the Major sitting up in bed while Bill sat nearby at an adjacent table.

The old man despite his ailments had a razor sharp mind and was a wonderful teacher and companion. From that moment on Bill found himself in charge of 8,000 acres and nearly two hundred African staff - it was an opportunity not to be missed! Luckily for him there were a number of competent and loyal overseers who had also been well trained by the Major.

The days were long and hard but still provided Bill with ample opportunity to hunt and he was able to keep the house and most of the estate staff well supplied with fresh meat - usually deer or warthogs.

It was a difficult decision but by midyear Bill decided to move on for his next six months of training to a very different farm located high up on the Western Rift Valley at an altitude of nearly 10,000 feet adjacent to a huge rain forest.

The area was extremely remote with no adjacent neighbours. Despite being on the equator temperatures at night plummeted to near freezing. The climate was also very different being much wetter and colder while the land was rich and arable.

The owners were a couple named Ritchie from Yorkshire who had taken the plunge to sell their English farm in order to settle in the Kenya Highlands. The farm was both dairy and arable.

There was a fine herd of Jersey cows whose milk was turned into cream and sold to a plant in Nakuru which produced butter and cheese for the local market and for export to England where butter was in short supply. The arable crops were barley, potatoes and Pyrethrum which was used in the production of DDT - now a banned substance.

It was a tough life but much enjoyed by Bill who loved the isolation. Up early at 5.00am to supervise the milking, followed by a hearty breakfast and then off with Mr. Ritchie to supervise the other farm activities.

The Ritchie's took to their beds early each evening so Bill was often to be found out on the farm at night ploughing. He loved the discipline of ploughing at night with just the tractor headlights piercing the dark and the challenge of creating the straightest possible furrows. A rifle was always kept on hand in the cab for protection The rain forest adjoining the farm was host to an abundance of wild life, in particular leopards and giant forest hogs. A strong and deep mesh fence had been installed along the entire forest boundary adjoining the farm to keep out "unwanted guests". These huge pigs, which can reach up to 600 lbs in weight, were a constant nuisance as they often launched nightly forays to dig up the potato crop. Bill spent many evenings in hides near the forest edge shooting the occasional hog for meat for the farm staff!

Leopards were also a major problem and a number of valuable calves were killed and eaten by them from time to time. During Bill's stay on the farm all efforts were concentrated on a very wily black leopard. Night after night the farmer and Bill stayed hidden in the loft adjacent to the calf pens equipped with a powerful lamp while an unfortunate goat was tethered in the nearby yard as bait. Finally the leopard took the bait and a broadside of heavy SSG shot accomplished the task.

Bill's college ambitions ended one evening when he received a phone call from his father to say that he was to be offered a position as a trainee in the head office of Kenya's leading coffee growers - a company called Socfinaf.

The offer called for Bill to make an important decision as Socfinaf's policy was to accept trainee managers prior to college entry as the company preferred to train its own managers "in house" over a two year period. He opted to accept the offer.

Socfinaf was part of a major international French farming conglomerate called Socfin with its head offices in Paris and Brussels and plantations located in Sierra Leone, Liberia, Ivory Coast, Nigeria, Congo, Kenya, Cameroons, Canada, Cambodia, Malaysia and Indonesia.

The Company's primary produce had been rubber and palm oil in Malaysia but after the war, they had branched out into Kenya where they acquired their first coffee plantations in 1950.

Socfinaf accounted for at least ten percent of Kenya's total coffee production at that time. It was by far the largest coffee producer in the country employing an African labour force of thirty five thousand who were overseen by a European management team of around fifty.

The Socfin Group was owned by two major French banks (Halle Bank and Caisse Privee) and was run with military like precision!

Having opted to join Socfinaf Bill soon found himself in a world totally removed from the remote farms of the past eighteen months. The company decided as an "experiment" to employ him in their Ruiru head office as an assistant to the French General Manager Michel Huas.

Michel some years later became a Director of the World Bank and was to be the man who inspired Bill to enter the business world.

He maintained his connections with Michel for many years and they were to meet up again in Washington DC.

Bill moved into a fully furnished company house near the Ruiru offices which he shared with the Deputy Company Secretary Taffy Enoch. They became good friends.

Ruiru was only around 12 miles from Thika, where Bill's parents lived, so he was able to visit them on a regular basis and was also within easy reach of Nairobi.

Transport was an immediate priority and as he could not afford a car a motorcycle was an obvious solution! Bill purchased his first motorcycle - a 250cc BSA.

At that time travelling in East Africa by motorcycle was a somewhat hazardous occupation to say the least. Most roads were just sand or murram tracks with little room to manoeuvre and either very dusty or very muddy depending on the seasons. Animals wandering onto roads and African cyclists were another hazard which Bill was soon to confront.

Coming back late one night from Nairobi a large buck ran across the road directly in front of him. Impossible to avoid a collision the motorcycle rammed into the side of the deer and Bill found himself flung over the bike to land on his head in the middle of the road.

Luckily he was wearing his crash helmet so other than minor concussion he was none the worse for wear! The same could not be said for his motorcycle which had suffered considerable damage.

Several weeks later he was able to collect his newly repaired bike from the workshop in Nairobi only to have another accident on his way home. Rounding a bend at speed he was confronted by two Africans pushing a bicycle across the middle of the road. In order to avoid hitting the Africans he aimed his motorcycle at the middle of the bicycle and yet again found himself landing on his head in the middle of the road. Luckily no one had any serious injuries but the motorcycle was a write-off!

He then proceeded to buy a much bigger and more powerful replacement - a BSA 650cc machine known as the "Super Road Rocket" -which at that time was one of the fasted road bikes in the world being capable of speeds well in excess of 100mph.

Bill took to "office life" at Socfinaf like a duck to water and was soon immersed in the business of estate management and finance. Over a two year period he was moved from department to department every four months in order to learn all aspects of the business. The company expected its employees to participate actively in the social life of the organisation with much focus on sporting activities.

With its own private club and sports centre in Ruiru and holiday apartments in Malindi on the coast the company cocooned its European managers in a very comfortable life style whilst they in turn were expected to devote their life to the well being of the organisation. In colonial East Africa at that time there was no fraternization with other races - strict social segregation was the norm and interracial sex was frowned upon!

This posed a particular problem for most young white men who often had considerable difficulty in persuading white girls to have sex with them unless marriage was in the air. Bill's close friend Eddie Palmer was concerned that Bill remained a virgin and was determined to "fix" the problem during one of his visits to Nairobi.

Ladies of easy virtue were to be found amongst the Somali community and it was with a Somali woman that the young man had his first sexual tryst. It proved to be a rather unsatisfactory encounter and the following weeks saw a daily self examination of his genitals to check for any signs of the "pox". Luckily he was in the clear and a blood test some weeks later by the Company doctor confirmed that nothing was amiss!

Most weekends he stayed with his parents in Thika where social life revolved around the Thika Country Club. It was there that Bill first met Morna Cochran - the first and probably greatest love of his life.

Morna was unusual in that she had never been to school having been educated at home by her mother who refused to allow her to attend boarding school. Slim, blonde and very pretty she was also an excellent tennis player so perhaps not surprisingly Bill was soon to be seen playing tennis on a much more regular basis at the Club.

Mrs Cochran seemed to approve of the young man and invitations to dinner on the Cochran Coffee Estate and weekend visits were soon extended on a regular basis. The couple were madly in love and before long the inevitable happened. Bill always stayed in the main guest bedroom which had a second door leading through to Morna's bedroom. Once Mrs Cochran was safely asleep Bill would creep into the girl's bedroom and they would make passionate love.

Sooner or later the love making was bound to be found out and sure enough some months later Bill's father received a call from a very angry Mrs Cochran requesting an immediate meeting to discuss their affair. She pointed out that Morna was a minor being still only fifteen years old and therefore legally Bill could be the subject of statutory rape charges. It was finally agreed, between the parents, that Bill would be forbidden to see or to make contact with Morna again until she was "older" while Morna, accompanied by her mother, would move to England in order to further her education.

The young couple were completely devastated but there was little they could do particularly with the threat hanging over their heads that Mrs Cochran would notify the police about Bill's "illegal sex with a minor". He was not to see Morna again for three years!

The Grange: P-H Family Home 1950

The Family at the Grange before Kenya 1951

Taverham Hall Prep School

Kilimanjaro expedition summit 1955 - Bill second from left

House at Limuru

Road barrier Kenya

CHAPTER 3

Kenya Years 1959-61

Bill worked at the Socfinaf headquarters in Ruiru for two years during which time he was able to see first-hand how a large multinational company operated. Reports had to be prepared for Paris each month on all the company's activities so deadlines and work pressure became the norm - excellent training which stood him in good stead in later years.

Then, quite by chance, an event occurred which would change his position in the Company and his outlook on life.

A visit to the company by two of the senior French directors - the Compte de Beaumont accompanied by his wife and Vicompte de Rives was to be an eye-opener for the young man. He was put in charge of all the local arrangements and told the budget was unlimited. One of the directors' wives - the Countess de Beaumont - had even requested that a personal European maid be at her beck and call, specified her own brand of soap which was to be used by her exclusively and that the soap be replaced each time she used it.

It was a great responsibility but also a good opportunity and one to be accepted with open arms.

He became a mixture of guide, travel agent and assistant as their itinerary was massive. They wanted to take in as much of what East Africa had to offer in a single trip.

Bill was to accompany the party at all times throughout their stay.

After a tour of some of the company estates the party set off for Tree-Tops hotel in the Aberdare National Park, famous for its tree-top big game observatory with a fine view of Mt. Kenya. The hotel had recently been rebuilt after being burned to the ground in 1954 by the Mau Mau.

Their stay was followed by a 250 mile journey south west to the Serengeti national park in Tanganyika where the party stayed at an exclusive private encampment.

This was followed by a weeks' rest before returning to Paris at the luxurious Socfinaf apartments located on the coast in Malindi.

Three boats had to be on stand-by for them the entire duration of their stay - a deep sea fishing boat, a glass bottomed boat and a native sailing boat.

The countess, who usually stayed in bed while the men were out fishing or sailing on several occasions ordered Bill to join her which provided his first experience of older lovers.

The entire trip was exhausting for Bill on so many levels but it was also his first experience of how the rich lived and it made him determined that one day he too would be able to experience a similar lifestyle!

During this period without his beloved Morna he spent much of his free time hunting extensively on the huge 35,000 acre Ruiru cattle ranch belonging to the Company. It became de facto his private game reserve and he was to be found there most weekends often camping overnight within its confines.

Game abounded throughout the ranch including large herds of zebra, wildebeest and gazelles. The Athi river which ran through the ranch at one point also fed several large reed lined lakes and swamps on the property. The fishing - mainly tilapia - was excellent and Bill was usually accompanied on fishing trips by a colleague from the office called Victor Mendoza. Victor and his family hailed from Goa. He was an accountant by profession, a former Olympic runner and keen fisherman!

Bill had been persuaded by Michel Huas to enter the company's annual sports day - he wanted a European to compete in the one mile event - so Victor was put in charge of his six month training programme this meant being up at 6.00 am most weekdays and long timed runs while Victor followed alongside on his bicycle with a timer! The training period paid off and Bill came second in the race.

The lakes were home to a substantial population of hippos who had migrated from the Athi and which presented a substantial danger to those who ventured into the swamps to fish while the river was home to numerous crocodiles always on the lookout for any unwary game who visited the river each evening to drink.

One evening, while fishing, Bill and Victor disturbed several hippos feeding in the reeds who fled into the water capsizing their small fishing boat and nearly crushing them in the process! The boat sank and they were forced to swim ashore.

Bill always hunted alone on foot but by now possessed an ancient but sturdy 1948 ex-army Land Rover which he used exclusively on the ranch for transporting dead game as it was not suitable for use on public highways having no lights and a battery that was unreliable to say the least.

In 1959 he decided to spend some of his annual leave on a long hunting trip in the wilder parts of the Ruiru estate moving each day to a different location. It was a perfect time to camp and hunt as it was the middle of the dry season and all the rivers were at their lowest levels thus making fording considerably less risky.

The second night of his trip he set up camp near the Athi River having carefully parked the land rover on a slope leading down to the river in order to be sure to start the vehicle the following morning. He retired to bed soon after nightfall but woke up around midnight to attend to a call of nature. The sky was partially overcast but a near full moon was straining to break through the clouds.

Just as he was finishing urinating he became aware of movement and slight noises around his campsite.

He slowly turned around to see the outline of a large figure in some sort of long overcoat and, before he could move, he felt a sharp blow to his chest which knocked him onto his back.

Several African voices could now be heard around him apparently discussing if he was dead or not. Someone started going through his pockets while another figure starting hacking in a random sort of way at his foot which luckily for him was protected by the sturdy boots he was wearing.

He decided immediately that his only chance to survive was to pretend to be dead and under no circumstances to move. Pockets emptied of anything valuable he became aware that the party were moving away in the direction of the river followed shortly by loud splashing and gradually their voices faded into the distance.

Bill stood up - his shoulder felt numb and he realised that his left arm was not functioning, he had been shot.

He could feel blood running down his chest and legs into his boots and knew the priority must be to stem the blood flow. He was able to walk slowly and quietly over to the parked land rover and pulled out several oily rags located under the car seat which he stuffed into his shirt over the entry wound area of his chest.

The key had been left in the vehicle ready for the morning start up so he climbed into the vehicle and prepared to start the engine. He decided not to risk using the starter motor as it probably would not work and, in any event, would make a lot of noise, instead he opted to risk a rolling start down the slope in the river direction.

The vehicle was standard right hand drive so engaging the gear was not easy as he had no movement in his left arm but reaching across with his right hand he was able to put it into second gear, turn on the ignition and release the hand brake. The vehicle started its run down the slope and when he judged, as well as he could that sufficient speed had been achieved, he let out the clutch and the engine fired up immediately.

However the vehicle was by now very near the water's edge and with no lights working it was very difficult to judge his distance from the river.

Bill knew the river at this fording point was very shallow so he concentrated on keeping the engine revved while he applied the brakes. A stall could well have been fatal as there would be no way to restart the engine and it was impossible to know how far away the gang had really moved!

The land rover rolled into the water and came to a halt while he frantically revved the engine with one foot and using the other foot for the clutch pedal while turning sideways, using his right hand, he was able to engage the reverse gear. He reversed as fast as possible backwards up the slope onto the wide shoulder of the river bank. Now he had to get help and urgent medical attention as he was still losing blood.

Luckily for him the combination of his extensive knowledge of the ranch, its tracks and the moon which was now fully out, enabled him to head towards the nearest cattle station, known as a boma, where he knew he would find some of the cattle herders who worked on the ranch.

His arrival at the boma, sounding his horn and revving the vehicle hard soon woke the astonished herdsmen two of whom agreed to accompany him to the nearest European house which was some five miles distant in a very isolated location. One of the men sat beside him holding a cloth over the wound while the other sat precariously on the bonnet clutching a torch as the only available headlight. Off they set and some fifteen minutes later were approaching the house in question when the Land Rover slid off the track into a ditch and stalled.

The men were too frightened to accompany him the final few hundred yards to the house as the occupants' guard dogs apparently had a vicious reputation. Bill trudged up to the front door of the house in the glare of the security lights with no sign of any guard dogs and hammered on the door. The master of the house emerged carrying a large pistol and was shocked to see this dirty and blooded apparition on his door step.

Bill was rushed inside and while the occupant's wife applied pads and a tourniquet to his chest, the husband called the local security forces on his radio.

A few minutes later they put him into their Volvo car and headed at high speed on the thirty five miles journey to the Nairobi General Hospital.

He was lucky - the bullet, which was a "dumdum" had entered the top of his chest a couple of inches above the heart, passed through his shoulder blade with the main part of the bullet lodged just under the skin in his back.

He had lost nearly three pints of blood. The nerves running into his shoulder and arm had been severely damaged and initially he had little or no feeling or sensation in the arm.

HIS LIFE SAVED — BY 2 IN.

EIGHTEEN - YEAR - OLD William Pellew-Harvey, of Thika, sat up in his hospital bed yesterday and said: "I suppose I am lucky to be alive. If that bullet had been two inches lower it would have killed me."

THAT bullet came from a .22 rifle — his own. It was fired by one of a group of Africans who attacked him while he was camping near the Athi River, 16 miles off the main Thika Road. The

pangas, he said. The raiders crept up as William sat outside his tent. One, carrying the rifle, shot him.

The raiders stole a 100/- note from him and left him for dead. He managed to crawl to his vehicle and reach the house of a European.

● A .22 rifle and 40 rounds of ammunition have been recovered by the police in a swamp near the spot where

Newspaper report of the shooting 1959

Dumdum bullets were developed by the British Army at the Dumdum arsenal in northern India for use on the north west frontier of that sub-continent in the 1890s.

Designed with a soft lead nose the bullets expand on impact and create a larger wound than a standard bullet. Outlawed for use in warfare by the Hague Convention in 1899 they remained in use for hunting and were also favoured by criminals and insurgents for the amount of damage they caused.

The surgeon wanted to remove the bullet fragments lodged in the shoulder and to remove the main bullet from his back but was dissuaded from doing so by the physiotherapist who was certain that any such operation was not necessary and would just further endanger the already damaged shoulder and arm nerves.

A three month hospital stay was accompanied by physiotherapy twice daily which proved to be the best solution. He gradually recovered the use of his arm but a lack of feeling in his lower arm, hands and fingers was to continue for at least eighteen months and the bullet in his back wouldn't be removed until several years later in London's Middlesex Hospital.

The Company meanwhile had decided that Bill's two year training as PA to the General Manager had readied him for a more hands on management role so upon his discharge from hospital he was promoted from trainee status to Assistant Manager on the company's Matungulu Estate.

Matungulu was a large coffee estate north east of Thika, further away from Nairobi and bordering the Wakamba Reserve which is now known as the Bisanadi National Reserve. As Assistant Manager he was provided with a comfortable fully furnished house on the estate and by this time he had sold his beloved BSA motorcycle and had purchased his first car- a dark blue Auto Union 1000.

Described at the time as a compact luxury car it was the first vehicle to carry the company's distinctive four ring badge on the radiator grill, a badge that these days is synonymous with Audi - the name chosen for the Auto Union when VW took control in 1965.

It was a major change from the confines of the head office and Bill was delighted to be involved in the day to day operations of a large coffee estate. The area was generally considered peaceful as the Wakamba tribe had not been involved in the Mau Mau uprising but there was another constant problem on the borders of the estate adjoining the reserve.

A river bed, usually dry, marked the border between the estate and the reserve. During the dry season the tribesmen would often wait until the late afternoon then quietly move small herds of their cattle onto the estate to graze hoping that their activities would go unnoticed by the estate guards and management. Bill's duties included, whenever possible, a check of the estate's borders every evening before sunset.

One evening he was on border patrol in his car accompanied by a guard when he came across a herd of around fifty cattle grazing well within the confines of the estate. He parked his car, grabbed his rifle, and accompanied by the guard gently approached the cattle in order to push them back across the river bed. However the young girl who was looking after them kept herding the cattle so that they remained on the estate's property with the result that the cattle just kept milling around moving first in one direction and the next moment in the opposite direction.

Bill decided to fire a warning rifle shot in the air in order to scare the girl off leaving him and the guard to move the cattle back. However the shot had the opposite effect - the girl ran screaming across the river bed and almost immediately angry shouts erupted on the Wakamba side. Very quickly a crowd of tribesmen armed with spears and sticks could be seen gathering on the opposite bank.

The crowd surged forward, crossed the river bed onto the estate and advanced up the hill towards Bill and the guard who were vainly trying to control the now very nervous cattle. Bill stood his ground but the guard turned tail and ran leaving him to face the crowd alone. They came to a halt about fifty yards from him and a man who appeared to be the ringleader approached demanding that the cattle be handed back.

Bill countered that they knew they were trespassing on private property and that the cattle were now under arrest and would be held in a company compound then handed over to the police until such time as they could be claimed by their owners which might well involve the payment to the police of a small trespass fine.

This reply was greeted in silence but then in response to a shout from the ringleader the crowd again surged forward.

It was an extremely tense moment which called for instant action and Bill fired two shots in rapid succession into the ground which kicked up puffs of dust in front of their leader. The crowd halted for a few seconds and then suddenly turned around and retreated rapidly and in complete silence down the hill and across the boundary back to their own side of the border.

Bill found himself with the herd of bewildered cattle but was soon rejoined by the guard who had emerged from wherever he was hiding and between them they managed to corral the cattle into a nearby compound. By this time it was nearly dark but he decided to report the events immediately to his manager whose first question was to ask if anybody had been hurt, to which he was able to respond truthfully that "nobody was injured".

His manager confirmed that he had acted correctly and that he would immediately notify the circumstances of the incident to the Thika police by radio. Bill went home, had dinner and retired to bed soon thereafter. He was woken up in the early hours of the morning by the sound of barking dogs and the sudden appearance of two vehicles in his driveway.

A searchlight was illuminating the front of the house and half asleep and blinded by the light he heard a booming voice from a loudspeaker telling him that he was under arrest, to lay down any weapons and to leave the house by the front door. Compliance was the only option so a few minutes later he found himself in a Land Rover sitting beside the local Chief Inspector of Police and several constables on the way to Thika Police Station.

Upon arrival he was formerly charged with causing grievous bodily harm to a Wakamba tribesman the previous afternoon. Bill's father had also been summoned and a discussion took place as to how Bill was to be held in custody pending a court appearance scheduled for later that morning. It was decided that as he was under 21 and there were no holding facilities anyway for Europeans at the Police Station that he should stay with a European family nearby who were "well regarded" by the police.

Later that morning Bill duly appeared in the local magistrates' court to answer the charge only to find that it had been amended to "unlawful wounding". He was accompanied by Norman Shaylor, a leading criminal lawyer who had been retained by Socfinaf for his defence. He entered a not guilty plea and was released on bail guaranteed by the Company.

Shaylor demanded and was given permission to see the wounded man in hospital to verify his identity and to see the actual wound. Bill and Shaylor then visited the local hospital and accompanied by a doctor were permitted to enter the ward in which the man was recovering. To their astonishment the man was not even in bed; he was walking around the ward chatting to other patients and the only sign of injury was a large bandage around his head and left ear.

The doctor was asked to remove part of the bandage so that Shaylor and Bill could "inspect" the wound. The man had a piece of his lower ear missing. Both were certain, as was the doctor, that the wound had not been caused by a bullet and a medical expert, subsequently retained as part of the defence team, confirmed during the court hearing that the wound had been caused by a machete or similar instrument.

Bill had the option of being tried in front of a jury or in front of a magistrate with the latter option being recommended by Shaylor as their best hope for a fair hearing. A trial date was set for some weeks hence and Bill was free on bail. He was not permitted to return to his duties and was suspended on full pay until the outcome of the trial had been established in order not to cause any "political embarrassment " amongst the company's employees bearing in mind that he as a white man had been charged with wounding a black man.

The trial duly took place in Thika with just two witnesses for the defence, the guard and the medical expert while the prosecution on the other hand called more than twenty witnesses. The prosecution case was that the tribesmen had accidentally allowed their cattle to wander onto the estate and that when they went to fetch their cattle to bring them back into the reserve that Bill had deliberately opened fire on their "leader" wounding him in the ear.

It was a complete shambles for the prosecution with each witness crumbling under Shaylor's tough interrogation by recounting numerous different versions of the event. Shaylor closed the case for the defence when the Medical Expert stated that the wound had been caused by a machete or similar instrument rather than a bullet.

Within minutes the Magistrate advised that he found no merit in the prosecution's case and that he therefore found the defendant not guilty and was free to leave the court.

Bill was reinstated by the company and returned to his duties. Unfortunately more problems were to follow!

Around this time he had attended a dance at the YWCA hostel in Nairobi where he met a South African girl called Ilene Bothma who was a student at a secretarial college. Ilene was a pretty dark haired olive skinned girl with full breasts and a great sense of fun. She claimed to be seventeen and they dated regularly with her often staying over at Bill's house.

During her half term holidays she accepted an invitation to spend her holiday with Bill rather than returning home to her parents in Malindi. Ilene had told the matron in the hostel at the college that she was staying "with friends" in Nairobi instead of returning home. Bill remained blissfully unaware of her real age!

A few days into the half term break he was driving home to have lunch with Ilene only to be confronted in his driveway by a large black car with a police woman at the wheel, the matron in the front seat and a weeping Ilene in the back. The matron advised Bill that he was in serious trouble as the girl was only fifteen!

The police woman added that statutory rape charges might well be instigated, Ilene's parents would be informed and more ominously for Bill that the Company would be notified that an offence or series of offences had taken place in one of the company's houses.

Several days passed with no news but the following Monday Bill was summoned to the Socfinaf headquarters in Ruiru by the Company Secretary Michael Ellis. Michael advised Bill that while he was well aware that Ilene looked and behaved like a consenting adult woman the company had no option but to take matters seriously as an official complaint had been made by both the YWCA and the Police.

He also advised that it would be best, under the circumstances, if Bill resigned and that the company would do its best to "settle matters" with the authorities. Michael's more personal advice was that Kenya had become "too small" for Bill and that a "prompt departure" by heading for the UK or America would open up better career opportunities rather than staying in Kenya.

Meanwhile Ilene's parents had arrived in Nairobi and told the couple that they must immediately get engaged and had even brought with them a diamond engagement ring for Ilene to wear.

Bill was speechless. His parents, who were totally against the proposed marriage, also felt strongly that his future lay elsewhere and that they would take steps to help find him a new career path if he made his way to London.

Within a month he had booked passage on a Compagnie Maritime Belge tramp steamer from Mombasa to Antwerp and slipped quietly away from Kenya never to return.

England was where his future lay and equally importantly would provide the opportunity to be once again near his beloved Morna!

CHAPTER 4

London – Early Years 1962-64

Once aboard the steamer and settled into his cabin Bill started to explore the somewhat elderly vessel.

It was a second world war Liberty Ship built in America and had no doubt been designed for convoy duties across the Atlantic. Many of these vessels were sold off cheaply to European shipping lines as part of the Marshall Plan in an endeavour to rehabilitate the decimated shipping industry and Western economies in general. Over 2,700 of these low cost cargo ships were built in 18 US shipyards during and immediately following the war. Not renowned for their comfort or speed these sturdy reliable vessels were widely used throughout the 50s and 60s. They were not designed for normal passenger use and CMB only permitted a maximum of six passengers per voyage in single or double cabins.

By an extraordinary coincidence three of the other five passengers on board were Bill's former history teacher, wife and son together with a Belgian priest and a South African businessman. Passengers ate together in the officers' mess but were otherwise free to roam the ship at will. Bill soon became friends with many of the crew - in particular the ship's chef known as "Cookie" and the First Officer who doubled up as the ship's doctor.

The first port of call after Mombasa was Port Sudan which at that time was renowned for its night life, bars and brothels. Many of the crew caught the "clap" during the stay in port so immediately after the ship's departure for Port Said, Bill was to be found assisting in the administration of daily penicillin injections to the unfortunate afflicted crew members.

Five weeks later on a cold and foggy February day the ship finally docked in Rotterdam and Bill disembarked in the company of Cookie who had invited him to stay for a few days. Unfortunately when the pair arrived at Cookie's house there was no sign of his wife who appeared to have decamped along with the entire contents of their home. They stayed the night in a sailors' hostel nearby and the next day Bill decided to take the first available ferry to England from Zeebrugge.

Prior to his departure from Kenya Morna's mother had consented to allow Bill to meet her daughter again and had invited him to stay with them in Tonbridge Wells while he went for his job interviews in London. Thanks to his father's assistance he had been offered an interview with Shell as a trainee manager and with Henry W Peabody, one of London's leading trading houses, as a trainee commodity trader.

Bill was offered a trainee position in both companies but decided to accept the Peabody offer to work in their head offices in London whereas Shell had planned to move him immediately to work in one of their Venezuelan operations. His salary was to start at £500 per year!

By the time he commenced work at Peabody's he had found a shared bedsit in West Kensington costing £2 per week. He was determined to "make do" on his salary and told his father that he needed no extra funds. He spent most weekends in Tonbridge Wells and, despite promises to Morna's mother to remain celibate, the pair had become lovers once again. However the relationship came to an abrupt halt several months later when Bill became involved in a fight at a party in London attended by Morna and her sister which, much to his distress, resulted in his being forbidden to see Morna again.

Life at Peabody's was very stimulating and the young man, after a period of training in the company's letter of credit department, was soon allowed to start to trade on his own under the strict supervision of the departmental director - the Hon Hugh Cohen. He was allocated a "ragbag" of accounts which the senior traders did not wish to deal with including a fledgling market retail company called Tesco. There he met their fearsome chief buyer Daisy Hyams whose opening remarks were invariably "you have 60 seconds young man to pique my interest" whereupon she would click on the kitchen timer prominently displayed on her desk.

Office hours were long and in the sixties the City also worked on Saturday mornings so "weekends" were much shorter than they are today! As part of his training he had to work for three months in Billingsgate Fish Market early each morning from 5.00am to 8.00 am and then, after a hearty breakfast, had to wash up and put on his city suit before spending a full normal day in the Peabody offices.

On other occasions he was despatched to Grimsby to supervise the unloading of frozen Japanese whale meat for delivery to Pedigree Petfoods in Melton Mowbray, part of the Mars Group and the major player in the British pet food market. In order to further increase his knowledge of the fishing industry he had to spend over a week at sea on a Hull based trawler fishing off the north Scottish coast for cod and halibut. It was an experience he did not wish to repeat!

The following year his father arrived from Kenya on a visit and was perturbed to see that his son's living quarters in West Kensington were cold and uncomfortable. There was no heating in the room and both young men were forced to use sleeping bags in order to keep warm. Budgets were discussed with his father and Bill moved into the Overseas Visitors Club in Earls Court for a few weeks in order to find a suitable flat in the area and three companions to share it with.

By this time Bill had renewed his friendship with his old school mate from Taverham - Victor "Mig" Temple - whose parents had recently moved from Kensington to rural Essex. Mig agreed to join him in locating a flat and soon two other Thames Rowing Club friends were on board. The young men found a suitable furnished flat near the Earls Court Exhibition Centre. Social life for Bill in London continued to revolve around the Overseas Visitors Club which had become a home from home for numerous "colonials" from East and Southern Africa and the Antipodes.

The "pill" had arrived on the scene; rock n' roll and the twist were all the rage. The Mersey sound was being led by the Beatles and London was soon to become the centre of world fashion and music.

Bill soon had a new girlfriend - the daughter of a French Army Colonel. Annie, together with her sister, was working in London to improve her English. The girls had a large bedsitter in Earls Court just around the corner from the Overseas Visitors Club.

Neither Bill nor Annie had much money so much of their free time was spent in bed. Annie would usually leave for work early in the morning and before long Bill had also been invited into the sister's bed for a quick tryst before he left for the office. Annie soon made it clear that she was quite happy to "share" him with her sister in a ménage à trois.

Some weekends he visited relatives in Dorchester and Guildford and on others he would travel with Mig as a passenger in his motorcycle side car to stay with his parents at their country house in Essex.

For four years Bill worked as a trader honing his business skills. He had also developed an in depth knowledge of the logistics industry or more specifically in what was known as "reefer traffic" of frozen commodities in particular fish, vegetables and fruit. Frozen foods were already well established in the United States - in 1959 Americans spent $2.7 billion but the industry was still in its infancy in the UK and Europe although developing fast. Bill could see the opportunities ahead and made sure he developed close relationships with the Company's main suppliers in the USA and Canada.

In mid 1964 he took the plunge to become a sole trader, resigned from Peabody and founded his own business known as W.B. Pellew-Harvey & Co. Ltd. Bill had no capital so he had approached a close business friend in Los Angeles, whom he had dealt with at Peabody, called James Lawless and secured an interest free loan of $2,000 in order to finance the start of the new company's operations. Hardly a fortune, the equivalent of around $35,000 56 years later, this "seed money" was sufficient for Bill to rent an elegant first floor flat in Cornwall Gardens which became both his residence and the first office for the fledgling company.

Jim also paid for him to fly to Los Angeles in order to visit the company's frozen fruit and frozen vegetable plants located in the Sacramento valley followed by a trip to Disneyland.

Since his arrival in the UK Bill had banked with Standard Chartered Bank and following his initial funding from the USA he was gradually able to gain the bank's confidence to the point where they were prepared to open Letters of Credit for him directly to his suppliers without additional security.

The business got off to a good start and cash flow was soon positive which enabled him accompanied by a close Norwegian friend - Len Alvestad - to embark on the first of his many business and vacation trips to North America.

Prior to his departure Bill had ordered a new E type Jaguar! Life was looking up!

CHAPTER 5

Discovering America, the Far East & Married Life 1964-66

The two young men flew from London to Seattle via New York where Bill met with the first of his soon to be frozen salmon suppliers Robert "Bob" Dignon. Bob was a leading supplier of Alaskan salmon who had been in the industry since 1935.

Alaska was home to the world's finest salmon dominated by the highly prized king (Chinook) salmon and Coho (Silver) salmon much sought after by Europe's top end salmon smokers. Alaska's three other types of salmon - sockeye, pink and chum salmon - were not considered suitable for smoking and were therefore destined to end up in any one of the numerous canneries located along the Alaska seaboard.

From Seattle Bill and Len drove to Vancouver to meet Canada's leading salmon exporter - Malcolm McCallum. Bill signed contracts to purchase a substantial tonnage of frozen salmon at fixed prices for delivery the coming spring and summer. The purchases were entirely speculative on his part as none of the fish had been presold.

This was the first of many financial risks - challenges he liked to call them - that he would take throughout his long and varied career. As he pointed out "if you are not ready to evaluate, speculate and put your money where your mouth is then don't call yourself a trader".

By this time the duo were ready for some fun so decided to visit Las Vegas a city that was a very different place than it is today.

It was rather small, dry and dusty with one main street, a few small casinos and burlesque clubs. The leading hotel was the Sands which Frank Sinatra had been headlining at for over 10 years. By 1964 he part owned the hotel and it had become a favourite watering hole of the Mob. It also had the best show in town featuring Sinatra himself, Sammy Davis Junior and Dean Martin. The show was rather informal almost to the point of being shambolic as Sinatra was drunk and appeared on stage, a glass of whisky in one hand and the Microphone in the other. The audience didn't seem to mind and happily sang along with many of the songs. It was an unforgettable evening and great fun!

The "boys" were getting low on funds and decided to make Miami

Beach their last port of call before heading back home. Bill had an idea on how to pay for this last part of their trip. He had been told that Miami Beach was a popular winter destination amongst many New York women who were quite happy to leave their husbands hard at work while they enjoyed the sun and for the more adventurous, the company of young men. The last of their funds were used to pay for two sea view rooms in the Coral Hotel one of the newest and most glamorous hotels on the Beach.

That evening found them sitting at the bar and sure enough before long they were to be found in deep conversation with two attractive middle aged women. Three very enjoyable days followed and Bill left the hotel for the airport with an extra $500 in his pocket for "services rendered".

Once back at base he started to sell forward some of the consignments of salmon he had purchased to well established clients he had built up a close relationship with over the years, primarily in the UK but also in Holland and Paris.

At the same time, several interesting business side lines attracted the attention of the budding entrepreneur.

He acquired a part share in a processing plant located in Port St Mary on the Isle of Man which purchased scallops and scampi from local fisherman. The scallops were "shucked" and then packed into special cartons ready to be air freighted off the island. The scampi were sorted for size with the large ones being packed for export and the smaller ones having their meat removed which was then frozen ready for sale to downstream processors who would bread the scampi for sale to the catering trade.

Almost all exports were destined for the Paris market where Bill had maintained friendships from his Peabody days with many fish dealers in Les Halles. Timing was critical and the production had to be shipped out by air on a daily basis. In the event Manx Airport was closed for fog or bad weather that days' production would be immediately frozen. The use of aircraft to transport fresh produce was an invaluable lesson for Bill and was soon to come in very handy for his later excursions into airfreight logistics.

Around this time Bill was persuaded by his Norwegian friend Len to accept a consignment of reindeer skins for potential sale to some of London's leading department stores. He did manage to sell several lots to Harrods but the remaining stock remained in a large pile in his flat destined to eventually be given away as gifts. In the meantime they provided a very unusual bed in front of the fireplace and his girlfriends were often invited to disrobe and to lie on the skins, purely in order to test their "quality" of course!

He was also starting business with a new supplier based in Portland Maine. His name was Philip Willard and they were to become lifelong friends. Philips family owned lobster farms and also operated a shrimp processing plant.

Philip was well connected with a major New England pharmaceutical wholesaler who persuaded Bill that the introduction and use of the "pill" had made women far more adventurous in their sexual activities including discovering the joys of cunnilingus. To capitalise on this an American company under the brand "Cupids Quiver" had recently launched a range of flavoured douches which were gaining in popularity.

Backed by a heavy advertising campaign in many leading American magazines including Cosmopolitan, Harper's Bazaar and Mademoiselle the product had been launched with four different flavours - Raspberry, Champagne, Orange Blossom and Jasmine. Other flavours soon followed including pineapple, lemon & lime, cherry, peach and even the exotically named Rum & tutti fruitti!

Bill could certainly see a potential market in the UK! Philip arranged for him to be sent an initial stock of samples and promotional leaflets. As a first step he decided that he should test the product at first hand on his girlfriends who were invited to participate in "quality control" sessions at his flat; another use for the pile of reindeer skins! Samples were also handed out to his male friends for testing on their girlfriends. The test market proved to be a resounding success and, armed with samples and the appropriate literature; Bill made an appointment with the Harrods Pharmacy Buyer.

The meeting did not go well. The Buyer was a large woman of indeterminate age who became more and more agitated as Bill made his sales pitch and explained the good results obtained in their London test market. An embarrassing silence followed the presentation until he was politely shown the door with the words ringing in his ears "Not a suitable product for Harrods young man"!!

During this time Bill had a number of girlfriends and even became engaged to one of them - an English girl called Lindy Ingle but the relationship was not to last and he was soon to be seen in the company of a beautiful German student called Brigitte who was on an exchange programme to London from Heidelberg University. Her home town was Konstanz located on the lake of that name in southern Germany bordering both Switzerland and Austria.

The couple were soon engaged and that summer drove down from London to Konstanz for Bill to be introduced to Brigitte's parents. He received a warm welcome but was somewhat taken aback when her father proudly showed him his copy of Mein Kampf which had been personally signed by Hitler.

Until now Bill had focused his attention on America but around this time he set off in the opposite direction on what was to be the first of his many trips to Asia. The first port of call was Bombay where he was met by his friend and Indian agent Narayan Day.

Bill based himself in the sumptuous Taj Mahal Hotel which overlooked the Gateway to India Archway.

The first hotel to have electricity in India and the first in Asia to have air conditioning, it was also the place where Lord Mountbatten announced Indian Independence and where Pierre Cardin held the city's first fashion show. Visitors have included George V and Queen Mary, Aldous Huxley, George Bernard Shaw, Jackie Onassis, The Beatles, Mick Jagger, Madonna, the Dalai Lama, Presidents Clinton and Obama and Oprah Winfrey.

This is where Bill "arrived" on the sub continent to do business and from where he visited various frozen seafood plants located on the outskirts of Bombay including a huge plant specialising in the processing of frog's legs.

It was a nauseating experience to say the least. The frogs were collected overnight from drainage ditches all around the city and brought to the plant in large hessian sacks. The production line consisted of three moving conveyor belts at floor level with the middle belt moving in the opposite direction of the two outer belts. Sitting on each side of the outer belts were scores of people sitting on the floor each equipped with a large wooden block and a "meat chopper". The frogs were removed from the sacks, had their hind legs chopped off and still alive were thrown onto the outer belts. Meanwhile the legs were carefully placed on to the inner belt which moved them to another part of the plant for freezing and packaging.

Thereafter Bill was never able to eat frogs' legs again!

From India he flew to Kuala Lumpur and then to Penang where he was met by Mervyn Andreas, his first boss from his early Peabody days. Mervyn had left Peabody's and set himself up in business on his own buying and selling frozen shrimp produced in Malaysia. Mervyn took him to a number of major shrimp farms and production plants and their business relationship took a new turn when his old boss became Bill's agent in Malaysia. Bill subsequently became one of the major importers of frozen Malaysian shrimp into the UK.

In Penang he was introduced to a Chinese girl and decided to take an extended holiday break. The couple hired a car and drove South staying in the beautiful city of Ipoh in the Cameron Highlands, then on to Malacca and finally Jahore Bahru across the straits from his next destination, Singapore. Here they had to part company as his girlfriend was unable to obtain a visa to travel onwards with him to Singapore which had recently been expelled from the Malayan Union that formed Malaysia.

From Singapore he flew on to Hong Kong where he stayed at the recently completed Mandarin Hotel. He spent his time in the colony visiting frozen shrimp processing plants located in the fishing port of Aberdeen. At that time Aberdeen was a major fishing port with literally thousands of fishing vessels based there. Today the fish processing plants no longer exist and have been replaced with luxury apartments while the few remaining fishing boats now form what is called the floating village and earn their livelihood as water taxis taking tourists around the harbour area.

Bill returned to London and the engagement to Brigitte was soon to come to an end when Bill started dating his future wife Maria who had been introduced to him by his sister Tassie.

They had much in common as Maria also hailed from East Africa, lived in Earls Court together with three friends and worked at the London offices of a well known New York Advertising Agency called Benton & Bowles now owned by the French group Publicis. Yet another engagement soon followed but this time it was for real and soon elaborate wedding plans were afoot.

In 1966 they married at the Anglo-Catholic church of St Stephen in South Kensington with the reception in the Hyde Park Hotel. Bill had just taken delivery of a new red E Type Jaguar coupe in which the couple set off for St Tropez for their honeymoon the following day. It was to be an eventful honeymoon in more ways than one.

He had decided to drive there virtually nonstop throughout the night and had taken several Benzedrine pills in order to keep himself awake. However while driving down the main road south from Beaune at around 2.00 am he fell asleep at the wheel! The car roared off the highway into the forest alongside the road. By a miracle neither were seriously hurt almost certainly because both of them had been wearing newly introduced seat belts which were not a compulsory feature of cars until the next decade.

An ambulance soon arrived on the scene and carted the couple off to Beaune hospital where, much to their surprise, they were permitted to share a room. Help was soon at hand as Bill's sister Tassie, having heard about the accident, immediately entrained for Beaune arriving there the following day.

After several days under observation at the hospital the couple were allowed to proceed on their way and accompanied by Tassie, finally arrived in St Tropez. Luckily Tassie and Maria were the best of friends so having his sister accompanying them on honeymoon did not pose any problems.

St Tropez was famous for its nudist beaches despite the fact that beach nudity was still officially banned in France. Daily visits to Tahiti Beach, which ultimately became the world's first nudist beach, were the order of the day and the threesome took to it like ducks to water. However some days later the Police raided the beach and arrested all the naked girls including Maria and Tassie. It was a scene straight out of a movie with several dozen good looking young women being escorted by police in full uniform to waiting vans with husbands and boyfriends left trailing behind.

Wedding Day 1966

Understandingly the Police appeared to be enjoying themselves enormously and were good humoured. The same could not be said for the girls who were rather alarmed at being arrested. They were not allowed to dress but soon started to see the funny side of the incident and some, including Tassie and Maria, even started to flirt with their Police escorts.

Upon arrival at the police station they were held in several of the station's offices, booked and then released into the care of their very embarrassed men folk upon payment of a small fine for "offending public decency". At the end of their stay they caught a BEA Comet back to London from Nice.

Honeymoon over it was back to business!

CHAPTER 6

The Business Grows

Maria was soon pregnant and it was obvious that the Cornwall Gardens flat would no longer be suitable as a joint office and residence. Adrian, their first born and only son, was born on July 21st 1967 at the Harley Street Clinic.

The countryside beckoned and the couple found an idyllic riverside house on the Thames in Bray - a small village just outside Maidenhead in Berkshire. It was a beautiful sunny Edwardian house with formal gardens fronting directly on to the river.

Meanwhile Bill had moved his company's offices to a spacious Georgian house situated on the Kings Road in Reading.

The Company was expanding rapidly and by now had a staff of seven. It was fast becoming one of the leading importers of frozen commodities into the UK representing a number of leading international frozen food processing plants.

Salmon and shellfish remained the most profitable parts of the business and Bill continued his annual spring visits to the West Coast of America moving between Alaska, Canada, Washington State down to the Oregon border where he usually ended his salmon purchases at Bumble Bee Seafoods followed by several days of fine fishing for King Salmon at the mouth of the Columbia River.

It wasn't just about the seafood, by now the company had also substantially increased its range of vegetables and fruit - all packed in bulk for further processing or ready packed for the wholesale catering industry.

Imports flowed in from across the world primarily into the ports of London and Liverpool where the company had leased cold storage facilities or from Europe by refrigerated truck or railway wagons through the channel ports.

This included salmon and king crab from Alaska, broccoli, spinach cauliflower and melon balls from California, peas from Maryland, shrimp and lobsters from Maine, strawberries from Mexico, salmon and vegetables from British Columbia, sweet corn from Ontario, lobsters and lobster meat from Nova Scotia, hake from South Africa, shrimp and frogs' legs from India, shrimp from Malaysia, Thailand and Hong Kong, asparagus from Taiwan and salmon and halibut from Hokkaido in Japan.

It was around this time that Bill decided to test the feasibility of supplying live fishery products to fish wholesalers in not just the UK but also Holland and Sweden using chartered aircraft.

Jet aircraft were becoming bigger, and so had greater capacity as well as being able to fly for long distances nonstop. Chartering aircraft for the first time was to be the trigger that started his lifelong interest in aviation and lead to his subsequent career in aviation.

Two products in particular were suited to this new form of rapid transportation, live eels to London and Holland and live lobsters to Sweden.

The eels came from New Zealand and were stunned using electric shock guns, packed into ice and flown as belly cargo by Air New Zealand trans Pacific then via New York to London. Upon arrival the ice was removed and the eels would gradually come out of their enforced coma to become "alive" again with no apparent damage or side effects. The key to the operation was a logistics time frame no longer than 48 hours. Any longer and the eels would never survive.

The lobsters, packed in wooden boxes with seaweed and ice came from Maine, were trucked to Boston thence flown to Stockholm by chartered TWA aircraft. At that time there were virtually no dedicated cargo aircraft so the seats had to be removed to make way for the lobster boxes.

The first flight as a test run of 10,000 lobsters was a great success with only 16 lobsters arriving dead at their destination.

Bill's father Edward had by now left Kenya and joined the firm, suggesting that they should also expand their activities to include the freezing of UK produced berries primarily in Scotland and Cambridgeshire. His father's knowledge of the fruit industry from his time in Norfolk and Kenya proved invaluable. New technologies were adopted and the company became one of the very first producers to use liquid nitrogen for the production of frozen strawberries and raspberries.

Bill also believed that in the future retail stores, selling only frozen products, could be successful and he decided to open a trial store in north London to test his theory directly on the public. The store known as Frozen Foods Unlimited opened in Swiss Cottage in 1968 and was the forerunner of similar Bejam stores set up by Bill's close friend John Apthorp.

Bejam, supposedly named after the first names of the Apthorp family, grew continuously and more than proved Bill's theory. They were eventually bought out by the far smaller Iceland chain in 1989, a move which netted the Apthorp family around £15 million, funds that were subsequently to acquire the company who became the Majestic Wine chain.

Frozen Foods Unlimited never made money but was an extremely useful tool to test market the frozen products that Bill was to pioneer in years to come.

CHAPTER 7

Potatoes 1969-71

Around a year after moving out of London to Bray, Bill and Maria decided they needed a bigger house so in 1968 they moved into a large Victorian house in Camberley and engaged the services of a full time Norland nanny - a formidable woman called Margot.

The couple had become interested in motor sports and were soon to be found at weekends racing their E Type Jaguar at various amateur race meetings. They became founder members of the British Drag Racing Association and were soon entering races at the Santa Pod Raceway in Bedfordshire.

The sport at that time was new to the UK having arrived first in 1964. The biggest problem was finding a suitably long piece of tarmac. The disused RAF Poddington airfield was purchased by the Association in 1966 and Santa Pod was born - a combination of the old RAF name and California where the sport originated. It was the first drag racing venue in Europe on a disused air base.

The Jaguar was sold and replaced by a custom built Marcos designed for the racetrack and a 1966 model Gordon-Keeble as their family car.

Both cars were rather unusual to say the least. The Marcos 1800 GT had a fibre glass body built on to a wooden chassis and at Bill's request the 1800cc Volvo engine was bored out to 2000cc, fitted with high compression cylinders and Weber carburettors. The car was extremely light, very fast and somewhat of a fire hazard.

Returning from a race meeting with the Markos on a hot summer's day the couple were caught in a traffic jam in North London and before long flames from the open Webers caused the engine chassis to catch fire. Bill had forgotten the fire extinguisher so Maria dashed into an adjacent off license and returned with a crate of lemonade. and, assisted by the onlookers who had gathered to watch, the fire was soon put out.

The Gordon-Keeble was very different - it was a fast and comfortable car. When introduced in 1964 it was the fastest four-seater car in the world with a top speed of 140 mph. The cars had a fibre glass body and were powered by a huge Chevrolet V8 5.4 litre engines designed for use in the Corvette Stingray. Only 100 units were ever produced and Bill had purchased number 49. They proved to be very reliable and there are still 90 of them on the road!

International jet travel had become much more the norm so the couple were soon spending long weekends in New York, in Maine with their friends the Willards and in Palm Beach Florida. Trips were made to Nassau in the Bahamas where they bought a building plot.

Meanwhile the business was growing but Bill wanted a greater presence in the frozen vegetable market - in particular the really high volume British basics such as potatoes and peas.

He cultivated a strong relationship with a major grower of peas in Yorkshire and arranged for the crop to be processed and stored in bulk one ton storage pallets at a nearby frozen food plant for subsequent packing under his own two labels - Chefs Choice and Angelus - or for other catering distributors under their label.

The market for frozen chips was also growing fast and the UK lacked processing capacity so he linked up with a major US producer based in Maine called Potato Services and started to import their potato products into the UK for sale to major independent distributors.

The Potato Services plant was situated in northern Maine adjacent to the Canadian border near the town of Presque Isle in Aroostook County and by the late sixties had become one of the world's largest frozen potato plants. The General Manager was a dynamic New Yorker of Greek origin from Brooklyn called Bill Angelus who, by a remarkable coincidence, shared the same surname as one of Bill's two vegetable brands!!

Mr. Angelus was not a man to be crossed. Bill had arrived from England for his first visit to the plant late in the evening and was picked up at the airport and taken to the local hotel invariably used by the Plant. They arrived about 10.00 pm and went to the bar for a quick nightcap only to be told by a rather abrupt barman that the bar always closed at 10.00 pm. Bill Angelus politely asked him to make an exception as his guest had just arrived that day from England and was in urgent need of a welcome drink. The barman refused whereupon Bill Angelus called the owner of the hotel, made him an offer to purchase the property which was accepted on the spot and guess what - promptly fired the barman and walked behind the bar himself in order to serve Bill his long awaited Scotch and water!

The two Bills got on like a house on fire and numerous escapades were to follow with the duo often accompanied by Bill's old friend Philip

Willard from Portland Maine.

When visiting Bill would usually fly into Portland and then Potato Services would send over their private aircraft to pick them up or if the weather was good the pair would drive the 300 miles to the plant.

Bill Angelus was crazy about horses - in particular Trotters or Harness Racing where the jockey sits on a light weight two wheeled cart called a Sulky. Many weekends were spent flying on the Company's aircraft to various race track venues around the North East with Philadelphia being their favourite. They always stayed at hotels situated within the vicinity of the race tracks. Long post race sessions would usually find the trio propping up the race course bar accompanied by women they had managed to "chat up" during the races to be followed by dinner and, if they were lucky, a romp in bed later.

Potato Services put Bill in a position to compete strongly in the UK frozen potato market with Harrison McCain's plant in Yorkshire presenting virtually his only major competition. Imports were inevitably however only a stop gap measure due to the shipping costs and he realised that the future lay in building his own potato processing plant in England.

How to achieve this aim and how to raise the money?

He decided to make the best use of his strong relationships with both Potato Services and Christian Salvesen who already provided his company with freezing facilities in Scotland for his fruit production together with cold storage and refrigerated trucking in other locations.

Christian Salvesen based in Leith and with a history dating back to its whaling roots in South Georgia had by this time become the largest provider of cold storage and refrigerated trucks in the UK.

Potato Services agreed to participate in the Project by offering to design the plant, supervise the building and to train the plant management. Christian Salvesen agreed to build the cold storage adjacent to the plant and to provide the freezing facilities.

Bill had by this time also established a strong links with two of Lincolnshire's largest potato growers Tony Keene and Jim Beelby who would be able to source and supervise the supply of raw material to the plant. His next step was to form a joint venture company with the farmers and Potato Services to be called Potato and Allied Services or PAS for short and to raise the necessary capital of £600,000 - a lot of money in the 1960's, the equivalent of £10 million in today's money.

Salvesen's introduced Bill to Kleinwort Benson - a leading merchant bank in the City. The Bank agreed to put up the capital required and the search was soon underway for a suitable site in Lincolnshire.

The criteria for the site was to have good access to the A1 highway which linked London to the South and Edinburgh to the North, an ample water supply and a nearby river into which clean treated waste water could be safely discharged. The perfect site was found near Easton just south of Grantham adjacent to the A1 highway.

The site was a disused iron ore mine - level above ground with lots of water available to be pumped from the mine itself and a northward descent leading to a perfectly located small river called the Witham. Work started in 1969 and by 1970 the plant was completed just in time for the main potato harvest.

That same year Bill relocated his Company and its staff to Lincolnshire where custom built offices were erected alongside the plant ensuring that everyone was "under one roof".

He leased a large country house at nearby Boothby Pagnell while his parents moved to the neighbouring village of Braceby. Bill and Maria happily settled into their new country life style and Bill was to be found at most of the local shoots during the season.

Life was hectic for Bill with two separate operations to worry about - as well as his own importing and distribution business he now had the challenge of supervising a major production plant and integrating its production into his overall sales structure.

By the following Spring it was obvious that the potato operations would require additional working capital. Christian Salvesen offered to purchase the plant leaving Bill's company to market the production.

Potato Services were against this move and Bill Angelus flew over to London with a cashier's cheques of one million dollars in order to pay off Kleinwort Benson so that the plant could remain independent but Bill and his two farming partners decided the risks were too great so they finally opted, albeit reluctantly, to sell the plant to Salvesen's.

To remain independent from the Salvesen operation Bill moved his entire operations to much larger offices in Grantham thus ensuring that he remained close to the potato plant and the cold storage warehouses from which he ran his national distribution while at the same time remaining fully independent from the Christian Salvesen operations.

The new offices represented something of a fresh start and enabled him to not only re-organise his administration and sales team but also to set up a better fleet management structure as his fleet of trucks now offered scheduled deliveries to the entire United Kingdom with distribution cost controls becoming of paramount importance.

What he needed was a state of the art logistics management system so he decided to invest in a Phillips computer system - one of the first ever to be used in Britain for logistic planning. The investment was huge for those times being over £100,000 in capital costs together with the additional costs of a dedicated air conditioned and humidity controlled computer room. Five technicians were required to operate the system. Today a simple PC costing a few hundred pounds would easily be able to fulfil the same function!

He needed more working capital and was able to negotiate funding from an old established City institution called Gray Dawes who were part of the publicly traded Inchcape Group.

Bill appointed a new national Director of Sales to head up his marketing team and to select, train and recruit a new sales team properly equipped and trained to present the company's ever increasing range of products to existing distributors and the new wave of Frozen Food Centres which were opening up across the country.

Noel Fletcher, the new Sales Director, brought with him a totally new marketing concept which he had successfully recently introduced into Young's Seafoods.

The existing industry system of area representatives visiting or calling wholesalers weekly for their orders was scrapped. A new national sales team of highly trained and motivated women operating from the Grantham Head Office was put in place to telephone each wholesaler on a regular schedule at the time and day most convenient to the wholesaler.

The Salesmen were no longer to take orders but to now focus purely on the promotion and introduction of the Company's products, listen to customer suggestions on new products or different packaging styles and to sort out any issues or problems that might be troubling the wholesaler.

The concept was a huge success and soon the Company became the largest independent national distributor of frozen foods in the country.

The range of frozen products the company now offered was dramatically increased to include a range of American style ice creams, cakes, pies and other bakery goods, prepared meals and exotic vegetables.

These products were no longer targeted specifically at the catering trade outlets but also the newly emerging frozen food retailers like Bejam whose sale of freezers in turn drove forward the ever increasing acceptance of frozen foods. This in turn stimulated public demand and soon the major stores such as Harrods, John Lewis and Selfridges were stocking the company's products.

The Company was being "noticed" and was soon destined to become the target of several take over propositions by larger players within the food industry.

CHAPTER 8

1970-1974

The early seventies were a period of considerable social upheaval in Britain marked by unemployment, strikes and power cuts on the one hand but massive increases in property values - both housing and land -had led to the creation of a new class of secondary banks and higher interest rates were fuelling the boom. Fortunes were being made in the city. New stores such as Biba and Habitat, night clubs, restaurants and bars were all the rage.

The jet age and the introduction of the first "jumbo jets" opened up a new lifestyle for those who became known as the "jetsetters". The Beatles and similar groups such as the Rolling Stones had reinvented the music scene. Wide use of the contraceptive pill had created an atmosphere of "free love" while Woodstock in 1969 had marked the epicentre of this new social culture to which so many aspired.

Pellew-Harvey & Co was booming and now employed an increasing number of attractive young women in the sale and administration departments. Bill was starting to participate in a life style which would ultimately prove disastrous for his marriage to Maria.

Noel Fletcher was of a similar ilk and between them they bedded most if not all the women in the company and numerous others whom they met in the course of exhibitions, business meetings and their excursions abroad to Europe and the United States. They often shared their women together - even swapping partners on the same bed.

Maria to her eternal credit chose to turn a blind eye to most of Bill's activities.

During this time Bill had met Tania Szabo at a function in London and they were to renew their friendship decades later by which time Tania had settled in Wales. Both her parents had been killed during the war. Her father, an officer in the French Foreign Legion had been killed in action in North Africa in 1942. Tania's mother, Violette Szabo whose mother tongue was French, joined the British Intelligence as a field officer in the SOE (Special Operations executive). She paid a terrible price for her bravery when she was captured at a German road block in France in 1944 and subsequently executed by the Nazis at the notorious Ravensbruck camp in 1945. She was posthumously awarded the George Cross which Tania had received on behalf of her mother while still a child.

It was an amazing coincidence as another war time heroine, Odette Hallowes, who was related to Bill via his mother's side of the family when she married Geoffrey Hallowes, had also worked for British Intelligence in the SOE was captured in France by the Nazis in the same period during 1943. Tortured and sentenced to death she was also despatched to Ravensbruck but survived.

She was also one of the only six women ever to be awarded the George Cross.

Throughout this period Bill started to present a more public persona.

Like his father he was a member of the Devonshire Club - later to merge with the East India Club - where he joined The "Thunderers" - a dining and debating Society within the Club.

He was invited to join the UK branch of the Young Presidents Organisation (YPO). Founded in the USA in 1950 the YPO has become a global leadership community of chief executives.

In 1973 he was proposed as a member of a City Livery Company - The Worshipful Company of Fruiterers and was made a Freeman of the City of London.

In 1974 he was elected President of the British Frozen Food Association.

He was invited to join the children's charitable trust known as the "Guild of the 19 Lubricators" whose unusual nomenclature originated from the founders members having oil industry backgrounds. Founded in 1936 during the Depression the charity raised substantial funds for underprivileged children's charity projects. Monthly dinners were held at the Belfry and the annual service at St Margaret's Westminster. Bill was to become the President of the Charity for 1976.

His interest in cars continued with the acquisition of a Jensen Interceptor and subsequently a Citroen Maserati.

For more formal occasions and visits to London Bill bought a large Mercedes and engaged the services of a full time chauffeur named Albert who was a former fire truck driver. His driving manoeuvres and constant use of the horn, if traffic was heavy in and around London, were highly alarming to say the least and Bill would be left slumped in the back seat hiding behind his newspaper while Albert appeared totally oblivious to the trail of irate drivers left behind!

The Company continued to expand and, at the suggestion of the Board, Bill and Maria took a sabbatical in the summer of '73 in Maine to stay with their friends, the Willards. Philip Willard, who came from an old Maine family, introduced Bill and Maria to many of his friends during this visit.

They spent time with the painter Jon S Legere. Jon was a truly larger than life character and a fine artist to boot. Today his paintings fetch very high prices. Jon worked for half the year and then spent the following six months "enjoying himself" which was his anachronism for entertaining young ladies.

In the summer months he was usually to be found on his own in his railway caboose which had been shunted into a very remote siding in the countryside where he painted. In the fall he would return to his loft apartment in Portland which featured a large double bed suspended from the ceiling by strong ropes. Here Jon would entertain his friends and girlfriends whom he always referred to as his models. Champagne was very much the order of the day and then the bed was duly lowered once he had persuaded his models to undress.

Despite his unusual life style Jon was an excellent husband and father. He adored his wives and could often be seen in Portland's main street shopping for clothes and shoes trailed by his current wife and teenage daughters who were all of a similar age.

Winter saw Jon established in Nassau where he would sell his paintings, produced during the previous summer, in a fine art gallery. Even in those days his paintings were fetching upwards of ten thousand dollars.

Bill and Maria together with Philip were invited by friends of the Willard family for weekends at the Hamptons and to the Palm Beach Estate of the Whitney Payson family, the American business and charitable dynasty.

Meanwhile on Britain's economic front dark clouds were gathering. By October 1973 bank rates had reached a record high of 13% and what became known as the "oil crisis" started the following month.

CHAPTER 9

The Secondary Banking Crisis & Potatoes Again 1973-1975

The secondary banking crisis of 1973-1975 saw a dramatic crash in British property prices that caused dozens of small "secondary" banks to be threatened with bankruptcy. Many of these banks had been borrowing heavily to support their loan portfolios. The sudden downturn in the housing market, ever rising interest rates and the oil crisis were the "straw that broke the camel's back".

The secondary banking market had also attracted a new breed of banking entrepreneur led by the likes of Jim Slater of Slater Walker & Co. These new bankers were not traditional City Bankers - they were tough ruthless risk takers from working class backgrounds who often derided their more cautious colleagues in the old established banks. The Bank of England bailed out several dozen of the smaller banks and intervened to assist thirty or so others.

No depositors lost their money but the cost to the Bank of England was substantial. The downturn was made worse by the stock market crash. Unfortunately for Bill his bankers Grey Dawes fell into severe difficulties and were soon scrambling for cash flow in order to remain afloat. Many "on demand loans" were called, including loans which had been advanced to Bill's company, early in the New Year of 1974.

The board were unable to raise new liquidity and the decision was made, albeit very reluctantly, to sell the business to Sears Holdings owned by the Clore family. Sears was acquired by Charles Clore in 1953 and within 10 years owned virtually every brand of shoe shop on the high street except for Clarks. Sears Holdings spent the 1960's branching out by taking over Lewis's, Selfridges, bookmakers William Hill and a major Liverpool based bakery chain called Reeces. By 1976 Clore had either sold or moved a number of his acquisitions including W.B. Pellew-Harvey & Co, Reeces Bakery and the jewellers Mappin & Webb into another of his financial conglomerates called AG Clothing - an eclectic mix to say the least!

In 1980 Sears sold the company by then known as P-H Foods to Kellogg's.

Bill had reached a private cash settlement with Sears upon condition that he would not compete directly with the company's frozen food distribution business for a minimum period of two years.

This did of course not prevent him from trading in frozen foods and left him free to go back to the roots of his business as a trader in food commodities.

In a matter of weeks he and Maria moved from Lincolnshire to a large 5 bed roomed flat in Albert Court Mansions adjacent to the Albert Hall and Kensington Gardens. Their son Adrian remained happily settled into life at Bill's old school, Taverham Hall in Norfolk.

Despite having no office Bill started to trade again - one of the first to establish a "home office". Business was soon thriving to the point where an office and small staff became essential.

Some friends offered him the use of the ground floor of their house in Holland Park just a short walk from home or a few minutes by car. There he installed a small team of traders.

Whilst business was on the up again his personal life was less successful and, and although he was shocked and disappointed, he realised that he only had himself to blame!

Maria had met Michael Denning who was to become her future companion and husband.

She told Bill that she had decided to leave him and to relocate with Michael to Richmond Virginia.

Amazingly enough they remained close friends and lovers right up to the day of Maria's departure from London to move in with Michael in the USA. There were no rows or disagreements - just a gentle sadness that this had come to pass and how essential it was to ensure their son's ongoing happiness and security. The friendship was to remain intact throughout their lives and Michael and Bill were to become close friends.

Whilst fidelity had never been his strong point Bill was now officially a bachelor again in the swinging London of the seventies with a beautiful apartment in one of the best locations in the city. His first steps were to become super fit again so he started a rigorous training routine based on an early morning swim every day, thrice weekly visits to the gym and off track motorcycling in Yorkshire on many weekends.

Philip Willard, who was also now a Bachelor again, became a frequent visitor to London and the pair would also weekend in New York at the Essex House Hotel on Central Park South. Philip would travel down from Maine accompanied by his current girlfriend together with a "blind date" for Bill whilst other times he would arrange for a couple of high-end escort girls to join them.

They would reserve a two bed roomed suite overlooking Central Park which they rarely left thanks to the hotel's excellent room service and the entertainment on offer. They always retained the services of a very discrete butler who never turned a hair even when asked to perform some unusual versions of room service.

There was a classic occasion when the boys persuaded one of the girls to lie naked in the bathtub while the butler was instructed to open a magnum of champagne and to pour the entire contents over the young woman which he proceeded to do without comment other than saying "excuse me madam, this may be a little chilly"!

Although he partied hard Bill also worked extremely hard and the wheel of fortune turned yet again in his favour.

In 1975 the summer drought reduced potato crops across Europe but Britain was hit the hardest with a drop of 2.5 million tons and by Christmas potato prices had tripled.

In response to this Bill travelled to Prince Edward Island, which produced over 25% of all potatoes grown in Canada, to meet Mitch Maclean who owned the largest potato processing plant on Prince Edward Island. Mitch was emerging as a competitor to McCain Foods who dominated the frozen potato chip or "French fry" market in Canada as the Americans liked to call them.

Mitch was having difficulty selling all of his production in Canada so was a willing seller when Bill arrived in his office. Bill contracted to purchase 50,000 tons of frozen French fries in 2lb and 5lb bags suitable for both the retail and catering markets for delivery over a seven month period.

The next matter to be addressed was how to ship economically this vast quantity of deep frozen goods from Canada to the UK and other North European ports. Bill contacted friends in London's Baltic Exchange and arranged to charter a fleet of Danish and Icelandic freezer vessels.

These ships, which had originally been designed for transporting frozen whale meat, were ideal due to their relatively small size so could unload in smaller ports with lower port charges. Each ship could hold up to 1500 tons of packed frozen French fries.

1976 was turning out to be even dryer than the previous year and potato supplies dried up. The few plants that processed potatoes in the UK were stopping production due to a lack of available raw material.

There was virtually no rainfall and by mid summer temperatures were reaching 32C on a daily basis, water was to become strictly rationed throughout the UK and even the use of outdoor sports facilities were limited due to the dryness of the ground.

The price of potatoes and potato products continued to rise! Bill started to make a small fortune by selling his Canadian supplies at a premium to all the major frozen food companies in the UK, Ireland and northern Europe.

He avoided the major ports and would choose any smallish port with decent facilities that suited his customers. Amongst the most popular were Hull, Grimsby, Newhaven, Bristol, Dublin and Eindhoven.

His sales strategy was simple. Discuss and agree with the client the quantity available, month of shipment and their preferred port leaving price to the very last.

In fact the market was so "hot" that he started to just politely advise the client the price he was going to charge on a take it or leave it basis.

It was a few hectic months with the entire quantity contracted to clients and the last shipments arriving in late August. In September it finally started to rain, the drought ended and potato prices started to return to more normal levels.

During this period Bill had started to investigate his ability to trade for the first time outside the food industry. His team took into their stride trades in almost any item that might be sold to the supermarket chains from lavatory rolls to distressed stocks of biscuits.

He had been introduced to two very smart electronics engineers, Mike and Paul Arnold the owners of a company called Guartel, who were developing products for electronic eavesdropping and related countermeasures specifically for use by security services - both governmental and private.

They had also developed a very powerful metal detector called the MD-4 which was capable of finding small metal objects at depths of up to 6 feet. Ideally suited for use by the security services it was to prove extremely effective in locating underground arms caches and mines.

This period was during the height of the IRA troubles and the Prevention of Terrorism Act was in place in Northern Ireland.

Bill could see the potential market and agreed to set up a separate company called Bonaventure Security to market abroad the equipment produced by the Arnold brothers on an exclusive basis. As part of the arrangement he agreed to employ a professional sales director and to open a USA branch sales office.

A new chapter in his future business career was about to unfold.

CHAPTER 10

Thailand 1976-1978

In the autumn of 1976 Bill had a meeting in London with an Israeli business man called Shaul Eisenberg.

Shaul was one of Israel's richest entrepreneurs with a huge business empire that stretched from the United States and Europe to Korea and Japan, he was also a pioneer in trading with China. A special law had been passed by the Israeli Knesset granting him tax immunity for a 30 year period. His companies sold everything from pig iron to food products to military equipment and were at that time extending their operations into Thailand.

The Vietnam war had finally ended the previous year but had left the area with communist rule in Vietnam, the Marxist Pathet Lao controlling Laos coupled with the Khmer Rouge in Cambodia. The Western powers, in particular the Americans, had become extremely anxious about the so called "domino" effect. Thailand was now on the front line!

Eisenberg had met with the Thai King and his senior military advisors some months earlier and the Monarch was understandably concerned over the long term stability of his dynasty in Thailand.

The previous year had seen the fall of the ruling families in neighbouring Laos and Cambodia following the fall of the Khmer monarchy five years earlier. Myanmar (Burma) also was in a state of unrest with warlords controlling much of the South and Eastern parts of country financed by the opium trade.

Many American service personnel had returned from Vietnam addicted to the opium based narcotics being grown in North Eastern Thailand - the so called Golden Triangle - and being transported into Burma across the totally porous border. Anti-Government student demonstrations had broken out in Bangkok the first week of October culminating in a massacre by the military on October 6th. Many students were arrested and martial law had been imposed.

Eisenberg had presented an interesting plan to the Thai leadership.

The plan involved the setting up of a special task force to substantially reduce opium production. In return the Eisenberg Group would be licensed by the Thai Government to build and operate food processing plants in the north of the country and to be given priority treatment for the supply of "security equipment" to the Thai Armed Forces.

It was to be called the Kings Programme sponsored by the King and operated under the auspices of the United Nations Drug Eradication Programme. The Israelis were to provide "security personnel" to guarantee the safety of those involved in the front line of the programme. The UN were to provide agricultural advisors and the Thai Government were to provide translators who were familiar with the various dialects spoken by the hill tribes. Air support would be provided by the Thai Air Force for both surveillance and firepower.

The Eisenberg team asked Bill to meet Shaul during one of his London visits to discuss "a project in Thailand". They had already been in contact with him about the supply of Guartel produced security equipment including "bug detectors", active bugging equipment and long range night vision scopes known as thermal imaging devices.

At the meeting the scope of the Project was explained in detail. It was designed to persuade the hill tribes of the Golden Triangle to discontinue the cultivation of opium poppies by offering them assistance and incentives to cultivate alternative cash crops, primarily vegetables, which would be suitable for food processing for ultimate export to the UK and Europe. Free seeds would be provided by the Government in the initial phases and guarantees were given by the production plants to purchase the produce.

The food processing complex being built between Chiang Mai and Chiang Rai was to consist of three plants - one for canned vegetables, a second for frozen vegetables and the third for dehydrated foods.

Bill was already travelling to Thailand on a regular basis visiting frozen shrimp suppliers so volunteering to join the programme was a logical step. He agreed to engage a suitable British General Manager to oversee the food processing plants while Bill himself was ideally placed to sell all the finished products to the food markets that he knew so well, on an exclusive basis of course.

Agreement was reached between the parties which appeared to offer a win-win situation for all concerned.

He quickly put in place an experienced General Manager who had worked for him before in Grantham to oversee the completion of the production plants. With that in hand he embarked on the first of his many "inspection" expeditions to the hill tribes accompanied by Mike

Arnold co- owner of Guartel.

The programme's operational base had been set up in Chiang Mai so the pair, travelled by road from there up to Chiang Rai. They formed an unusual group, two Thai girls for companionship, two UN Translators and a local guide. The latter were also fluent in the two main languages of the hill tribes - Akha and Karen.

The distance between the two towns was just under 200 kilometres - a journey of about 3-4 hours at that time and thence up to the Burmese and Laotian border area a further 200 kilometres north. They drove north beyond the small town of Chiang Saen a few miles from the Laos border. Having parked their vehicle at a Thai Army Rangers camp they then set out by foot up into the hills to visit villages which had been selected by the UN team as being "suitable" for the crop replacement and poppy eradication programme.

Some larger villages had road access which would be essential for the collection of harvested crops for the food processing factories but many villages were extremely remote with no roads or possible access by any type of vehicle. The only access was by foot or by helicopter in emergency although even these had a very limited use as landings were difficult due to the heavily forested topography.

One of the tasks ahead was to set up a supply chain from these remote villages to the nearest road.

Each village was ruled by a chief or elder who answered for the actions of the entire village. They had little contact with the outside world and were entirely self sufficient. The villages were usually located in forested valleys with fresh springs or streams providing year round water supplies.

Adjacent forest areas had been cleared for growing crops for food and in many cases opium poppies.

Each village harvested its own opium resin which was air dried and stored for subsequent use as a medication for cuts and wounds, smoking and for sale to the Burmese opium traders.

It was very unusual for any of the villages to become involved in the actual processing of the opium into heroin but not totally unknown. Harsh punishment was meted out by the Thai authorities if processing facilities were found including the bombing of the facility and the arrest of the village headman together with any others who were supposedly involved in the refining process.

After visiting several nearby villages, the UN inspectors and their guide suggested that they should climb high up into the hills to visit more remote locations. They set out early the next morning with their two female companions, translators and guide and headed for the hills. After a strenuous days' climbing they set up camp in the late afternoon on a remote hill side near a thermal pool they had discovered.

After their long climb Mike, Bill and the girls stripped off and started to relax in the warm murky waters. Suddenly they realised that they had unexpected visitors! A group of camouflaged and heavily armed soldiers had emerged in total silence from the forest and were advancing on the encampment. A short exchange of words with the translators and the officer leading the patrol followed and, much to their relief, Bill and his entourage were advised that a troop of Hmong soldiers had decided to investigate the presence of "strangers" in their territory.

Most of us have never heard about the Hmong and therein lies an interesting piece of history.

The Hmong people have never had a country of their own. They were originally from the mountainous regions of what is now Southern China. In the 1600s Chinese authorities started to persecute them and many migrated to neighbouring countries.

During the Chinese civil war in the period 1927 -1950 they had allied themselves with Chang Kai Chek's Nationalists and had fought tenaciously against the Communists throughout that period.

By 1949 the Chinese Red army had finally won the long drawn out civil war and the Nationalists withdrew their forces to Formosa later renamed as Taiwan. However a number of Nationalist divisions including the Hmong had become cut off from the main Nationalist Army and were forced by the advancing communists, together with their families, to flee south and west across the borders into Laos, Vietnam, Thailand and Myanmar.

The Thai Government backed by the Americans and French had welcomed the presence of these virulently anti communist forces on their border. Communist insurgency was becoming rife throughout the region with the French battling Ho Chi Min in Vietnam, the British in Malaya and Burma and the Dutch in Indonesia.

Following the outbreak of the Korean war in 1950 United Nations forces were soon confronting the North Koreans and Chinese in a war that ended in a truce dividing up the country between North and South.

A year after the truce in Korea the French left Vietnam in 1954, after five years of fighting and that country too was divided into the communist North and democratic South. Within a year the fiercely anti- communist

Ngo Dinh Dien seized power in the South and started a purge against alleged communists and 100,000 people were rounded up, tortured and executed.

Not surprisingly the communist north took exception and another war broke out that was to drag on for 20 years spreading into Cambodia and Laos. The Americans were soon to become involved in sending advisors and later troops to prop up the anti-communist Government of South Vietnam.

The American intelligence agencies realised that they had a potentially valuable fighting force well versed in guerrilla warfare sitting on their doorstep on the North East Thai border. Thus a deal was struck with the Thai Government and the Hmong - its status quo remains until today.

In 2019 it was estimated that more than half of their 7 million population was spread across those countries with many others as far afield as Australia and America. In Thailand the greatest concentration of the Hmong people remained in the heavily forested hill country by the boarders with Laos and Myanmar.

Bill and his little party were permitted to continue their journey and they trekked ever higher through thick forest and finally just before nightfall arrived at a remote and hidden village located in a small valley under a canopy of trees. Their arrival roused much curiosity and they learned from the translators that they were the first white people that many villagers had ever seen.

They were given a friendly greeting by the village chief and shown to a raised hut which was to be their accommodation. The village was remarkably well organised and totally self sufficient as it had no contact with the outside world.

They even had running water! It was piped to each hut from a stream via an ingenious system of overhead piping using hollowed out bamboo poles to function as the pipes. Holes at various points in the system plugged with bamboo encased in pieces of cloth ensured fresh cold water was instantly available "on tap". All you had to do was to remove the plug and you could instantly fill your water urn or take a shower!

There was even a village forge adjacent to a vein of iron ore for the production of hand held agricultural implements, metal cooking pots and other metal oddments. The little smelter was heated by charcoal with the pressurised air produced by a foot operated animal skin bellows.

Currency, for any type of financial transaction, was based on King George V florins which had a 92% or 50% pure silver content depending on the year of minting. These coins had been in wide circulation in Burma and throughout parts of South East Asia since the 1920s and remained as a currency of choice amongst the hill tribes throughout much of the 20th century.

The coins were also used by the women of the tribe to make necklaces. Tiny holes were made in the centre of the coins which were then strung together and worn around the neck and sometimes around the waist. They were very highly sought after and a woman's status within the tribe was dictated by the number of coins she wore.

The next day the party set out on a tour of inspection accompanied by the Chief who had assured them that any nearby arable plots were being prepared for food crops only - not for opium poppies!

Little did the Chief know that Bill had in his possession maps and aerial reconnaissance photos supplied by the Royal Thai Air Force which showed more distant hillsides with a number of suspicious looking plots that were probably poppy fields. Following inspection of the arable plots the party requested a further inspection of some of these more remote fields.

The Chief became very uneasy but could hardly refuse so they set off using the photos and a compass to guide them. Sure enough an hour or so later they eventually located several large poppy fields in a small valley. It was obvious from the maturity of the seed heads that the plants had already been "cut" prior to "milking".

The Chief apologised profusely for their "mistake"!

Given that the programme was still in the very early stages the UN inspectors decided to take no further action but warned the Chief that any repetition could well result in his arrest and severe penalties being imposed on the village. It was in reality a somewhat idle threat as the village was so remote as to be virtually immune from any form of policing or governmental control.

It made Bill realise that from a practical point of view the economics of growing cash crops for processing as opposed to opium poppies would have to be restricted to those areas that had sufficient road access, however remote, to the crop collection points for subsequent delivery to the food processing plants.

Two days later the party were back in Chiang Mai for some R & R followed by debriefing meetings in Bangkok and then it was back to London.

Many trips followed and Chiang Mai became de facto Bill's second home for a time, he directed his business via telex from his office in the hotel and his son Adrian spent part of his school holidays there. Adrian loved Chiang Mai and spent a lot of time with Bill's Thai girlfriend May and her family who lived in a small village some miles outside the town. He would travel around on the back of May's motorbike.

By the early spring of 1977 the processing plants had been completed and the first vegetable crops - primarily green beans and sweet corn - were starting to be delivered by the growers. Bill organised the first of a number of visits by senior supermarket buyers from the UK to Thailand.

The trips of course proved to be highly popular as he paid all the expenses and provided "local entertainment". The visits had a fairly set formula which worked well for all concerned.

The first few days were spent in Bangkok sightseeing during daytime with after dinner visits to a high-class massage parlour followed by visits to the red-light district of Patpong for further "entertainment". Patpong was always thronged with foreign visitors and US military personnel on R&R and provided very raunchy entertainment including extraordinary feats of vaginal muscular demonstrations. Throughout the trip, starting from the moment of their arrival, the visitors were provided with twice daily heavy doses of penicillin to ensure they did not take any "unpleasant gifts" back to their wives or girlfriends!

The party would then fly up to Chiang Mai to inspect the production facilities followed by more "local entertainment" and most importantly for Bill the signing of purchase contracts he had prepared in advance for product shipment to the UK over the coming months. The entire production output of the plants was invariably signed up in a matter of hours!

Then it was back to Bangkok for a three day visit to Pattaya - a coastal resort famed at that time for its beaches and entertainment. It can best be described as Thailand's equivalent of Brighton!

Thailand had enabled Bill to rekindle his love of hunting and expeditions into the wild harked back to his Kenya years. He had become extremely keen on hunting wild boar having arranged a wild boar hunting trip in Austria the previous autumn inviting his friends Gerald Wombwell, John Apthorp and Nigel Balcombe to join him.

In 1978 he decided to mount a hunting expedition in the far North in the area near the Thai Laos border; he invited the same hunting friends to join him. Gerald was unable to come but both John and Nigel were happy to join the expedition.

Something else that took Bill back to his days in Kenya was that the border area was still considered dangerous despite the official end of regional hostilities. Banditry, kidnappings and attacks by Pathet Lao rebel forces, who had taken refuge in the area, were common so it was essential to have good personal protection.

The local military commander in Chiang Rai agreed to provide several platoons of heavily armed troops, commanded by a major, to accompany the party. By the time all concerned had assembled for the expedition Bill and his friends were amazed to find that the group was nearly one hundred strong. They set off in trucks provided by the army and later that day disembarked from the vehicles and set off on foot in a North Easterly direction led by the army major who reputedly knew the best hunting areas.

The party were issued a variety of firearms by the major - Bill was given an M16 which was not the most ideal weapon for a hunting trip That first night they camped in a clearing in the forest, guards were posted and a hunting group set off to "provide supper" as it appeared they had only been supplied with rice, water and strawberry jam for some strange reason and were expected to "live off the land". This was easier said than done as for sure any deer or other suitable game they might have shot en route had certainly been frightened off by the noise of the party as they trekked to the camping area.

By the time the hunters returned it was completely dark, a huge cooking pot of hot water was simmering over a fire in readiness for the "feast". However the party was very concerned to see that the hunters had returned with a strange selection of somewhat unappetising game including dead parrots, several monkeys and what looked like large rats.

The animals were then gutted, skinned and chopped up and the entire mixture, bones and all, were thrown into the pot. The resulting stew looked and smelt so awful that the party decided to eat only the boiled rice with a little jam for dessert!

The following day the group headed out across the Laos border and trekked for hours finally arriving at the entrance to a large valley dominated at the far end by thick jungle and steep slopes rising up into the hills. The hunting party were despatched to the far end of the valley and positioned on high points looking down into the valley. Once in place the army personnel at the lower end of the valley were used as beaters.

They fanned out on the valley floor and started beating their way through the heavy scrub and forest towards the slopes where the "guns" had been positioned. The noise was stupendous and soon birds were rising up over the guns while larger animals could be heard running in front of the beaters but the vegetation was so dense that it was almost impossible for the hunters to see what exactly was running towards them.

The first animal to emerge was a black bear of some sort but it was left in peace while the hunters waited for the arrival of the expected wild pigs or deer. Suddenly a large elephant emerged just in front of Bill who had to rapidly jump behind a tree to avoid being trampled on. The animal had on a large length of broken rope around one ankle and no doubt had been left to feed in the valley by its owner.

Finally some deer did break cover but the hunters all held their fire as by then the beaters were getting quite close and it was impossible to see where they were. The risk of accidentally hitting one or more of them was too big a risk to take and it did occur to the hunters later that having beaters in full army camouflage had its drawbacks!

The guides couldn't understand the decision not to fire and were very puzzled at the strange behaviour of the foreigners when presented with so many good targets!

The party trekked back towards the Thai border and that night made camp on a dry river bed.

Everyone was exhausted and soon fell asleep after another supper of boiled rice and jam only to be woken up in the early hours to find their camp awash due to unexpected heavy rains in the hills, it was most definitely not a dry river bed any longer!

The Major had been able to contact base on his radio and soon after daylight, much to their relief, transport arrived to pick up the Party and return them to Chiang Rai. Bill decided it was perhaps better to seek alternative countries for wild boar hunting!

Meanwhile back in London his social life had started to take a new direction.

The original Austrian hunting trip - in the vehicle Gerald Wombwell and John Apthorp, Bill by the passenger door

CHAPTER 11

Back in London, Malta & Rome 1978-81

As a young single man in London with a beautiful apartment and plenty of money to burn Bill was leading a carefree bachelor life style. He embarked on numerous affairs often with married women and was to be seen at Arthurs, Hippopotamus and Studio 54 in New York and at Annabel's in London.

Two of these relationships produced offspring which have remained a secret throughout his life but need to be acknowledged.

The first was an Englishwoman - the wife of one of his employees, but it isn't as sordid as that might sound. Her husband was sterile and they desperately wanted a child so, at their request, she bore a baby boy by Bill. He was the boy's godfather and maintained a good relationship with the family including the provision of an insurance policy for the young man which matured on his 21st birthday. He attended his wedding in Torquay and was happy to follow his career in the Police.

The other relationship was far more complex.

He had met and became totally infatuated with a stunning Philippines woman in Bangkok the previous year. She was a well known singer and toured with her orchestra to many major venues across Asia including Tokyo, Hong Kong, Jakarta and Singapore. He was determined to bring her to London and after several months was finally able to arrange a visa for her to visit the UK.

Much to their consternation Bill took her to visit his parents in Lincolnshire who were worried that he would marry her. Despite their views the affair continued and several months later she was pregnant. Bill tried to persuade her to have the pregnancy terminated but she was adamant that she was going to have his child. She moved out of his apartment to a nearby hotel in Kensington and then flew back to her family in Manila to have the baby.

She refused all offers of help from Bill and refused to maintain contact. To this day he does not know her whereabouts and has no details of the child.

Soon afterwards however he was to finally settle down with his bachelor days destined to become just memories.

He had received a phone call from a friend in California asking if her younger daughter, who planned to visit Paris and then London could stay in his apartment and perhaps "he could keep an eye on her"!

Barbara was a beautiful Texan redhead of Irish American extraction who was living in San Francisco, had started a successful modelling career and was much in demand from several major advertising agencies. She modelled for Chevrolet, Avis and various fashion magazines.

The plan had been for her to stay for a few days in London and then to return to California.

However Bill persuaded her to stay on in London; to move in with him and soon marriage plans were being discussed. It had all happened so quickly that problems were arising with Barbara's now to be ex boyfriend in California who was bombarding both her mother and Barbara herself with frantic phone calls.

Bill decided to deal with the situation by calling on the services of his old friend Mike Pascall.

Mike, a former marine sergeant and secret service agent was a formidable individual standing 6'6" and weighing in at over 300 lbs. He had recently moved from Boston to Los Angeles to set up his own private detective agency. He specialised in working primarily for corporate clients collecting debts by seizing movable assets such as aircraft and ships and also for private clients whose children had been inducted into religious cults such the Unification Church also known as "the Moonies".

Bill had met Mike through his friend Philip Willard and he had already used his services successfully the previous year in Thailand. Bill and some Thai Associates had invested in a ruby purchasing and sales operation run by an American expatriate who claimed to have access to legally mined rubies which were subsequently to be cut in Bangkok for onward sale to the jewellery market.

The American had made the mistake of absconding to the USA with a batch of rubies belonging to the partnership. Mike had little difficulty tracking down the culprit to a house in San Diego. The rubies had already been sold but Mike had successfully "persuaded" the individual to hand over the sale proceeds in cash.

Bill asked Mike to "pay a visit" to Barbara's boyfriend in order to "discuss" his annoying phone call habit. Needless to say the calls stopped immediately and much to the couple's amusement the ex boyfriend was soon advising Barbara's friends that she was marrying a "gangster".

The couple decided to get married in the September of that year (1977) and arranged an elaborate wedding at the American Church followed by a reception at the Houses of Parliament with the couple arriving in a horse drawn carriage. The bridesmaids' dresses were created from pure silk purchased by Barbara in Thailand who had started to accompany Bill on his visits to make sure he was not "led astray"!

Barbara was soon pregnant and their first born, Warren, arrived in August of the following year. Meanwhile interesting developments were taking place on the business front.

The Irish troubles were in full swing at that time and the Arnold brothers had developed a new mine detector which met the latest requirements of the security services. The IRA would bury weapons and explosives deep underground, often in graveyards or woods, down to depths of 6 feet which were beyond the capability of most current mine/metal detection equipment.

The new Guartel units produced by the Arnold brothers for sale by Bill's company Bonaventure could easily penetrate down to this depth to reveal concealed weapons.

At this time Britain and other Western countries enjoyed close trade relationships with Libya. Oil prices were high and the Gaddafi Government had embarked on a spending spree acquiring both military equipment and consumer goods. The Libyan Government also had an on-going problem with World War II mines. Camels, goats and local tribesmen were continuously wandering into mine fields by accident with awful results.

Libya had probably the world's biggest minefield problem ever at that time with literally hundreds of thousands of mines - most of them still live - buried in the sand dunes all along their Northern coastal areas. The situation was confounded by the location of many of these minefields not being properly recorded or else the records had been lost or never handed over by the Allies after the war.

The period 1940-43 had seen the continuous movement of armies - Italian, German and British moving in both directions along the coastal plains. Numerous minefields were laid during this period. The problem had been compounded by the Libyans themselves laying large defensive minefields during their border "wars" - in reality "skirmishes" - with Egypt in 1977.

To counter this problem the Libyan army planned to make a large purchase of mine detectors. A business friend of Bill's, John Rossiter, who was a man with excellent connections in Libya had heard of the plan which was to purchase 1,000 units and he used his connections to invite Bill to compete for this huge order. The competition came from a well known British company Plessey Electronics which was subsequently sold to GEC and Siemens.

It was a somewhat David and Goliath situation!

Both companies submitted their mine detectors for live trials and testing in Libya. Plessey came second and Bill's company, Bonaventure, was awarded the contract which involved not only the supply of the detectors but also local training of the Army Corps of Engineers. That corps was headed by the soon to be famous Colonel Radwan Salah who later was to lead Libyan forces into Uganda in aid of Idi Amin and subsequently the Libyan occupation of Northern Chad.

The contract was in excess of £1 million - a small fortune at that time.

Bill headed to Libya and returned several weeks later with the signed contract in hand.

In addition to the supply of the mine detectors he had agreed with the Libyans to approach the British Ministry of Defence to see if he could obtain any additional mine field maps relating to the 1940-44 period which could well be very helpful in identifying unknown hidden minefields on Libyan territory. The Ministry of Defence were very helpful and with Foreign Office approval, were able to provide some very detailed maps for use by the Libyan Army Corps of Engineers.

Several months later Bill was again back in Tripoli, maps in hand, to negotiate a second major contract with the Engineering Corps for 100 remote controlled tracked robots similar to the units used by the British Army to locate and to defuse bombs coupled with a large quantity of periphery equipment, produced by his friend Teddy Sas. Additional training programmes were arranged using ex British Army personnel to run the courses.

Bill had learned great patience in his dealing with the Libyans.

Colonel Radwan had kept him waiting for 5 weeks before seeing him and awarding the second contract. Every day Bill would arrive at the Engineering Corps camp in Tripoli with book in hand and would be invited to wait in an armchair in the Guard House at the camp entrance. It was June and the heat was tremendous in the Guard House - no air conditioning, no fans, nothing! No one could tell him when the Colonel might arrive - it was always "inshallah" and come back again tomorrow.

It was all part of the game to test his endurance and determination to go after the business.

A second and even larger contract was awarded to Bonaventure for the SAS equipment.

Bill had taken the decision to delegate the food trading activities to his staff in London and to concentrate most of his attention to Libya but still keeping a close watch on the business in general.

Bonaventure had by this time moved to Jermyn Street into prestigious but somewhat cramped offices on the 4th floor of an office building near Piccadilly Circus. The offices were owned by his friends and minority shareholders in his company, Leslie and Harold Bolsom, who had made their fortune from Carmen Hair Curlers.

Much to his delight the Bolsom's agreed that he could rename the office "Bonaventure House" a name that remained for many years thereafter.

Bill found commuting between London and Tripoli increasingly stressful and soon after the birth of their son Warren in August the couple decided to move to Malta which was just a 30 minute flight from Tripoli. This enabled him to fly home most weekends thus leaving Tripoli each Thursday afternoon and returning on Sunday mornings for the start of the Libyan week.

The couple rented a charming old house in the centre of the island and started to look for a permanent home. By late 1979 Barbara was pregnant again with their daughter Alix so they needed additional space for the new baby and a nanny.

They purchased an old Palazzo in Mdina directly opposite the Cathedral. The building was huge with well over 20 rooms and a basement area on the street side that was home to two Maltese families who had sitting tenant rights under Maltese law and only paid a peppercorn rent.

The palazzo had stood empty for many years and required major renovation in order to become habitable. It was also a somewhat macabre tourist attraction as the torture scenes of a major movie called "Midnight Express" about an American caught in possession of drugs in Turkey had been filmed there.

By this time Bill had an additional Libyan partner called Mohammad Zayan. Zayan was a cultivated man, married to an Egyptian doctor and had a background as a journalist. His connections in Libya were extensive, to say the least, but his political differences with the Gaddafi regime meant that he had been forced to live outside the country. He had moved to Rome where he had an office in the EUR complex - famous as the location of the 1960 Rome Olympics.

On the strength of this partnership the couple decided to move from Malta to Rome, where Bill was invited to share Zayans's EUR office. They both adored Rome and for Bill it was the start of a lifelong love of Italy and its people.

Rome turned out to be an ideal business location as there were excellent air connections to both Tripoli and London and many Libyans visited Rome on a regular basis. Libya, as a former colony of Italy, also had a long-standing and extensive trade relationship with its former colonial master.

Barbara found a beautiful apartment for them, on a hill-side in Trastevere, within an easy drive of the centre of Rome, the offices and the airport. The apartment came with its own car as part of the rental arrangements and Bill was to be seen speeding around in a tiny Mini-Cooper which was ideal for Rome's narrow streets and limited parking.

Rome at this time, was a potentially hazardous place in which to live in the late seventies. Since 1969 left wing demonstrators had been becoming more and more active leading to the formation of various communist groups who would become the unified Red Brigade and be responsible for many terrorist acts. Not to be outdone neo-fascist groups had also sprung up. The activities of the Red Brigade and a general rise in crime in Italy were to become known as the 'years of lead'.

1978 had seen the kidnapping and murder of Aldo Moro, a former prime minister and leader of the Christian Democrats. 1980 heralded a year of multiple assassinations and kidnapping of a number of major industrial leaders. In May a bomb exploded in Bologna station, killing 85 people and wounding hundreds more. Women went out or shopped without jewellery or watches and even handbags due to the activities of motorcycle gangs impudently assaulting them and snatching off watches and jewellery and grabbing handbags.

Later that year major problems arose for his partner Zayan who had run further afoul of the Libyan authorities with his political views and he was placed on their arrest list which meant he could not return to the country.

Soon word reached him that he was to be assassinated in Rome. He, his wife and child took shelter in Bill's apartment, while a safe house was found for them. To protect them Bill arranged for round the clock security, having engaged the services of former SAS personnel from an international security company.

A somewhat amusing incident occurred at this time involving his brother in law, David Gore, who arrived in Rome from Tripoli carrying a roll of carpet for Bill, which he had left behind from his last trip. David had arranged to stay with them and had taken a taxi from the airport which dropped him off at the entrance of Bill's driveway, where upon he proceeded by foot towards the apartment. The SAS guys had been watching David with some concern once he got out of the taxi. He was very tanned, black haired and could easily have passed for an Arab. They also saw that he was carrying a rolled up carpet that could have contained a weapon. They emerged from the bushes, tackled poor David to the ground and told him he was under arrest. The matter was of course soon sorted out but it illustrates that tensions were running high.

Bill decided to start looking elsewhere to settle in a location that was both crime-free and tax friendly.

By this time Bonaventure's sales were running into many millions and Bill was becoming a rich man.

As he resided outside the UK for more than 6 months per year he was not subject to UK taxation, which at that time was very high. Matters had improved under Margaret Thatcher when she reduced the top rate of tax from 83% to 60% following her 1979 election victory and was finally reduced to 40% in 1984. In any event, Bill still found the rates extortionate and was determined not to have to share his increasing wealth with Her Majesty's government!

He was now commuting between Rome, London and Tripoli.

At other times he would fly directly from either Tripoli or Rome to London in order to catch up on the company's food trading activities and the expansion of the electronics business with Guartel.

They were developing a range of sophisticated concealed electronic listening devices more commonly known as "bugs" for secret surveillance and long range thermal imaging telescopes for night time surveillance of both land based, ship to shore and general night time maritime surveillance purposes.

The "bugs" were miniature voice activated radio transmitters with a microphone and transmitter small enough to conceal in everyday objects such as light bulbs, ash trays, telephone "jacks", pens and the like or could be "planted" behind picture frames etc.

He formed a separate company called Bonaventure International Security to market this product range. He recruited a UK based sales manager to handle British and European sales and had appointed his old friends Philip Willard and Mike Pascal to oversee sales into the American markets.

The aim was to concentrate on selling this equipment to the Military, Police, Intelligence services and security sectors. In view of the sensitivity associated with the sale of such equipment Bill instigated a system internally of very accurate record keeping of every sale and end user. This decision was subsequently to prove exceedingly useful in the months to come when some of the equipment started turning up in the wrong hands!

CHAPTER 12

Libya 1979-82

The New Year of 1979 heralded a major expansion of the Bonaventure business and the engagement of many more staff primarily for the Libya operations. His younger brother Steve and brother-in-law David Gore, still talking about the brush with the security men in Rome, had joined the Company. The Beach Hotel, where Bill and his team initially stayed in Tripoli, was becoming increasingly crowded and the food was awful. A nearby villa was rented from one of Zayan's local contacts.

It was a large villa but soon proved to be inadequate to house the stream of company personnel both British and European engineers coming out to service equipment. A second villa was rented primarily for visiting engineers. Three Fiat cars were purchased for transporting staff and a mobile workshop van was imported for the engineers' use.

The supply contracts for both the mine detectors and robots stipulated long operational training courses; in some cases as long as two years. Bill engaged a small team of retired ex British Army officers to undertake the training for the Libyan Army Corps of Engineers.

Given the political climate in the country most companies, except the Italians and Maltese, were generally nervous about visiting or opening offices in Libya. It was illegal to have a local agent other than a government institution which, in the case of all purchases by the military, was called the Africa Company. The Africa Company was in fact a front company for the Libyan Intelligence services.

The company pretended to act as the exclusive agent of the military contractors, charged the suppliers a "fee" on all contracts and owned its own hotel specifically to accommodate and monitor the activities of "important suppliers". Bill and his senior managers, including David Gore, were soon encouraged to stay there while regular staff were expected to stay elsewhere in the rented villas.

Their fellow guests at the "Africa Hotel" were a strange bunch to put it mildly but it was a comfortable and secure place to stay. It also enabled David in particular to glean a lot of intelligence information - in particular details of suspected IRA agents staying there - which was subsequently discreetly passed on to MI6. At one time quite a few so called Irish "businessmen" were to be seen in residence but who were in fact quite obviously connected to the IRA.

Colonel Ghadaffi, Libya's self appointed leader, had published his Green Book a couple of years earlier setting out his personal philosophy of government by central committee. It rejected both capitalism and communism. He ruled Libya with an iron fist via his so-called Peoples Committees. Anyone suspected of plotting or speaking against the regime was subject to arbitrary arrest, interrogation, imprisonment or worse as evidenced by the treatment of Zayan in Rome! In general foreigners were not harassed but great care had to be exercised at all times in order to avoid suspicion of spying or anti regime activities.

In this socialist utopia Libyans were not permitted to conduct business or accept commissions or any form of payment so all meetings with foreigners were conducted in great secrecy at night in supposedly secure villas. Foreigners suspected of paying illegal commissions were subject to arrest, deportation or imprisonment.

In addition to its existing military contracts Bill negotiated for Bonaventure to become the exclusive representative of a significant number of major UK and European manufacturers including:

JCB, VOLVO BM Earth Moving Equipment, Lancer Boss Forklifts, Alvis armoured car maintenance, Marconi Training Ranges for anti-aircraft guns, HP computer hardware, Freuhof tank transporters and trailers, Fairy Marine Naval Target Boats, Bridport Gundry Camouflage nets, agricultural netting, fishing netting, Linguaphone Language Reading Tapes, NCK Rapier Cranes, Arms and Armour Defence Library Books, Chubb NBC vehicles, Ferranti Technologies and Oerlikon Contraves SPA anti- aircraft defence systems. By far the most important agency from a cash flow point of view was Lancer Boss owned by a larger than life individual - Sir Neville Bowman-Shaw and his younger brother Trevor.

Lancer Boss was one of the world's top 10 forklift truck manufacturers. The Company produced a range of forklift trucks but specialised in giant forklifts with a lift capacity of up to 130,000 lbs specifically designed to lift and transport fully laden 40 foot sea containers. Each unit sold for anything up to $200,000.

Bill was able to secure almost all the orders from the Libyan Ports Authority by not just offering the best equipment but equally importantly implementing a fully integrated spares system, mobile workshops and employing a team of expat technicians to carry out not just the servicing but also training local Libyan engineers. Orders ran into the millions and Libya became for a time Lancer Boss's biggest and most important export market.

Bill and Barbara had become close friends with Neville and his wife Georgina who owned the Toddington estate in Bedfordshire and lived in Toddington Manor - a lovely Gothic style country mansion with extensive gardens, croquet lawn, cricket pitch, orchard, fishing lakes and acres of woodlands. Neville and Bill had a lot in common outside of business - sons of the same age as Adrian and they both loved shooting. Many a weekend over the winter months were spent either at Toddington or on Bill's shoot that he rented in Anglesey.

During the summer Neville and Georgina were to be found staying with the Pellew-Harveys in Monte Carlo. Neville, who was to be knighted in 1984, was closely associated with the Conservative party and a strong supporter of Margaret Thatcher. He was also a close friend of Enoch Powell who was to be in the "political wilderness" by 1987 having lost his seat as an Ulster Unionist MP.

Around this time Neville decided to introduce Bill to Powell, who was bedridden at the time ensconced in a nearby hospital. Although alcohol was not permitted, Neville and Bill would smuggle in bottles of cold Laurent Perrier hidden in an ice box and take up stations around his bed. Discussions invariably turned to politics and immigration and there seems little doubt now - forty years on -that Powell was right - race is the basis of identity. The increase in the immigrant population of Britain classified as non-white is now 14 per cent of the population - even surpassing Powell's prognosis!

Further representations followed as Bill started to extend his dealings in Libya to include consumer product supplies to the Libyan State owned Building Supplies Organisation.

Trade with Libya was at that time strongly encouraged by the British Government and ECGD (Export Credits Guarantee Department) who bent over backwards to offer guarantees to British manufacturers that exported to Libyan State Corporations.

He became close friends with the Chairman and Purchasing Director of the Building Supplies organisation and arranged some of the largest UK exports ever recorded of several products including:

100 sea containers of green paint to be used for painting all the major buildings in Tripoli green in honour of Ghadaffi's Green Book, 400,000 packs of Super Glue and 10,000 air compressors. Bonaventure's

security business was also expanding into Libya with the supply of Italian manufactured secure encrypted communications equipment to the Army Headquarters.

Not all equipment presentations were plain sailing! A demonstration of Italian military radios by David Gore at Army Intelligence Headquarters was to be vetted by their "foreign advisors" all of whom turned out to be North Koreans. The system was turned down after they picked up just a single clear word in one of the many scrambled communications.

Another time Bill and his brother Steve, who by now had joined Bonaventure, were demonstrating anti riot control equipment which included live fire tests of rubber bullets, tear gas balls, wooden baton rounds and grape shot rounds. Steve had volunteered to be the "guinea pig" after assurances had been given by the British manufacturer Teddy Sas that all the rounds were strictly non lethal.

Before he started to fire at Steve's chest Bill was asked by the Range Officer to fire a baton round into a test dummy which simulated the impact on human flesh. The penetration of the round was found to be so deep that it could well have inflicted a mortal wound. Much to his relief Steve stood down and all the tests were conducted on the dummies.

Due to the ongoing mine clearing contracts and extensive dealings with the supply of radio and encryption equipment to the Military, Bill spent much of his time in Tripoli visiting the Military Procurement Contracts Office.

The waiting room often contained some very dubious and larger than life characters including Frank Terpil and on a regular basis Edwin Wilson.

Terpil was a former CIA agent who had joined the Agency in 1965 working in the "Technical Services Division" which specialised in weaponry for covert operations. He had been fired by the CIA in 1971 for "irregular activities" and had turned to supplying "military equipment" to Libya, Iran and Idi Amin in Uganda.

Bill found out that he was "the competition" for a potential supply contract of silencers which he had been evaluating and testing with a Danish factory. The silencers had been classified for civil use on "pigeon shoots". Perhaps it was for the best that the contract was awarded to Terpil!!

Later that same year of 1980 Terpil was arrested in the USA, charged and then convicted of selling a large consignment of machine guns to Libya. However he skipped bail and fled to Lebanon.

In 1981 he was sentenced in absentia to 53 years in jail. Soon after his arrival in Lebanon he offered his "services" to the PLO and their leader Yasser Arafat. He also visited Syria where he was jailed for some months by the Assad regime on suspicion of being an American spy which was rather ironic. Upon his release from jail he returned to Lebanon but his stay was soon cut short when Israel invaded Lebanon in 1982.He was given refuge in the Cuban Embassy in Beirut after brandishing a personally signed visiting card from Fidel Castro who Arafat had introduced him to. A call was made to Havana and his safe passage to Cuba was arranged. He subsequently flew to Havana where he settled down under the alias of Robert Hunter reputedly working for the Cuban General Intelligence Directorate.

Terpil went into partnership with another American fugitive called Robert Vesco who had carried out a $200 million securities fraud. Although officially under house arrest Terpil was permitted to live a comfortable and peaceful life by the Cubans. He died in Cuba in 2016 aged 76 after a long battle with diabetes.

Edwin "Ed" Wilson was impossible to miss and was regularly to be seen in the military contract waiting room in Tripoli. Standing at 6'5" Ed was an imposing figure, often rude and aloof with a somewhat unsavoury reputation amongst the Army's foreign contractors.

A former Marine he joined the CIA in 1956 and was seconded to the Office of Naval Intelligence in 1971 and left a few years later to set up his own Companies. He was reputed to be extremely rich and by 1976 had become an important arms supplier to the Libyan Government.

He had a large estate in Virginia, houses in Europe and when in Tripoli resided together with his wife in a villa just outside the Beach Hotel where he was often spotted by Bill and his staff.

Under constant scrutiny by the FBI but claiming to be working for the CIA he was finally convicted in a US court of illegally smuggling from the USA large quantities of weapons and 20 tons of Semtex explosives to Libya.

Enticed by the CIA to a meeting in one of the Caribbean islands he was arrested and extradited back to the USA and sentenced to 15 years in prison which was subsequently increased by a further 24 years after he was accused of attempting to arrange the assassination of six prosecution witnesses and his ex-wife. He had always claimed that he was working for the CIA, maintained his innocence and in 2003 his conviction was overturned and he was finally freed in 2004. He maintained that he was "left in the cold" by his own Government and in 2007 sued the US Government albeit unsuccessfully.

Articles from the time of his arrest labelled him very much as the villainous spy wronging his country and breaking the law. Ironically articles, often in the same journals after his release, talk of him running companies that were in fact CIA fronts.

Ed Wilson died in 2012

Many people ask what it was like living in Libya during the Ghadaffi regime and in particular when the Green Revolution was at its height around 1980.

The answer is that life could be surprisingly pleasant if one took advantage of some of the stunning desert scenery and some of the most isolated and best preserved Roman cities that existed in the world. The two best known locations within easy striking distance of Tripoli were the ancient cities of Leptis Magna to the East and Sabratha to the West not far from the Tunisian border.

Ancient Tripolitania - literally Three Cities - consisted of what became the modern city of Tripoli, Sabratha and Leptis Magna. All three were originally settled by the Phoenicians in the 7th century BC and later by the Carthaginians around the 4th century BC. The Romans arrived in 200 BC and stayed for 600 years.

When the Romans left Leptis Magna became a regional capital of the Byzantium Empire before the Arab conquest of 642 AD when the city, which housed 25,000 people simply stopped being used.

Buried by sands until the early 20th century it somehow survived WW2 unscathed and remains probably the best preserved Roman city in the world. Leptis Magna and Sabratha were declared UNESCO Heritage Sites in 1982.

Most Libyans were friendly and courteous to Westerners. Alcohol was strictly forbidden but that did not stop people trying to smuggle in the odd bottle of Scotch. The black market price for a bottle of Scotch was $100 - a lot of money at that time. Some expats resorted to making home brewed alcohol with very mixed results to say the least. It was considered a serious offence and any expat found to be distilling, brewing or trading in alcohol was subject to imprisonment and deportation.

Bill had brought over to Libya several team members from his London Office including his PA/ secretary Rosemary and his excellent telex operator Sid. Telex was the forerunner of email, it allowed the exchange of text messages in real time via telephone lines and could be encrypted if necessary. Sid loved his tipple and unbeknown to Bill had set up a still in the bathroom of one of the villas. Unfortunately Sid's still exploded one evening destroying not only the bathroom but part of the villa roof collapsed caused by the lavatory bowl being blown up through the ceiling and roof to land a good 50 yards from the villa.

The fire brigade were called and soon the police arrived as well. Luckily no one had been hurt and the distribution of some "baksheesh" calmed the situation somewhat but Sid had to be put on the first flight in the morning to London to avoid arrest!

As part of the "deal" with the Chairman of the Building Supplies Organisation Bill had agreed to arrange for his two teenage sons to attend an English language college in Bournemouth in addition to the opening of a UK bank account into which commissions were paid.

To facilitate meetings with suppliers Bonaventure funded visits to the UK to enable Military teams and the Building Supplies Organisation's senior team to meet with Bonaventure suppliers in order to place additional orders on the spot. The visits by Military teams posed no problems - they were model citizens and always behaved in a most discreet and proper manner with no drinking or night club visits.

However the same could not be said of the Building Supplies team and one visit will be imprinted on the memories of those involved until their dying days.

Bill's brother Steve arrived at Gatwick Airport in a Rolls Royce to collect the delegation.

Unfortunately several of the delegates had been drinking on the aircraft and within a few minutes of leaving the airport started to vomit in the Rolls. Not a good start to the visit but worse was to follow.

Rooms had been booked in the Hilton Park Lane, call girls invited and following an excellent dinner in the roof restaurant of the hotel the delegates settled in for their 6 day stay. All appeared to go well the first night but the following morning the hotel management called to ask that the guests be removed for "unacceptable behaviour".

It seemed that several delegates had mistaken the maids for call girls and had attempted to have sex with them. Steve then arranged for them to move into the Berkeley Hotel in Mayfair extorting them not to molest the maids.

However their stay in the Berkeley was equally short lived as the hotel had refused to allow the call girls up to their rooms and the next morning a similar request was received from the hotel to remove "our guests" for behaviour that was not considered compatible with "accepted guest norms".

In desperation it was decided to move them to the Holiday Inn in Swiss Cottage and at the same time to rent a large flat near the Gloucester Road for "entertainment purposes". This proved to be an ideal solution!

Finally, after the longest 6 days anyone could remember, the visitors departed, laden with expensive jewellery paid for by the company. The biggest sigh of relief came from Kate, the company receptionist, as she had been responsible for hiring the nightly call girls. A challenge in itself made harder by the delegates insistence on having "new" girls every night.

By 1982 declining oil revenues had dramatically reduced government revenues and caused a serious decline in economic activity with Libya. To make matters worse for Bonaventure a purge on corruption was instigated and had led to the arrest and torture of many senior executives of the state owned companies including the Building Supplies Organisation.

Bill was in Libya when both the Chairman and Purchasing Director were among those arrested. He was staying as usual at the Africa Hotel and received an anonymous phone call late one evening advising him that his name was going to be added to the arrest list the next day, that he must leave immediately on the first available flight out of the country and advise no one, including his own staff, about his departure.

He left the hotel early the following morning with just his briefcase in hand advising the receptionist that he had an early appointment and drove to the airport. He booked a seat on the first flight out with Olympic Airways to Athens and headed to passport control. There was a long queue at each of the three booths and each passport was being carefully checked against a list.

Bill remained calm but was deeply worried and hoped he would be passing through before the updated arrest list arrived at the airport. He passed through immigration without being stopped only to find that the aircraft departure had been delayed by an hour. The departure lounge was unusually quiet and the wait became increasingly nerve racking. Finally boarding started but his initial sense of relief evaporated when he saw that there was an additional passport check at the aircraft door by plain clothed security men. His passport was examined again against their list and he was waived through to his seat.

No one spoke and just as the last passenger was waived through two more security men arrived with another paper in hand and proceeded to move slowly down the aircraft examining each passenger carefully. It appeared that they were unable to identify the person they were looking for and finally departed. It was almost possible to hear the sighs of relief inside the aircraft as the doors closed and the engines started.

However Bill was well aware that the ordeal would not be over until the aircraft had left Libyan air space as, on several occasions in the past days, flights that were already airborne had been radioed to return back to Tripoli and passengers forcibly removed.

Finally the aircraft landed in Athens, Bill disembarked and booked himself on the first flight to France which turned out to be Marseilles. Upon arrival there he rented a car and drove to Monaco arriving home in time for dinner much to the surprise of Barbara and the children.

The Libyans had an unusual way of dealing with these situations. Bill's staff were permitted to remain in Libya and to continue their work as normal while he was to remain "outside" until he was advised that he could return but in the interim he was to instruct his bankers in London to return to the Central Bank of Libya those funds that he had given as gifts to any Libyan national.

He was also instructed to send back to Tripoli the two sons of the Chairman of the Building Supplies Organisation whom Bonaventure were educating in the UK at the company's expense as both boys were due to be inducted into the Libyan Army to undertake their national service obligations.

Bill complied with these requests and several months later was informed that he was free to return to Tripoli without fear of arrest.

Meanwhile storm clouds were gathering in the middle east as Saddam Hussein planned his imminent invasion of Iran encouraged by unofficial support from the West who wanted to see the overthrow of Khomeini and his mullahs.

Iraq invaded Iran on the 22nd of September 1980 in order to gain full control of the Shatt al-Arab waterway. Despite early success by Iraq the war ground to a stalemate that was to last 8 years and claim an estimated one million lives.

The repercussions were soon to be felt throughout the Middle East and the major Western powers!

Bill at Leptis Magna, Libya

CHAPTER 13

Monte Carlo 1982-84

In 1980 Barbara had given birth to their first daughter whom they named Alix. It was also the year that the Bonaventure offices in Jermyn Street were proving to be too small and new accommodation was becoming urgent. A more prestigious location was called for to cater to the increasing numbers of overseas visitors and delegations connected to the Libyan Government and clients of the security business who had started to visit the Company. Bill had retained his team of traders but was devoting much less time to their activities. They continued to trade in almost any food industry related products and occasionally got themselves in hot water with unsuitable clients.

One amusing incident occurred when they sold three containers of Canadian canned salmon to a distributor in the Midlands who was making excuses not to pay for the product which by this time had already been delivered to their warehouse. Bill decided to call on the services of a well-known wrestler called Giant Haystacks who was based in Lancashire. His real name was Martin Ruane and as a side line to his professional wrestling career he arranged debt collection services using a team of Liverpool dockers as his assistants. A huge man - he stood nearly 7 feet tall and weighed in at around 700 lbs - he was in fact a gentle giant, a devoted family man who ran a respectable and well organised business.

The distributor was by this time refusing outright to pay Bonaventure so Bill rang him to advise that the Company would have no option but to arrange for the collection of the goods. He put a call through to Haystacks, arranged with him to collect the goods and then truck them to a warehouse in Liverpool. The operation followed with military precision. Haystacks and his team of dockers drove to the Distributor's premises located in a very remote and isolated village, cut the telephone wires and proceeded to the warehouse gates. Entry, as expected, was refused whereupon Haystack's team attached chains to the gates and gained immediate access to the warehouse. The warehouse staff started to protest but one look at Haystacks and his dockers was enough to shut them up. The goods were loaded into the two trucks and duly delivered to the Liverpool warehouse.

Bill had arranged with Haystacks to meet him in London at the Bonaventure offices in order to pay for his services in cash. The arrival of Haystacks at the office entrance also coincided with the arrival of Bill's friend and shareholder Harold Bolsom who had decided to pay a visit to the offices. Harold was a small man, neatly dressed with a well trimmed beard. He squeezed into the lift with Haystacks and having enquired which floor he wanted was very perturbed to hear that Haystacks had an appointment with Bill. Harold decided he had" urgent business" on a higher floor and watched anxiously as Haystacks got out of the lift at Bonaventure's floor. Bill was very amused as he sat together with Haystacks over a cup of coffee to receive an urgent call from Harold on the floor above enquiring if "all was ok." He assured him that all was fine!

In 1981 Bill purchased the lease on a large 5 storey town house in Charles Street in Mayfair with a rear mews flat and garage providing spacious office facilities in the lower and ground and first floors together with a very elegant apartment for Bill and his growing family on the two upper floors for when they visited the UK. Bonaventure personnel occupied the two lower office floors with the upper floor ballroom being rented out to a Lebanese friend of Bill's for use as his office.

By now Bill was commuting between Tripoli, Rome and London with considerably more than 6 months being spent outside the UK in each year so, on the advice of his accountants, he and Barbara decided to apply for official residency in Monaco where no income taxes were applied to residents.

As soon as their residency was granted the family moved to Monte Carlo in early 1982 while still retaining the Charles Street house for their London visits and their (still empty) Palazzo in Malta.

They leased the entire fifteenth floor in Le Formentor - a prime location in Monaco on Avenue Princesse Grace overlooking the sea. Designed as two apartments they created a single large apartment with two kitchens, separate staff quarters at the rear and a 4 car garage in the basement. Three Filipino staff cleaned and looked after the children while their private Chinese chef cooked for them when they were at home.

Constantly increasing revenues flows from the business operations enabled the family to enjoy a lavish lifestyle and they soon made friends with other rich tax exiles living in Le Formentor and parents of the children's school friends.

Close friends and dinner companions included World Champion racing driver Jody Schecter and his wife Pam, billionaire Baron "Heini" Thyssen Bornemisza and his Spanish wife Tita. They attended all local functions including the Red Cross Ball and the Cirque de Monaco.

Heini was a fascinating man, born in Holland to German father and Hungarian mother - the title was from her side - he had amassed an immense fortune and an equally immense art collection which he kept in his Swiss villa. In the early 1990s the Spanish Government paid over £240 million for the 800 or so paintings and donated the Villahermosa Palace in Madrid to house the collection.

Bill purchased a 25' power boat which he kept moored in Monaco's smaller harbour of Port de Fontvieille. On many weekends the family powered down to Ste Marguerite, an island off Nice, to meet up with friends for lunch and water skiing.

On one occasion however, when his brother Steve and wife Annie were staying with them, Bill had a narrow escape from disaster. He had failed to check the weather forecast properly and set out for a trip to Ste Marguerite. The sea was calm but most unusually there were no other boats in sight.

Virtually without warning high winds caused by a "Mistral" whipped up the sea and heavy rain reduced visibility - a large wave broke over the rear of the boat, the engine cut out and no amount of trying would persuade it to re- start. With no engine to control it the boat started to drift towards a very rocky part of the shore with sheer cliffs behind.

Bill put out an emergency mayday call which luckily was picked up by the Monaco Life Boat which battled out to rescue them towing their stricken boat safely back to Monaco.

It was a very frightening experience and a lesson well learned - thereafter for all boat expeditions the weather was very carefully checked before they set off anywhere down the coast!

Bill set up the first of his home offices in Monaco but spent much time commuting to Tripoli and London for business meetings. In view of the growing sensitivity of some communications and the deteriorating political situation in Libya he installed a special Italian made telex encryption system operating between the Tripoli, Monaco and London Offices which could be used for confidential communications.

Life became a strange dichotomy - it was as though he was living in two completely opposite worlds - the opulence of Monte Carlo and the harsh life of an expat in Libya.

He realised that his Company was becoming too reliant on its Libyan operations so took advantage following his enforced "exile" from Libya to look at other markets.

He had close friends in the Sothern Rhodesia Air Force which was in the market for a new STOL aircraft suitable for supplies and paratrooper drops. The country was about to become independent and in April 1980 formally changed its name to Zimbabwe but the Air Force continued to be managed by white personnel.

He was able to arrange for Bonaventure to represent in Southern Africa the former Spanish Government owned aircraft manufacturer - Construcciones Aeronautica ("CASA"). The company had just been privatised and subsequently acquired by the French conglomerate EADS which in turn became absorbed by Airbus Defence and Space.

CASA produced the ideal aircraft for the newly named Zimbabwe Air Force called the CASA 212. It was and remains a truly multi role aircraft with its rear ramp. The aircraft can be used for transportation of cargo, passengers, surveillance, search and rescue, supply drops, troop infiltration, sky diving etc.

Many of these aircraft are still flying and its successors - the C235 and C295 - larger and more powerful models remain in production and can be found operating the world over under the most rugged conditions.

It was agreed that Bonaventure would fund the cost of flying the aircraft from Spain to Harare the newly named capital of Zimbabwe and thereafter the operational costs would be borne by CASA. An extensive series of trips to demonstrate the aircraft had been arranged by Bonaventure in addition to Zimbabwe including Botswana, South Africa and Lesotho. South Africa was officially under embargo by many countries including Spain so the visit to Johannesburg was classed as a technical stop!

Bill decided to fly on a commercial flight to Harare and then link up with the CASA crew.

The Zimbabwe demonstration flights were a great success and an initial order was agreed for 10 aircraft.

One of the aircraft's strengths is its ability to fly at low altitude so, on the journey to Botswana, the crew decided to fly en route at low altitude over the Victoria Falls with the rear ramp down. The view was incredible but somewhat scary as Bill and the crew took it in turns to sit on the edge of the ramp securing themselves from the slip stream by chest ropes tied to bolts in the floor.

In Botswana the aircraft's arrival was greeted by Brigadier Ian Kharma whose father Sir Seretse Khama was the President of Botswana. He had made headlines in the British press some years earlier by marrying a white English woman called Ruth Williams. Ian Kharma himself was subsequently to become the 4th elected President of Botswana.

At the end of the trip Bill flew home from Johannesburg rather than accompany the aircraft on its ferry flight back to Spain.

Col. Ghadaffi had publicly announced his strong support for Iran soon after the Iraqi invasion started in September 1980 and decided that Libya would actively assist Iran in its war with Iraq which was strongly backed by the US, Britain and France - de facto most of NATO.

Libya was unable to send troops to Iran as its armed forces were already stretched to the limit defending Libya's land border with Egypt, its occupation of northern Chad not to mention its deadly excursions into Uganda the previous year in support of Idi Amin so its main contribution would be limited to money and military supplies.

Libya's assistance to Idi Amin was of particular interest to Bill who had not only visited Uganda a number of times during his Kenya days but perhaps more interestingly the Libyan Expedition into Uganda in April 1979 had been led by his good friend Colonel Radwan Salah.

Col. Radwan was commander of the Army Corps of Engineers and had awarded Bill his initial mine detector and robot orders for the Libyan Army. He was an unusual man and Bill was happy to consider him a friend. The son of a Nubian servant he was coal black while many Libyans - particularly the officer corps - were white or pale brown. He was one of the very few high ranking black officers in the Army.

Long periods of sponsored training with the US Army Corps of Engineers and training in Britain ensued that his views and outlook had become very pro-western. Bill visited the Colonel regularly in Benghazi and was often invited to his house in open disregard of the rule that the regime did not permit inviting foreigners to visit Libyans at home without official sanction. In addition, despite the total ban on alcohol consumption in Libya, Radwan seemed to have an unending supply of Johnny Walker so he and Bill would usually consume a bottle over dinner during these visits to his home.

Radwan was always very circumspect in what he said but during their private discussions it was impossible not to notice his disdain for the Leadership and his concerns about the increasingly anti western direction his country was taking under Ghadaffi.

By April 1979 Idi Amin was starting to lose control of Uganda. The previous month Libya had despatched 2,500 militia and armoured units to prop up the Regime. Tanzania was preparing to invade Uganda in order to overthrow the Amin regime who had appealed to Ghadaffi for additional military assistance.

In great secrecy Col Radwan was asked to assemble a special battalion consisting of 500 black Libyan troops who would be flown in Libyan C-130 aircraft from Maaten al-Sarra air base in Southern Libya to Entebbe Airport with instructions to establish and retain full control and security of the airport. The troops all had to undergo parachute training as a precaution in case the airport had already been occupied by Tanzanian troops before the Libyans arrived.

The first wave of troops in three aircraft arrived safely and the aircraft returned back to Libya to ferry Col Radwan and the remaining troops to Entebbe. The second flight was a disaster with one of the three aircraft running out of fuel before it could reach Entebbe. The pilots, once they realised they could not make it to Entebbe, had decided to lower the rear ramp of the aircraft and have the troops "jump out" in order to save themselves.

The unfortunate and ill trained paratroopers landed in dense forest some 50 miles short of Entebbe. Many died or were severely injured but some eventually were able to make their way on foot or in commandeered vehicles to rejoin their comrades. Entebbe Airport fell to the Tanzanian forces on April 9th and Kampala itself the following day. Many Libyan troops died defending the airport and those who survived, including Col Radwan, retreated to Jinja and were eventually repatriated via Kenya and Ethiopia.

By the Autumn of 1982 Bill had been given all clear that he was free to visit Libya once again and that his safety and security would be guaranteed by the erstwhile Africa Company.

During his enforced exile from Libya, Bill was busy negotiating with James Edmiston to acquire his company - the Sterling Engineering Company based in Dagenham. Sterling were renowned for their manufacture of the Sterling sub machine gun widely used throughout the second world war. Extensive discussions took place but James finally decided not to sell!

It was to be the start of some of the most extraordinary years of his life and the start of the transformation of his company Bonaventure from a trading and agency company into a fully fledged military supply and logistics organisation.

Bill pictured in Monte Carlo 1982

Bill and Barbara on a shoot in Wales

CHAPTER 14

The Transformation of Bonaventure - the move to Geneva - Iran, India & Iraq

By the Summer of 1983 the Iran - Iraq conflict had reached a strategic stalemate and had become a war of attrition with conditions on the front line not unlike the bloody battles of the First World War. Artillery and mortars had become the "king" of the battlefield! Most of Iran's artillery was US made including their towed and self propelled 155 howitzers.

Oil prices had peaked in 1982 reaching nearly $40 per barrel and Libya's spending spree had continued unabated despite warnings in the financial press of an impending oil surplus and reduction in pricing.

A year later prices fell rapidly to around $28 per barrel as it became apparent that the oil market was becoming glutted and prices were heading downwards to levels that would seriously curtail the purchasing power of the Libyan Government. The decline continued and by 1986 prices fell to an all time low of $10 per barrel.

Bill was visiting Libya again with regularity in 1983 and spending considerable time with the Africa Company trying to drum up additional business. It was around this time that he was invited by the Africa Company to meet with the Iranian Military Attaché.

The meeting took place in a villa just outside Tripoli - no notes were taken.

The Libyans had large stocks of 155mm ammunition which had been supplied by the US and Britain during the days of King Idris and the early days of the Ghadaffi regime. This ammunition was no longer of much use to them as they had phased out their 155mm howitzers having replaced them with Russian artillery of mainly 122 mm, 152mm, and 203mm calibres.

The Iranians were in desperate need of artillery ammunition and were scouring the world in an endeavour to obtain supplies. Their situation was made even more difficult for them as most Western countries had instigated an arms embargo and were now discretely backing the Iraqi Government.

The Libyans wanted Bill to negotiate the sale of their surplus 155mm ammunition stocks and in return Bonaventure would receive "favourable treatment" for the promotion of its business in Libya. The Iranian Military Attaché asked Bill to fly to Tehran for more "detailed discussions".

He flew out the following week via Damascus and thence on to Tehran where he was met on the aircraft steps by two representatives from the Ministry of Defence who whisked him directly through the airport avoiding the long immigration and customs queues which was a relief as immigration was under the control of Revolutionary Guards who were often hostile and rude to foreigners.

Accommodation had been booked for him in the Intercontinental Hotel and discussions took place over a 3 day period and Bill then returned home to Monaco via Paris - happy and relieved to be back home. The family assumed that he was just back from Libya!

Shortly thereafter Bill was contacted by the South African born General Manager of the Italian shipbuilder, Intermarine, and asked to visit their shipyard in Sarzana near La Spezia. Intermarine had become a world leader in the construction of large Glass Fibre Reinforced Plastic (GRP) naval ships - in particular the construction of Mine Countermeasure Vessels.

GRP has many advantages over traditional steel or wood hulls - reduced weight, less maintenance and most importantly in a minesweeper less likely to set the mines off.

The company had orders in hand and had already commenced the construction of a number of these vessels for the Iranian Navy but found itself in considerable difficulties as the Italian authorities had implemented a temporary export ban on the vessels due to the ongoing hostilities with Iraq. Intermarine were claiming that as their vessels were unarmed they should be treated as a civil sale despite the fact that their client was the Iranian Navy.

They asked Bill if he was willing for an attractive fee to act as the shipyard's advisor and representative in Iran in order to negotiate with the Naval Authorities modifications to the contract documentation which might enable the Italian Government to lift the export restrictions which had been imposed. He was also assured that he could rely on the Italian Embassy in Tehran to assist in any way possible to clear the way for the delivery of the ships.

Bill agreed to act for them as he could then combine visits to Tehran on behalf of Intermarine with other possible supply contracts. On his return to Tehran his first meeting took place with the commercial attaché in the Italian Embassy.

The attaché briefed him fully on the updated local situation and it appeared that the political situation between Iran and most major Western countries was deteriorating even further with growing support being given to the Iraqi regime. Decisions and negotiations with the military and MOD, including the Navy, were being stalled with these institutions losing their power in favour of the Revolutionary Guards known as the IRGC. Furthermore the security situation in Tehran was deteriorating as Iraqi air force bombing raids were becoming more intense.

Bill stayed at the Intercontinental again but was offered shelter in the basement of the Embassy if required. The Embassy had set up an extensive facility - a sort of large dormitory in the basement well stocked with food and supplies for embassy staff, visiting Italians and "friends" of Italy.

Bombing raids, although frightening, were spectacular and in many ways similar to a giant panoramic son et lumiere. The best views were from the roof of a high rise hotel on the outskirts of the city. Bill would taxi there for dinner and then, along with some other hardy expats, go up on to the roof to watch the "fireworks".

The Iraqis were usually very punctual and around 22.00 the sirens would start to caterwaul; searchlights would start probing the sky soon followed by bright bursts of antiaircraft fire. Tracer rounds intermingled with the normal proximity fused ammunition ripped into the sky.

It was impossible to see the incoming aircraft as they were always flying very high and they appeared to drop their bombs more or less at random as small explosions could be seen across a wide area, often outside the city. The noise was incredible but mostly it seemed that little damage was done.

Discussions with the Navy were proving difficult. The only possible way to get around the export ban revolved around their agreement to accept the Intermarine vessels without any form of periphery armaments - none in fact - which would then enable them to be classified as civil and/ or humanitarian vessels which might exclude them from the export ban. However despite his best efforts little progress was made and Bill was soon back at home in Monaco.

Meanwhile back in London Bonaventure's main trading and security equipment activities continued to be based in the Charles Street residence in Mayfair. Bonaventure Security had expanded its sales base in the USA thanks mainly to the activities of Bill's old friends Mike Pascall and Philip Willard.

Sales of night vision scopes increased as did the sale of sophisticated "bugs" but, despite keeping careful export compliant records, some of the equipment fell into the wrong hands.

A major scandal occurred in the Massachusetts State Assembly where the Governor's office was found to be bugged with the company's equipment. To make matters worse the US Coast Guard had captured drug smugglers in the Gulf of Mexico using high speed power boats equipped with the company's night vision equipment supplied by a Florida dealer who was selling the equipment ostensibly for use on fishing boats.

Shortly afterwards Bonaventure received visits from Scotland Yard to Charles Street at the behest of the US Embassy to investigate Bonaventure's security equipment sales to US Distributors.

Bonaventure's export records were found to be fully in compliance with UK legislation but the police investigation made the staff uncomfortable to say the least.

The final straw occurred when the Bonaventure Security sales director was arrested during a visit to the USA on a charge of "passing off" forged US bank notes. The company's lawyers were able to obtain his release from the American prison and arranged for him to be deported back to England to face the charges there. He admitted his currency crime and after being fired by Bill, was turned over to the Police and formally charged with being in possession of forged currency. He subsequently agreed to become a Crown witness against the forgers, pleaded guilty to the charges and was sentenced to jail in his home city of Bristol.

Bill was becoming increasingly worried that problems associated with the sales of security equipment via civilian outlets was in danger of affecting Bonaventure's business reputation so it was decided to concentrate on Government sales only going forward.

Around this time Bill had become friendly with a Swiss lawyer called Martin Loseley who had some very interesting connections in the Middle East particularly with the wealthy Saudi arms dealer Adnan Khashoggi whose yacht was often to be seen in Monaco harbour.

Martin's wife was one of Adnan's several mistresses, an arrangement which he seemed to accept.

She was sometimes able to pass on interesting projects to Bill via her husband. One such tip off resulted in one of his more unusual trips around the Arab world.

The Indian Army was in the process of phasing out its Centurion L7 main battle tanks and around 150 units were scheduled for sale by the

Indian MOD. Bill had been introduced to a leading Indian agent with close connections to the MOD who invited him to Delhi for discussions relating to the possibility of Bonaventure selling the tanks to countries approved by the Indian Government.

Terms and conditions were agreed and the discussions then turned to the logistical problem of physically moving the tanks each weighing 52 tons and 10 metres in length from their main base near Delhi to the port of Mumbai and thence for shipment to the Middle East where it was assumed they were to be sold.

Meetings took place with the Indian Railways in Delhi who agreed that the tanks could be moved on railway flat wagons to the port for loading by heavy duty cranes on to a ship's deck. However subsequent discussions with the port authorities demonstrated that the safest and most economical solution would be to drive the tanks under their own power from the railcars in to either a large ocean going towed barge or roll-on-roll-off vehicle ferry.

Having discussed the logistics Bill prepared to fly back to Delhi only to find upon arrival at Mumbai airport that all flights had been cancelled for an unspecified period of time due to bad weather. He found himself sitting in the airport next to another Brit who turned out to be a Professor of Ornithology from Manchester University also trying to get to Delhi. He was an expert on vultures and had been invited to Mumbai by a group of Parsi priests who were concerned about the increasing lack of local vultures to eat corpses.

Parsi funerals consist of carrying the cadaver up to special flat roofed funeral towers - known as Towers of Silence - where the body is left for consumption by vultures.

The pair discussed travelling by rail to Delhi but this involved a two day train journey so they decided it was best to seek hotel rooms and to stay in a comfortable seaside hotel well away from the city but not too far from the airport.

The professor invited Bill to visit the Mumbai Towers of Silence to witness himself the funeral rites.

It was a somewhat macabre experience to say the least.

They arrived at the "cemetery" about 10.00 am and waited for the first funeral cortège of the day to arrive.

However it was not a normal cortège but an open cart drawn by two water buffaloes decked out with flowers with the corpse lying exposed to the elements. The body was carried to the top of the tower and just dumped on a sort of wooden rack.

Finally Bill was able to depart back to Delhi once the weather had improved to have his meeting with the MOD. Now that the logistics matters appeared to have been sorted out the next and equally important phase of the project needed to start - the actual sale of the tanks.

Martin believed that he had just the right customer in Abu Dhabi so they arranged to meet there.

Bill flew in from Delhi while Martin flew in from London to meet up with the "middle man" who was supposed to be the key to the business. It soon became apparent that the client was not to be the UAE Government as had been suggested, but was in fact to be the Palestinian Liberation Organisation.

In 1982 the PLO had relocated to Tunis after being driven out of Lebanon by Israel during the first Lebanon War.

Bill immediately terminated the discussions and the duo set off for Khartoum where Martin was by this time hopeful that the Sudanese Armed Forces would be the ideal potential client. The meetings were inconclusive and after several days stay at the Nile Hilton they returned to London.

Bill was determined not to give up and was soon on his way again - this time without Martin - to Sanaa - to meet the Minister of Defence of what was then North Yemen, Saleh Muslith Qassem.

At that time North Yemen was considered to be "pro western" whereas communist South Yemen was heavily backed by Russia.

Sanaa lies over 2,000 metres above sea level in a fertile bowl. It had been continuously inhabited for over 2500 years and, at that time, had over six and a half thousand houses built before the Normans invaded England in 1066! The history of the city could be dated back to 5000 BC making it likely to be the oldest constantly inhabited city in the world.

It was a fascinating place to visit in the early eighties being totally unspoilt with no modern hotels or buildings. The city's houses were almost entirely built of hard earthen bricks with the most incredible multi coloured hand crafted glass windows. It was a living museum.

It had a wonderful souk where donkeys could be seen pulling rotating open air grinding stones to produce flour - it was like being transformed back to biblical days.

The local paper currency was distrusted by many shop keepers in the souk so payment had to be made in dollars or silver coinage. Solid silver coins had been the only stable currency of choice for centuries amongst

Yemeni tribes was the Maria Theresa thaler being at one time the official currency of the Hejaz, Yemen, Aden and Oman!

After nightfall the city became eerily quiet with virtually no vehicles or pedestrians to be seen - just the occasional military patrol. Bill would take his walks in the evening to avoid the heat but found himself being trailed by packs of stray dogs which made such excursions an uncomfortable experience to say the least.

The discussions with the Ministry of defence were positive and a MOU for the purchase of the tanks was signed subject to the relevant export licenses being issued by the Indian Government.

Indira Ghandi (soon to be assassinated) was the Prime Minister of India during this period and had close links with Russia. It was feared that the supply of a large quantity of battle tanks could only be used with one purpose in mind - the invasion of South Yemen by the North. Relations with the Marxist South Yemen were precarious and civil war erupted in 1986 with unification finally being agreed only in 1990.

The Export license was never approved!

On another occasion Martin introduced Bill to one of Brazil's leading generals who was in London to negotiate the purchase 155mm howitzer ammunition for the Army.

Brazil had been under military rule since 1964 and in the early 1980s was still under de facto military control. The United States had provided strong political support culminating in Operation Condor in the mid seventies intended to eradicate communism throughout much of South America. However during 1977 Brazil had renounced military aid from the United States due to the dispute over Brazil's intentions to develop its own nuclear capabilities and was now looking elsewhere for its armaments.

The meeting took place in a London hotel suite and it was agreed that Bonaventure would arrange the supply of shells from an Italian plant with whom Bill had an existing relationship.

The General, who had demanded at the start of the meeting to see Martin's passport, then announced that he would retain it as surety for the contract! He was finally persuaded to return it the following evening after a very expensive visit to a night club!

Business with Libya was declining rapidly as the lower oil prices kicked in and Bonaventure's revenues were dropping - urgent action was required to save the business.

In addition the behaviour of the Libyan Government was becoming more and more erratic and their relations with the British Government was deteriorating fast. Matters came to a head with the murder of a police woman outside the Libyan Embassy in St James Square, London on the 17th April 1984.

With falling income there was also a need to make economies at home. With four young children the couple felt a move to the country was sensible - well away from the social distractions and expense of Monte Carlo. They put the lease of their apartment in the Le Formentor up for sale and before long closed a deal with a wealthy American client of the Hotel de Paris in Monte Carlo.

In order to maintain their Monaco residency status they leased a smaller apartment in Monte Carlo overlooking the harbour.

They already had friends living near Geneva and Bill had extensive and well established banking connections there so they decided to move from Monaco to the Lake Geneva area but remain on French territory. The family settled in the countryside near the small village of Ballaison adjacent to Douvaine with a fine view of the lake and the Jura mountains. It proved to be a very convenient location in every way being just a 15 minute drive across the frontier to Geneva with its banks and international airport while at the same time offered the advantages of living in rural France adjacent to Thonon-Les-Bains and Evian. The house was a large bungalow style villa with a big garden, swimming pool and servants' quarters. An English couple were engaged to help look after the children. He was also able to secure a mooring for his boat in the picturesque port of Nernier. Bill had previously arranged to share the Geneva office of his old friend Heinz Pollman - a long established Swiss based arms trader. Heinz was considering semi-retirement and was keen to see if his business could be integrated in some way with the activities of Bonaventure.

A former second world war tank commander in the Waffen SS Heinz had excellent relationships with a number of European armament manufacturers including both Bofors and Carl Gustav in Sweden. This colourful character had only recently been permitted to legally enter France again after a ban imposed by the French Government following an incident in Morocco.

Since 1957 Morocco had claimed sovereignty over Western Sahara (formerly Spanish Sahara) as its Southern Province in the face of fierce resistance from local militia known as the Polisario. As a result a guerrilla war had broken out which eventually lasted until a ceasefire was negotiated by the United Nations in 1991. The Polisario were backed by the Algerian Government who supplied both arms and funding to the militia.

France and the United states had sided with Morocco but it was not until 1977 that France intervened directly following the kidnapping of a number of French technicians near the border with Mauritania who had also laid claim to the territory following the discovery of large phosphate deposits.

The Algerian Government had placed a substantial order with Heinz for Swedish produced weapons and ammunition for delivery to an Algerian air force base near Tindouf bordering Western Sahara. Heinz chartered a Boeing freighter to fly the consignment from Sweden to Algeria and had decided to travel on the aircraft himself to supervise the cargo unloading and safe delivery to his client.

Unfortunately for him French intelligence had got wind of the transaction and he was awoken over the Bay of Biscay by the pilot to be advised that the aircraft had been intercepted by two French air force Mirage fighters. Looking out from each side of the cockpit the fighters could be seen positioned alongside each wing tip of the aircraft!

The freighter was forced to land at an air force base near La Rochelle and the cargo was confiscated.

Heinz was arrested but was released without charges after extensive "debriefing" and upon the condition that he was banned from stepping foot again in any French Territory.

Heinz had agreed to see if his business could be merged in some way with Bonaventure - a sort of joint venture. However it was not to be as they soon discovered that their management styles were very different. Heinz would close the office for long lunches with friends which Bill was expected to attend and would not keep the offices open into the early evening irrespective of the workload.

After a few months Bill decided to move out and work from home where he had outfitted a basement office complete with telex and fax communications with his housekeeper doubling as his secretary/PA.

He continued to maintain an excellent working and social relationship with Heinz and they collaborated closely on a number of deals together in the Middle East. Bill and Barbara would often meet up with Heinz and his wife Sarah for Sunday lunch on Lake Annecy at their favourite watering hole - Auberge du Père Bise in Talloires - which had one of the finest wine cellars in Europe!

A fresh start and business planning for the future was called for.

Bill had meanwhile closed his London offices, sold the remaining lease on his Charles Street property and, with much regret, made all his London based staff redundant. It was time to transform Bonaventure into a full scale military sales organisation to take advantage of the ongoing military conflicts in the Middle East and Afghanistan.

He realised that political focus was essential to his planning and that to succeed he would need to align his business with those of NATO and in particular France where he now resided and Switzerland where he planned to have his permanent offices.

He would need to create a "new" Bonaventure entity as his original organisation was de facto a Panamanian holding company.

Retaining exactly the same name - Bonaventure International - he established his "new" operation in the British West Indies which offered the best of both worlds - the protection and respectability of a British Company but with no corporate tax obligations.

At the same time, in order to comply with Swiss regulations, he created a new Swiss company called Bonaventure SA which would be used as the vehicle to employ staff and to pay local bills relating to any business expenses arising in Geneva.

During the closure of the London offices and subsequent disposal of the Mayfair property Bill had met a man named Patrick Benson - known as "Irish Pat" to all his friends.

A tough Cockney with a legal and accounting background Pat was just the character he was looking for to take care of his new Bonaventure base in Geneva thus freeing Bill to travel extensively - sometimes for months on end - arranging contracts and supplies of military materials to foreign Governments.

They became lifelong friends and met regularly over the years long after their business relationship had passed. Sadly, Pat died in 2016 from cirrhosis of the liver.

The next question for Bill was where and how to arrange suitable offices in Geneva with the minimum of overhead. The solution was soon to present itself.

Bill had been friends for some time with Mehmet Karamehmet, the owner of the Swiss traders Baytur Trading which was itself a subsidiary of the Turkish banking conglomerate Cukurova Holdings based in Istanbul.

Cukurova in addition to its Turkish banks also owned several banks in Switzerland. Cukurova Holdings is, to this day, still owned by Mehmet Karamehmet and his family. In 2010 Forbes estimated his personal wealth to be around $4billion. Bill had developed a close friendship with Emin Sirin - the General Manager at Baytur Trading. Emin had agreed with Mehmet to be released from Baytor so that he could set up his own commodity trading activities while still retaining a close working relationship with his old company. Emin was looking for a suitable company to share his offices who would complement and not compete with his commodity trading activities.

Bonaventure was the ideal candidate and soon arrangements were settled for Bill together with Pat Benson, now ensconced in his role as Bonaventure's finance director, to move into Emin's new Geneva offices. The arrangement worked well for all parties. Around this time Bill and Barbara had met socially another British couple whose two children attended the same school. Neil, who was also ex Baytur had set up his own commodity trading business and it was in Neil's office that Bill was introduced to an American commodity trader called Randy Kreiling who had recently arrived in Geneva. An outgoing and likable character he and Bill were soon to become close friends. Their characters were very similar in many ways - both had a long history of successful trading, both were risk takers, both had made and sometimes lost fortunes and, as it turned out, shared a close interest and fascination with the procurement and sale of military equipment.

Yet another new chapter of his business career was to open for Bill involving him in some of the most extraordinary military and political events of the 20th century post World War II.

The family at Ballaison, France

CHAPTER 15

Egypt & Afghanistan

On December 24th, 1979 the Soviet Union had invaded Afghanistan in an endeavour to "prop up" Afghan's Communist President Nor Tariki. Insurgent groups known as the Mujahedeen fought a long and ultimately successful guerrilla war against the invaders finally forcing the withdrawal of Soviet forces in early 1989.

The Mujahedeen were backed primarily by the USA, Saudi Arabia and Pakistan - it was de facto a proxy Cold War. The Mujahedeen began to receive massive amounts of aid and military equipment financed by the USA and Saudis. The CIA played a very important role in providing US military assistance to the Mujahedeen primarily channelled through Pakistan.

Iran, which shared a common border with Afghanistan, was totally preoccupied with its war with Iraq following the Iraqi invasion in September 1980 but by 1985 its relationship with the communist regime in Afghanistan had also deteriorated as Iranian Shia groups supported the Mujahedeen and by default became participants in driving out the Soviet forces.

In the mid 1980s, when Bill was first introduced to Randy Kreiling, the Soviet presence had grown to over 108,000 troops and the level of fighting was increasing. For the first time pitched battles were taking place and with each successful engagement the Mujahedeen were capturing large quantities of Soviet weapons, artillery and even tanks.

However the Mujahedeen had difficulty getting their hands on suitable ammunition to use in their captured weaponry as the Soviet troops were usually able to destroy ammunition stocks when they withdrew from their positions rather than permit them to fall into enemy hands. Their preoccupation and those of their American allies was to find the means to obtain suitable Soviet designed ammunition with which to utilise these captured heavy armaments.

America, Saudi Arabia, Pakistan and other Western allies were all equipped with NATO calibre armaments which were of no use for the captured Russian calibres. It became essential for Russian designed munitions to be sourced and secretly shipped into Afghanistan. Being landlocked the only option was to truck supplies over the border with Pakistan which was a logistics nightmare in every respect.

As it turned out Bill and Randy were ideally placed to participate in this potentially lucrative business. Randy was 6 years younger than Bill and also had experienced an extraordinary career or to be more accurate a series of careers.

Randall Kreiling was born and raised in Peoria, Illinois. A fine athlete, he played football, was a swimming and diving champion and won a national black belt at Karate. He attended Southern Methodist University in Dallas earning an honours degree in Economics followed by a law degree at SMU. By the age of 30 he was an internationally renowned commodities trader.

In Dallas he had met and married Helen Hunt - daughter of Nelson Bunker Hunt scion of Haroldson Lafayette Hunt owner of Hunt Oil who at the time of his death was one of America's three richest men alongside Howard Hughes and Paul Getty at the time of his death.

Herbert, brother of Nelson Bunker Hunt, hit the big time in Libya in the 1960s when his company Placid Oil discovered the Sarir oil field with reserves estimated at 11-13 billion barrels. He went on to own oilfields in the Philippines and Mexico as well as numerous skyscrapers, ranches and mines around the world. In the 1970s he was reckoned to be worth up to $16 billion. At one time Herbert had 1,000 race horses!

Randy was welcomed into the Hunt family and invited to join the Hunts in what was to become the biggest gamble ever made by an individual family.

In 1973 Nelson, together with Herbert, attempted to corner the world silver market.

Randy was soon to become an important player in this mammoth "game of poker". As the "family commodities expert" he started to purchase silver futures on a scale never seen before. Even more extraordinary was that the Hunts insisted on taking physical delivery of the silver they purchased.

Within a year they had accumulated 55 million ounces of silver - 8% of the world's supply. They insisted upon physical delivery and storage on their Circle K Ranch under Randy's management despite the potential danger of robbery. Eventually Randy was able to persuade the family that it might be wiser to store their silver in Switzerland. Aircraft were chartered to transport the silver to New York and thence to Zurich for storage in the vaults of Credit Suisse and Friedlager.

In 1975 Bunker had visited Tehran to meet the Shah's brother and then to Saudi Arabia for talks with members of the Royal Family. The discussions resulted in the Saudis forming a joint venture with the Hunts called the International Metal Investment Company which became the main vehicle for ongoing purchases of silver in the commodities markets. Throughout 1974 silver prices rocketed and by 1979 the Hunts and their Saudi partners had virtually cornered the world silver market with around 66% of the world's supply and the price for silver over this period had jumped from $6 to $48 per ounce but by March 1980 prices collapsed back to just $10 per ounce.

The Hunts inevitably found themselves unable to meet their obligations which caused panic in the silver markets so The US Federal Reserve Board intervened by granting the Hunts a billion dollar credit line. When the oil prices followed suit that same year the Hunts were forced to file for bankruptcy in order to protect the family assets and a major Federal investigation was launched.

Randy wisely decided it was perhaps time to leave the United States. He purchased a property on Hydra in Greece and restarted his commodity trading activities. Helen did not wish to move with their three daughters from Texas to Greece so the couple had agreed to divorce much to the disapproval of the Hunts.

In 1975 Randy had visited China and had been able to arrange a meeting with Chairman Mao's de facto second in command - Deng Xiaoping. China had continued to suffer severe food shortages following the so called "Cultural Revolution" but was still a major rice exporter in order to obtain hard currency.

Following his meeting with Deng, Randy had been able to negotiate lucrative purchases of Chinese rice together with certain other commodities including silver and rare earth metals. Deng had strong ties to the Military and had directed Randy to discuss the possibility of potential armament exports with several major Chinese Exporters owned and controlled by the Military of which the two most important were Norinco and Poly Tech.

Chairman Mao died in 1976 and the following year Deng had become the supreme leader of China. He had started to instigate far reaching economic reforms which heralded the start of the so called Chinese economic miracle.

Randy had continued to maintain his strong links with China

throughout this period but had not really been able to exploit the export potential of Chinese armaments controlled by Norinco and Polytech.

Bill meanwhile had been developing his own close connections with armament manufacturers in Italy and France but also with Warsaw Pact countries in Eastern Europe in conjunction with Heinz Pollmann - in particular Poland, Hungary and also Romania which was not a Warsaw pact member but produced its own Soviet calibre munitions. Following a meeting in Geneva with an Egyptian Agent with close ties to the Ministry of Defence Procurement department Bill visited Egypt. He was soon to learn that much of the Egyptian MOD purchases were being funded by the CIA as a conduit for the supply of ammunition to the Mujahedeen via Pakistan.

Egypt with its large army was the perfect cover for this supply route as it had an existing huge inventory of Soviet artillery, mortars, rockets and RPG launchers and could therefore be seen by the press and public to be a totally legitimate and credible buyer of such equipment on a continuous basis.

Bill and Randy decided to pool their military contacts and the pair were soon headed to Cairo where they took up residence in the Sheraton Hotel on Gezira Island. It turned out to be a long stay with both of them commuting back to Geneva every month or so.

In his spare time - and there was plenty of it - Bill was encouraged by Randy to become really fit and the pair took over the use of the small gym in the hotel basement. Randy acted as Bill's trainer and was soon to introduce him to some more hard core skills including both offensive and defensive unarmed combat.

Guided by their Egyptian agent and the retired General hired to assist them they commuted most days to the Procurement Department at the Ministry of Defence located about 30 minutes taxi ride from their Hotel. They soon became familiar figures in the waiting room!

Either by accident or design the Egyptians put all their potential suppliers for each contract in the same waiting room and then summoned them in one by one to make their technical and commercial presentations relating to each specific purchasing requirement.

Many times the same few faces were to be seen day in day out with the main competitors being the North Korean delegates who could be easily identified by their badges with the face of their Supreme Leader Kim Il Sung, posthumously now called the Eternal President of the DPRK.

All contracts placed by the Egyptians were for shipment to Red Sea

Ports and most if not all suppliers had to use specially chartered vessels as the munitions could not be shipped on normal cargo ships for safety and security reasons. Officially that was their final destination but in reality the munitions were unloaded, stored dockside and then reloaded on ships destined for the Naval Base in Karachi.

Once the supplies arrived in Pakistan they were unloaded for storage by the Navy under the control of the Directorate of Military Procurement until such time as they were loaded onto fleets of trucks for clandestine delivery across the border to Helmand Province in southern Afghanistan.

The Soviets continuously monitored border crossing activity with aerial patrols so once they approached the border the trucks were dispersed to various locations and the convoys were reassembled under cover of darkness then proceeded slowly to move across the border with all lights off.

One of the senior KGB officers posted to Helmand as part of the Russian border forces responsible for intercepting these supplies was Major Anatoly Kaleshnikov.

Neither Bill nor Anatoly could have possibly conceived that their paths would cross again many years later in Bishkek, the capital city of Kyrgyzstan where Anatoly not only introduced Bill to his future wife Irina but also became godfather to Bill's daughter Justine.

Small world!

Bill's first order was for 20,000 rounds of 130 mm artillery ammunition each one consisting of a separate projectile and loading charge. He negotiated the purchase of the shells with the Polish MOD and arranged for an Egyptian delegation to inspect the inventory and test fire 6 rounds at random prior to shipment from Gdansk to Egypt.

The Egyptians nominated two Army Generals as their inspectors who flew to Warsaw where they were met by Bill and Barbara who had accompanied him on his visit. The following day Bill and the Generals were collected from their hotel by an army car and driven some 50 miles or so to a large ammunition storage facility while Barbara remained in Warsaw to take a look around the city.

It was February and exceedingly cold so the generals were in a hurry to complete the inspection. Six rounds were picked at random from the ammunition stockpile and taken by truck to the firing range where several 130mm field guns were lined up. The party were issued with ear protectors and the range gunners successfully fired two shells at 10 kms, 2 rounds at 20 kms and 2 rounds at the maximum range of 27 kms. The party returned to Warsaw and Barbara joined them for a celebration dinner followed by a visit to a strip tease show, much to the amazement of the generals!

Meanwhile Randy had agreed to concentrate on monitoring orders to be sourced and shipped from China.

Orders were placed there including 82mm mortar rounds.

These were followed by a large order for Rocket Propelled Grenade (RPG) ammunition which Bill again sourced in Poland. These were based on the newly developed Thermobaric rounds suitable for anti-personnel and urban warfare.

Another potential supplier for Bonaventure was Romania and with his growing reputation as a trusted and reputable armaments supplier Bill was not surprised to be contacted by the regime.

Romania was still ruled by the iron grip of the Ceausescu family and backed by the Chinese. The country had become a major manufacturer and supplier of armaments and munitions - all reverse engineered from Russian designs.

Marin Ceausescu - the President's elder brother and Head of the Romanian Trade Mission- was based in Vienna.

Marin, via a mutual friend Hans Pragler, invited Bill accompanied by Pat Benson for a private meeting at his villa on the outskirts of Vienna.

Bill trusted Hans' business acumen as the previous year he introduced him to an Austrian company that had a major contract to supply certain components classified as "civilian" under Austria's export regulations to an Iranian Research institute.

The Austrians were having difficulty in fulfilling the order for some very special and expensive components which they had been unable to source on an industrial scale.

The components in question were tiny washers of the types used in clock making to be made of pure gold which then had to certified by an approved Swiss inspection agency prior to shipment.

Being based in Geneva Bill was confident that he could source the washers legally in compliance with Swiss regulations and agreed to supply the entire quantity on a profit sharing basis with the Austrians.

He located a specialist workshop near Zurich known as a "movement maker" who agreed to produce the washers.

The Swiss asked no questions but Bill was curious as to the possible use of the "washers" which seemed to be intended for some sort of applications in an environment that was hostile and subject to corrosion.

Silver has the highest thermal conductivity of any metal so why use gold? Gold has much higher corrosion resistance than silver or copper so what item could possibly be so focused on corrosion as to go to the expense of using pure gold washers?

He concluded that the "washers" application had to relate to fuse mechanisms - in particular proximity fuses - used in missiles, rockets and artillery shells where component corrosion arising from storage was of critical importance. Ironically he would be on the receiving end of some of these "components" before too long.

Marin asked Bill if he was willing to visit Romania, as a guest of the Government, to inspect their locally manufactured munitions production capabilities and to discuss possible contracts with the Minister of Defence. Bill was soon on his way to Bucharest accompanied by Pat Benson.

Upon landing they were greeted at the aircraft door by Ministry officials and whisked through the airport to the Intercontinental Hotel.

Bucharest had been a beautiful city but at that time was a sad and miserable place completely stripped of its former glory with almost nothing to purchase in any shops, virtually no street lighting, no cars and virtually no people to be seen on the streets except those hurrying between work and home. Even the hotel - supposedly the best in the country - was ill lit and very cold.

Almost every dish featured on the restaurant menu was "not available today"

Bill had brought with him his own Guartel radio microphone detector and much to his amusement following a detailed sweep of his room located 6 "bugs". Pat Benson's room was similarly compromised so they agreed to hold any private talks via written notes retained on their person at all times during the visit. The following day they were taken to what looked like a park near the city centre.

However this was no normal park as it was encircled by a high security fence and the entrance was manned by armed guards in military uniforms. Inside the park were a series of buildings and bunkers sunk deep underground and covered by topsoil and vegetation.

The road from the entrance led directly underground into a large garage - exceptionally well lit and clean totally in contrast with the rest of the city.

The underground complex included a large reception area, several meeting rooms and a carpeted passageway leading to a series of large underground show rooms containing an array of armaments and military vehicles from heavy machine guns to armoured vehicles. It was a splendid and astonishing display of the countries indigenous military production capabilities. Following the tour of the show rooms a small reception and luncheon was held in one of the conference rooms.

Bill submitted a list of military equipment that Bonaventure wished to offer to their clients.

The following morning they were driven to the VIP facility at the airport for their return flight to Geneva.

Bonaventure subsequently placed orders for mortars and ammunition which were then shipped from Constanta to Adabiya - part of the Port Suez complex on the Red Sea used by the Egyptian navy.

All connections with Romania had ceased by late 1989 following the start of the Romanian Revolution but Bill was to return to Bucharest many times in the following decade en route to Moldova.

The President - Nicolae Ceausescu - and his wife Elena were executed by firing squad on Christmas Day 1989 following the collapse and overthrow of his regime three days earlier.

Four days later on December 29th, 1989 Bill's contact Marin Ceausescu - the President's brother was found dead in his Vienna office - his body was found hanging from a heating pipe in the cellar under his office according to police reports. He was also said to be armed so many speculated whether he had really committed suicide or had been "assisted" by third parties.

By 1987 and early 1988, following the signing of the DRA, USSR, US and Pakistan peace accords the Soviets started to withdraw their forces from Afghanistan, their 10 year tenure of "helping" the country had cost over 15,000 Russian lives.

By then Bill had already shifted his main focus to Iraq and the ongoing hostilities with Iran.

A new chapter of his career and life had, once again, opened with participation in one of the most extraordinary periods of history in modern times.

CHAPTER 16

Iraq

During 1987 Emin Sirin, with whom Bonaventure were sharing office space, introduced Bill to a Milan based Iraqi national called Kassim Abbas who appeared to have very close connections with the Iraqi Ministry of Defence. His speciality was the procurement of machinery and components for supply to Iraq's burgeoning Defence Industries.

Iraq under Saddam Hussein's leadership was determined to become as self-sufficient as possible in the production of military equipment including locally produced armaments, munitions, bombs and missiles based on a "reverse engineered" locally produced version of the Scud.

This policy was encouraged by the United States and all the major European powers who saw this as an opportunity to defeat the Iranians and of course offered lucrative contracts for their defence related industries.

The war with Iran was grinding on with ever greater emphasis being placed on local armament production.

Kassim had created a quite substantial business sourcing specialised metals, machine tools etc primarily in Italy but lacked the contacts and knowledge to source throughout Europe whereas Bill and his team at Bonaventure had developed extensive contacts and substantial expertise in this field. In addition and most importantly Bonaventure enjoyed and had developed an excellent trade banking relationship with Barclays International in Geneva.

Kassim drove to Geneva for an initial meeting with Bill, Emin Sirin and Bonaventure's Finance Director Pat Benson.

An agreement was reached whereby Abbas would introduce Bill personally, as the owner of Bonaventure, to all the main armament plants in Iraq as a "trusted supplier" in return for a specific fee payable on each transaction successfully completed.

The next step was to organise a visit to Iraq with Bill's visa to be issued by the Iraqi Embassy in Rome. By then he was holding three passports all of which had been authorised by the British Authorities in view of his extensive continuous travel to countries, primarily in the Arab world, which required visas.

At that time in order to apply for an Iraqi visa it was necessary to declare if the applicant had previously visited Iran so he was very careful to use a passport which had no evidence of his previous visits to Tehran! He was soon on his way to Baghdad accompanied by Kassim.

Baghdad was a real eye opener for Bill and quite unlike any previous Arab country he had visited.

The airport was clean and efficient - no tips or bribes - and within 30 minutes of landing they were on their way to the Al Rasheed Hotel which was to become de facto Bill's residence for the next several years. Abbas always stayed at his family villa located in the nearby Al Mansour district.

The Al Rasheed was a fine 18 storey hotel much favoured by "visiting dignitaries" and the military and was set in magnificent gardens with a swimming pool and tennis courts.

Whilst the hotel had a properly functional business centre including fax facilities all communications, both incoming and outgoing, were copied and then passed on daily to the SSO (Special Security Organisation) for checking and filing. All telephone calls were recorded for subsequent checking.

The next morning Kassim and Bill set off to visit the first of the armament plants that Bill was to deal with over the coming months. They were to have a formal meeting with each Director General.

Over a ten day period Bill visited most of the Plants that were to subsequently become his clients.

He had no idea at that time that unwittingly he would end up as a participant and role player in what was to become the largest UN military operation since the Korean war.

Each Plant had an individual name many of which sounded somewhat exotic to Western ears and included:

Al Kadesiah, Hutteen, Al Qaqaa, SOTI, Nassr Al Faruk and the more prosaically named Precision Casting Factory!

The Iraqis had a very different procurement system than most countries at that time and quite certainly very different from Bill's previous experiences in dealing with military contracts.

At that time Iraq was devoting at least 40% of all oil revenues to military related procurement. Unlike other countries each factory was allowed to enter into its own supply contracts providing the orders related to the production output of their specific military product range. Each contract was negotiated and agreed on a face to face basis, there were no tenders or bidding involved.

The Plant buyers were however very knowledgeable and had a very good idea of the realistic costs of each product or piece of equipment so there was little point in attempting to pull the wool over their eyes. They expected and received fair prices from their trusted suppliers and always allowed them to make a decent margin with the result that many suppliers developed a loyal and protective attitude towards the plants and their management.

Overall control of the Plant programmes was centrally managed by the Ministry of Industry and Military Industrialisation known as MIMI.

MIMI was headed by Hussein Kamal al Majid, Saddam's son-in-law and second cousin who was also head of the Secret Service Organisation (SSO). His key deputy was Colonel Safa Al-Habobi who was also the Director of Hutteen, the facility which ultimately was suspected of contributing to Iraq's nuclear weapons programme.

Hussein Kamel and his brother Saddam Kamel, who were both married to daughters of Saddam Hussein, defected to Jordan with their wives in August 1995. They co-operated with the CIA and MI6 but the secrets they thought would make them wealthy and safe were not considered that valuable by the West. They were persuaded to return to Iraq in February 1996 when they were to be "forgiven". However upon their return they were ordered to divorce their wives, denounced as traitors and executed.

Bill was to meet with Hussein Kamal regularly at Hutteen and Safa also visited Bill in London at the Bonaventure offices as head of the Iraqi MIMI delegation and visited several UK equipment suppliers represented by Bonaventure.

All the military industrial facilities in Iraq were also encouraged, particularly following the ceasefire with Iran in August 1988, to utilise their plants to produce civilian products as well as armaments.

The Al Kadesiah plant specialised in the production of small arms including Beretta 9mm pistols under an existing license agreement with Beretta in Italy who at that time was under the leadership of Dr. Hugo Gussali Beretta.

With a history dating back to the early 16th century Beretta is unquestionably the oldest firearms manufacturer and the oldest family owned company in the world having been under continuous family ownership and management since 1526. Beretta, whose first order was to supply the Venice Republic with a quantity of arquebus barrels, has since supplied weapons for every major European war since 1650.

Ironically some 20 years later Dr Beretta and Bill's paths would again cross in a totally different context as Bill, in his capacity as President of Ocean Airlines, was to meet regularly with Dr Beretta the President of Brescia Airport.

In 2000 Bill was to live for several years in Gardone Val Trompia near Brescia in a penthouse apartment located just down the road from the Beretta Plant!

His two younger daughters, Justine and Katy, were both born in the Gardone Val Trompia Hospital.

In addition to the production of Beretta pistols Al Kadesiah also produced the renowned AK-47 assault rifle based on Yugoslav drawings known as the Tabuk AK and a 7.62 Russian design semi auto sniper rifle based on the AK called the Tabuk Sniper Rifle and the Al Kadesiah Sniper Rifle.

The Hutteen plant manufactured ammunition including aerial bombs and heavy artillery shells for Iraq's conventional weapons programme.

Al Qaqaa produced the SCUD B Al Hussein class missiles.

The State Organisation of Technical Industries known as SOTI was responsible for procurement of certain components destined for military plants but whose use was never revealed to suppliers.

Nassr, with its multiple sites, produced components for the SCUD B Al Hussein missiles and as it subsequently turned out, although unknown to Bill and his subcontractors, was to be used as the prime facility to produce what became known as the "Supergun".

The Al Faruk facility specialised in the manufacture of transporters and launchers for the long range missile programme.

Before long the factories started to place trial orders for components with Bill in order to "test" Bonaventure's capabilities as a potential supplier.

Bill could see the enormous potential to become a trusted supplier to MIMI and decided to base himself in Baghdad, a move which was welcomed by the authorities.

He settled into a five week routine. He would normally spend 3 weeks in Baghdad and then return to Geneva for 2 weeks of family leave and to oversee order progress with his staff and to meet suppliers.

He engaged one of the hotel taxi drivers, who had security clearance to drive him to the various plants, as a de facto chauffeur. The most important issue was to make sure during summer months that the vehicles air conditioning was working properly as temperatures in the desert areas, where the factories were located, could easily reach 50C.

This arrangement was no doubt convenient for all concerned providing Bill with reliable transport and entry to the facilities while at the same time allowing the SSO to keep track of his visits and movements.

Baghdad at that time was a very pleasant city in which to reside. It was safe, the people were friendly, the shops had everything one could wish for and there were many picturesque open air restaurants located along the Tigris which specialised in barbecuing the excellent Tigris carp.

Alcohol was freely available upon request and the Al Rasheed hotel had an excellent wine cellar!

Bill felt it safe enough to bring his eldest daughter Alix with him on one of his trips. They had a fine time together first flying to Cairo where Alix, who was horse crazy, joined him on a wonderful early morning ride around the Pyramids and then on to Baghdad where she stayed with the family of a friend of her fathers' who was Head of the Iraqi Olympics team.

The Iraqis worked hard and most were totally dedicated to their families. There was only one day off work per week - Fridays.

Military personnel were not permitted to socialise with foreigners without special permission except when abroad as part of a delegation which suited Bill just fine.

No commissions were ever requested which was a most welcome change. This was hardly surprising as any military person suspected of bribery faced execution.

While commissions or gifts to any Government official were strictly prohibited there was one notable exception - the "Boss".

In early 1990 as a mark of the importance of Bonaventure as a supplier it was mentioned by several senior government personnel that the gift of a couple of Arabian Oryx to Saddam's private zoo would be much appreciated.

These rare animals were bred in captivity in Texas so Bill located a reputable breeding farm and paid $20,000 for a pair which he arranged with Lufthansa to ship from Houston to Baghdad via Frankfurt. The animals arrived safely and in good health!

One dreads to think of what may have happened to them the following years after the US led coalition invasion of Iraq.

The heroic rescue of many of the animals by a small team of dedicated Iraqis and South African born Lawrence Anthony are faithfully recorded in his book Babylon's Ark.

On Fridays Bill could usually be found in the hotel swimming pool or in the shade nearby reading. On occasions he went on excursions down the Tigris to Babylon or other towns located along the river.

The ongoing hostilities with Iran usually seemed very remote but Fridays, during that period until the ceasefire was declared on August 20th, 1988, could be somewhat unnerving as the Iranians seemed to choose Fridays as their "missile day" - perhaps they had nothing better to do!

The Scud missile attacks usually started around 10 o'clock in the morning with the first signs of the impending attack being the wailing sounds of the sirens. As soon as the sirens stopped everybody would suddenly become very still and very quiet - you could almost hear a pin drop! The next sound would be the explosive impact of the missile either nearby by or some distance away depending on the impact location.

In general the Scuds were not very accurate and it was just a matter of pot luck where they landed - a bit like the German V2 rockets of WW II. Surprisingly the collateral damage was minimal as the warheads had a limited explosive capacity and impact fuses.

Baghdad's terrain was very sandy soil so usually the missiles would impact the ground prior to exploding with the result that almost all the shock waves were absorbed downwards into the soil. It was not unusual following an attack to see a large crater 5-10 metres deep but the houses nearby with hardly a shattered window. Of course anyone who was unlucky enough to be in the line of a direct hit was blown to smithereens!

The regime, unlike most other Arab countries, tolerated Christianity and de facto the Christians were regarded as natural supporters of the Sunni minority who made up the majority of the Baathist regime under Saddam's leadership. The 70% Shia majority were generally not trusted and often suspected by some Iraqis to be an Iranian backed fifth column!

Most of the Iraqis that Bill came to know were totally secular and appeared to have little or no interest in religion. They enjoyed what was at that time the best free health service in the entire Arab world, excellent education, good universities and the opportunity to study abroad. Most were Sunnis but there were also many Christian engineers who held positions of authority and were trusted and tolerated by the regime.

Tariq Aziz, the Foreign Minister and Deputy to Saddam Hussein who was to become the "face" of Iraq following the Kuwait invasion, was a Christian born as Mikhail Yuhanna and a member of the Chaldean Catholic Church!

The 1987 census - Iraq's last - counted 1.4 million Christians (8 % of the population) - mainly Catholic Chaldeans, Nestorians and Eastern Orthodox. On several occasions Bill attended Sunday services at the Presbyterian church.

Life in Iraq was very simple for everyone including foreigners - support the regime and keep your nose out of politics! Bill maintained no social life of any sort in Baghdad - he kept himself to himself and did not mix with any of the Expatriate European community at all.

He would occasionally fly out a technical expert to accompany him for meetings at the plants if it was necessary but these visitors were never permitted by him to meet the Plant Directors or to be privy to financial or contractual dealings.

This ensured absolute confidentiality for both the Plants and for Bonaventure which, being Geneva based, was well protected by Swiss privacy legislation.

It was a somewhat lonely existence but his work kept him exceedingly busy and he always brought with him a good supply of books.

Bill's hard work soon paid off with more and more orders being placed and letters of credit being opened in favour of Bonaventure by then considered a "trusted" supplier by the regime.

By early 1990 the Iraqi Plants had placed numerous contracts and his outstanding order book at the start of that year exceeded $10,000,000.

Bonaventure's suppliers were mainly based in the UK and Italy but also included China, Austria, France, Switzerland and even Australia.

There was however a major exception when Bill was asked to arrange for an Iraqi delegation visit to South Africa for discussions with the Armscor Corporation for the supply and technology transfer of long range155 mm artillery shells.

The South Africans had developed with the aid of Dr Gerald Bull a much improved 155mm artillery round known as the extended range base bleed shell.

Dr Gerald Bull, a Canadian, was the world's foremost artillery expert who by then, unknown to most people, had been secretly engaged by the Iraqis to head up a special related project which Bill was to become entangled with the following year!

The maximum standard range of a 155 howitzer is 30 kms whereas the Armscor base bleed rounds had a range of 40 kms and they had recently developed, with the assistance of Dr Bull, an even longer range rocket assisted shell capable of reaching 50 kms known as the V-LAP round.

The Iraqis were very keen to get their hands on these shells for use on the Iranian front.

Bill, who was friends of the Swiss based Armscor representative, was able to arrange the visit and he flew the Iraqi delegation via Switzerland to Johannesburg for the meetings followed by a live fire demos of the South African produced G5 howitzer using these extended range shells.

The South Africans also arranged a demo of another new item - an anti tank device using a special shape charge.

This devise could be hidden in a bush or buried on a known tank route and was triggered by a magnetic sensor or wire as the tank passed by.

The delegation witnessed this demonstration from close quarters in an underground bunker equipped with special cameras. The noise and vibration was incredible!

On another occasion Bill was asked to arrange the supply warhead cones.

He was provided with a set of drawings of a missile warhead cone which was to be machined from a special aluminium alloy.

He headed for Austria to meet an old friend who operated a suitable machine shop.

The cone was duly produced and Bill headed back to Baghdad via Amsterdam having checked in the missile cone as extra large luggage.

Upon arrival in Baghdad there was no sign of the cone and no one could explain its absence.

The next day Bill returned to the airport to meet the next KLM flight accompanied by two military personnel and much to his relief there was the missing cone.

It had obviously been opened and tucked inside was a little note which read "be careful what you ship" - somebody had a sense of humour!

As a French resident, Bill was expected to report to the French Military Attaché in Baghdad on a regular basis and had started to develop a close working relationship - encouraged by the Attaché - with some of the leading French defence equipment suppliers.

Bill always made sure that Bonaventure acted as the principal in all transactions. That way he could control the profit margins in total confidence and privacy. All commercial transactions and banking were undertaken in the name of his primary off shore company Bonaventure International.

Back in Geneva Pat Benson had reached an agreement for Barclays to handle the Bonaventure account, receive and confirm letters of credit, issue where necessary performance bonds and to open letters of credit to the factories supplying Bonaventure.

Bonaventure Services was operating efficiently for all equipment procurement, quality control, inspection and testing, shipping, accounting and letter of credit documentation preparation.

However the Company was not just focused on Iraq. As an example his back office team which was a polyglot mixture of nationalities - British, Swiss and French including two ex British Army personnel - a former General and Sergeant who were both small arms experts engaged on a non Iraqi project relating to muzzle stabilisers for automatic assault rifles and sub machine guns.

Bonaventure had acquired the sales rights of these American designed muzzle stabilisers for a number of locations including Egypt.

The Company was asked by the Egyptian MOD to arrange a live fire demonstration at their main small arms factory just outside Cairo.

The Bonaventure team flew to Cairo and the demo commenced with Peter, the firearms specialist, located inside the indoor shooting range while the Egyptians, Bill and the General watched through the reinforced glass ports.

The General had noted ammunition boxes stacked up against the side of the range and was concerned but their Egyptian hosts assured him that all was totally safe.

All proceeded well with Peter firing short 3 round bursts but soon after he started firing on full automatic a blue and yellow flash streaked down the range with the interior engulfed in flames. The Egyptians all scattered leaving the General and Bill to open the range door and haul out a badly singed Peter. They ran for their lives out of the building.

Luckily the fire had extinguished itself as the General had closed the range door thus cutting off the oxygen supply.

It seemed that when Peter was firing on full automatic that the fire had been caused by hot ammunition cases dropping on the floor igniting cartridge powder dust.

It was obvious that the factory had failed to keep the indoor range properly cleaned and dust free!

Immaculate records were kept by Bonaventure both as an internal discipline and to ensure legal compliance with all applicable Swiss and country of origin export licenses. Bill was also careful to retain the services of his Geneva and London based lawyers who had both been close personal friends as well as his corporate advisors for decades.

All equipment was shipped to Iraq on a door to door basis by truck using Swiss freight forwarders. The usual trucking route was via Romania and Turkey into Iraq and then southward to the Baghdad area where the plants were located. Bill's obsession with maintaining good records was to be a key protective factor for him as the dramas of 1990 started to unfold.

CHAPTER 17

1990 Year of the Metal Horse

Chinese mythology describes 1990 as the Year of the Metal Horse - the strongest willed and bold to succeed and a term suitably applicable to the events of 1990.

In the Autumn of 1989 Bill had been asked to attend a meeting at Hutteen relating to the supply of equipment for a new "oil refinery" to be built by the State Oil Company with certain "piping and pressure tanks" to be built locally by State enterprises.

During the meeting he was introduced to a British engineer called Dr Christopher Crowley who headed up the refinery design team for a Belgian company called ATI. He was surprised to learn that the owner of ATI was none other than Dr Gerald Vincent Bull.

In March 1990 Gerald Bull was returning to his Brussels apartment when he was killed by an unknown assassin with two pistol shots to the head at point blank range. The highly professional killing was taken as a warning to Iraqi suppliers, who were convinced that it had been arranged by Mossad, not to supply equipment which could harm Israel despite ongoing NATO support for Iraq.

Bonaventure had been selected to arrange the manufacture of high pressure bolts which would be used to connect the high pressure pipes to be used for the new oil refinery.

It all sounded very normal with only one unusual aspect being that the bolts were to be made using a very specific maraging steel.

Maraging steels possess superior strength and are used in the aerospace industry for rocket and missile skins, armouring of ships and vehicles and also has many diverse civil applications including the nuclear industry, fencing blades, surgical and engine components.

Maraging steel production is closely monitored in most countries including Britain and America due to its suitability for use in gas centrifuges for uranium enrichment. Enriched uranium is essential to fuel nuclear power stations and is also used in nuclear weapons. Once back in Geneva he instructed his team to purchase the 20 tons of maraging steel that would be needed. He contracted the production of the bolts to his old friend Angelo Prati who had suitable machining facility at his Valtro small arms factory in Gardone Val Trompia , a small town near Brescia renowned for its production of small arms.

Bill had used this Italian facility, which had the very latest high precision CNC machine shop tools, in the past to produce ultra high pressure valves for Nassr. Their intended usage was a matter of much speculation amongst the Italian engineers and it was only later discovered that these valves formed a vital part of the fuel system for the Iraqi produced Scud missiles.

The specification for the steel was just below the MIL standard which therefore did not require an export license from the British Authorities so the order was placed without any export restrictions with Forge Masters in Sheffield.

Delivery to Italy was due to take place the following spring.

On April 11th, 1990 Bill and Barbara had flown over to New York on Concorde for a weekend break at the Plaza Hotel and were watching CNN in the lobby while waiting for their room to be ready when a newsflash appeared about a "supergun in Iraq" and the seizure of steel pipes by the British customs at Newcastle docks from Forge Masters in Sheffield.

A spate of investigations also took place around Europe as other suspect parts of the so-called super gun were intercepted.

Bill immediately realised that the contract for maraging steel bolts in all probability was also to be part of the supergun components. He knew that the truck destined for Brescia with the steel on board would by now be somewhere between the UK and Italy.

He immediately called Geneva and arranged to have the truck stopped at the Swiss Italian border when it reached Lugano. The office also alerted the Italian customs who duly intercepted the truck and then accompanied the cargo to Brescia where it was placed in a warehouse under customs detention.

Meanwhile other suppliers from all over Europe making components for the "oil refinery" were being visited by customs agents including Angelo Prati at Valtro where the bolts were to be made. No arrests were made.

The real facts were only later to emerge on what this supergun was intended to be. The operation was called Big Babylon and there were two different sides to the story. The Iraqis claimed that they were preparing its use for firing into space a locally manufactured satellite. Dr Bull had been working on the idea of a gun that could fire craft into space since the early 1960s but the same gun would have a range of many hundreds of miles firing an explosive shell.

There is no evidence to suggest that Dr Bull didn't know that the Iraqis more likely target was Israel and other countries within range rather than satellite launches but he was assassinated before he could give any evidence of its intended usage.

The gun he had designed was simply huge and had a barrel length of 156m (512 feet) and a bore of 1 metre.

The completed device would have weighed over 2100 tonnes and would have been built into a hillside to support the barrel. It will never be known for which purpose it was being made - for space travel or heavy bombardment at a great distance or both.

However around this time Bill had been shown at Nassr drawings of a huge shell which was supposedly to be used in a new long range artillery piece. It was only later that he started to realise that this shell was probably destined for use in the supergun. The British and Italian press had a field day with lurid headlines about "superguns", much of which had little basis in fact for the simple reason that there were no facts known at that time. Reporters were telephoning Bonaventure's Geneva offices requesting interviews. Bill decided to remain in New York for the following few days until matters had died down somewhat but he realised that Bonaventure and his future activities would be carefully monitored.

Once back in Europe he returned to Baghdad together with several British based equipment suppliers to discuss the supply of major testing equipment for the University of Baghdad.

Soon after his return to Geneva in early June Bill received some very unexpected visitors.

It was a warm summer night and around 4.00 in the morning he woke up to hear his dogs growling near the front door and looking carefully through the blinds he saw two cars in the drive out of which a number of shadowy figures were emerging.

There was a loud banging on the door followed by shouts of "Police - ouvre la porte".

He immediately opened the door and six armed men dressed in black with balaclavas rushed into the hallway followed by a man in civilian clothes.

Bill and Barbara were both naked but were permitted to get dressed under the watchful eyes of two of the police team who also started to search the bedside drawers.

Everyone was very quiet and very little was said throughout the search. Bill's loaded pistol, which was in the top drawer, was quickly checked and the magazine removed.

Once dressed the couple were told to move to the sitting room where the nanny and Bill's driver/ bodyguard Tony, who had also been roused from bed, were sitting quietly on a sofa guarded by two policemen. The children meanwhile - luckily - had remained asleep and were totally oblivious to the unfolding events.

The civilian, who spoke good English, introduced himself as Pierre. He told Tony and the nanny to return to their quarters to look after the children as normal and to take them to school while Bill and Barbara were to be taken in separate cars down to the Commissariat de police in the neighbouring town of Annemasse for interrogation.

Bill asked repeatedly why they were being arrested and was finally told by Pierre that it was in connection with three assassinations in Athens.

It all seemed pretty strange as neither Bill nor Barbara had visited Athens in recent years and he thought to himself that perhaps this was a "set-up" of some sort. He asked if he could contact his Geneva lawyer only to be told that this would not be permitted as French police are authorised to arrest and detain incommunicado for a limited period of time any person suspected of committing or attempting to commit a criminal offence!

Pierre then asked Bill to open their walk-in master safe in the basement of the house so that they could inspect his firearms all of which were correctly licensed except for a Steyr 30-08 hunting rifle which had recently been presented to him by Steyr in Austria.

He also asked both of them to hand over their personal phone books.

Upon their arrival in Annemasse they were kept apart and told that each would be interrogated separately. Later that morning Barbara was released from detention and driven home by the police with "apologies" for disturbing her and that no charges were to be levelled!

For Bill it was a different situation. The Police interrogator advised him that at that very moment the Swiss Authorities were raiding his Bonaventure offices in Geneva but no explanation or details were given.

He then produced Bill's phone book and at the same time the police brought in a translator to assist.

It turned out that the translator was not only Arab but had very limited English so Bill requested that he be removed and said that he was ready to answer all their questions in French.

Everyone appeared to be relieved as Bill knew that many of their questions could well relate to some very sensitive topics being discussed which would not be suitable for an Arab's ears!

The interrogator, with Pierre listening silently, started to "plough" through Bill's extensive phone book pausing to ask questions about any person in whom he seemed to be taking a particular interest. Much to Bill's amazement very little was asked about his current business in Iraq - the focus was almost entirely on his Libyan connections and in particular the Tripoli based Africa Company. The questioning continued throughout the day and by 1700, over 13 hours after his arrest everyone was exhausted and it was agreed to continue the following day.

By this time the atmosphere had become much more relaxed and the interrogation became more of an interview. However Bill was not permitted to return home but was told that he would be held in a cell over night ready for the following day's interrogation. He was permitted one call to Barbara in order to request her to deliver some food for him to the Commissariat.

During the call she told him that all was "calm" in the Bonaventure offices and that the Swiss officials had only removed some files and drawings then departed and that Pat Benson was working with their lawyers to secure his release.

The Police cells at the Commissariat were deep in the basement and uncomfortable to say the least. Bill's cell had a plain wooden platform set in concrete with a thin folded duvet for a bed and a lavatory in the corner. His supper - a pizza and a bottle of water - were delivered to him in the cell. Sleep was hardly possible as throughout the night drunks, drug addicts and criminals were put in the adjoining cells.

The next morning the interrogation continued finally finishing around mid afternoon. Barbara was called by the Police to collect her husband who was free to return home but that he was to remain in the area on standby for further "discussions" with Pierre during the coming days.

During this second day Bill was finally able to discover in more detail why he was being investigated or at least the official reason which seemed rather farfetched to say the least!

He was told that three political opponents of the Gaddafi regime had been assassinated in Athens a year earlier and that Interpol had tracked the chief suspect, a Libyan national who worked for the Africa

Company - to an address in Stockholm. The Swedish police raided the apartment but were too late - the suspect had escaped and was probably on his way back to Tripoli.

During an extensive search of the apartment the police had found one of Bill's old visiting cards with his Monaco address. Details were passed to Interpol and then to the French DGSI (Direction Generale de la Securite Interieure) who then had proceeded to set-up an extensive surveillance of Bill and Bonaventure's activities in conjunction with the Swiss BAP Federal intelligence service based in Bern. Bill established that Pierre was DGSI. These intelligence services were working on the assumption that because Bill was well known to have extensive Libyan connections to the Africa Company for the supply of military equipment that he was in some way "involved" in the supply of arms to the Libyan Intelligence services and was therefore a suspect in the supply of the weapons that had been used in the Greek assassinations.

It all sounded very implausible as he had long ceased any business with Libya and in his opinion was just an excuse or cover to find out his extensive current dealings in Iraq which therefore had to include the Swiss authorities being asked to raid his offices in Geneva. The files and drawings taken from the office had nothing to do with Libya.

Bill's staff, although shaken by the raid on the Geneva offices by the Swiss authorities, continued to work as normal and had presented a totally united opinion to the Swiss authorities that Bonaventure was a successful company with nothing to hide and that all its business activities were in full compliance with Swiss law.

Bill was soon back in Baghdad accompanied by several of his project technicians and his projects moved ahead without further interruption.

August holidays were soon to arrive and Bill arranged for his technicians and staff to take their annual leave at the end of July ready for a restart on site in September.

He returned to Geneva on August 1st, 1990. A few hours after he left, around 2.00a.m. on August 2nd the first wave of Iraqi troops rolled across the border into Kuwait.

From the Valtro brochure of the time

CHAPTER 18

The Phony War

The Iraqi invasion was quick and effective.

Just after midnight on August 2nd 1990 Iraqi armoured units crossed the border into Kuwait meeting very little resistance from Kuwaiti forces. Within 48 hours Kuwait became the "Republic of Kuwait" only to be renamed three days later on August 29th as the 19th province of Iraq with Kuwait City renamed "Kadhima".

The Kuwaiti forces were quickly overrun and were either captured or retreated across the border into Saudi Arabia and Bahrain. The West was stunned at this unexpected but long threatened event.

There is in fact little doubt, following the public disclosure in 2011 of the conversations between the US Ambassador April Glaspie and Iraq's Foreign Minister, that Saddam thought that he had been given a "green light" to invade or at the very least take over the disputed oilfield on Iraq's Southern border with Kuwait.

Bill was in fact privy to the tape recording of the conversation between April Glaspie and Tariq Aziz -the Iraqi Foreign Minister - during his visit to Tunisia some weeks after the invasion had occurred.

Luckily he and several of his suppliers who had spent July in Baghdad had already left the city for their summer holidays the previous week as the Iraqis closed all their airports to civilian traffic on August 2nd - the very day when a French Technician, who was the only remaining member of the Bonaventure team, was due to fly home to Paris but had been turned away from the airport. He was told to return to his hotel and to remain there until further notice.

Bill kept in close contact with the Technician's wife via the French Foreign Ministry. She had, understandably, become extremely alarmed that her husband could become a hostage.

After several days the Ministry advised that if a payment of $10,000 could be paid to the French Government then their embassy in Baghdad would ensure that the corresponding amount in cash would be handed over to the technician along with verbal instructions on how best to arrange his escape from Baghdad across the border into Jordan.

The plan worked well and within 5 days Bill received confirmation of his safe arrival in Amman and within hours he was on a plane to Paris!

Immediately before and in the days following the invasion Bill had several million dollars worth of goods en route to Iraq. No one really knew what was happening but on August 6th - just 4 days later - the UN Security Council imposed draconian economic sanctions against Iraq. Even Switzerland - a non UN member - agreed to comply with the embargo.

Bill and his team had no option but to "freeze" all exports to Iraq and to endeavour to try to arrange for the return of all transit shipments. This was easier said than done because the trucks en route were stuck throughout a chain of countries stretching from Western Europe to Turkey and within Iraq itself. It was often impossible to contact the drivers who in some cases had their cargoes and even their trucks impounded.

The authorities in Bern requested a full declaration from Bonaventure detailing all goods in transit and all goods ordered but not shipped. The company's bankers, Barclays Bank, who were the recipient of all the letters of credit issued to Bonaventure by the Iraqi banks - had to make similar disclosures.

The details are included at the end of this chapter and amounted to over 10 million dollars.

Meanwhile the Iraqis were frantically trying to make contact with all their main suppliers including Bonaventure. Numerous telexes (which Bill was tipped off as being re-routed via Washington) arrived from all the Iraqi factories being supplied by Bonaventure requesting details about their expected shipments. It was assumed that all communications were also being intercepted by both the Swiss and French Authorities.

The company was only permitted by the Swiss authorities to give a standard reply and nothing more! " All shipments to Iraq are subject to the sanctions imposed by UN Security Council Resolution 661". In addition to the telexes the Iraqis were continuously telephoning the Company requesting to speak to "Mr. Bill".

At the same time Bill was contacted by Pierre from the DGSI requesting an urgent meeting. Pierre visited Bill at home that same day to ask him if he was ready to fly to Paris for a meeting with his counterparts at the DGSE and that a suite would be arranged for him to stay at the George V in Paris which would also be where the meeting would take place.

Pierre advised that two British "representatives" would also be present as observers but Bill was given strict instructions not to communicate with them - only with the French DGSE officers who would attend the meeting. He also reminded Bill that as a resident of France he would be expected to report only to the DGSE - not the British and furthermore that he was entitled to the protection of the French State. He would be given a 24 hour emergency number to call in the event he felt in need of protection and a permit to carry a concealed firearm. He was also to report to Pierre on a daily basis advising him of his movements and whereabouts.

No indication was given about the topic of the meeting but Bill assumed that it related to Iraq. The following morning he flew to Paris, checked into the George V, one of his favourite hotels, in preparation for the meeting that was scheduled for the next day. To ensure privacy the meeting was to be held in the suite which had been arranged by the DGSE. The DGSE team accompanied by the two British "representatives" arrived for the meeting the following morning. Bill was asked if he was ready to co-operate and to assist the French State and its allies with regard to Iraq.

The Allies had information that the Iraqis were preparing to hold all remaining Westerners trapped in Iraq as hostages for use as "human shields" in order to protect Iraqi military production plants from attack. The DGSE were well aware that Bill had an almost unique knowledge of most, if not all, of the key production facilities and their internal layout. He therefore held the key for the Allies to understand in which parts of each military complex hostages were likely to be held.

As an example he was shown an aerial photo of the Hutteen Establishment taken just the previous week and was asked to locate the main office building, the meeting rooms, personnel accommodation, the kitchens and the main ammunition production areas of the factory.

The DGSE confirmed that they were monitoring all incoming calls directly from Iraq or from Iraqi embassies to Bonaventure's office, calls which Bill had so far declined to accept. Going forward however they asked him to accept all the calls and to appear to be willing to assist in every way. It was made clear that only he personally was to take the calls in private in his office - none of his staff were to be involved nor to be briefed as to the nature of the calls.

They also confirmed that it was highly likely that the Iraqis would ask to meet for face to face discussions about ongoing or new supplies of military equipment despite the total embargo imposed by the United Nations. Bill would be required to agree to the meetings, advise Pierre, attend the meeting and subsequently report back to Pierre upon his return for debriefing either locally or in Paris.

The office staff and his family were to be told that all his "overseas meetings" were with potential new clients - not related in any way to Iraq. Given his knowledge of the plants he would also be required to attend meetings at short notice in Paris on an ongoing basis to assist in the evaluation of military factory layouts and new aerial photos.

It was agreed that all meetings in Paris would continue to take place in the George V, as this is where Bill normally stayed and so would raise no questions, with the hotel costs to be paid by the French authorities thus avoiding any queries or suspicions within the Bonaventure offices or possible "shadowing" by persons connected to the Iraqis.

And so Bill became a spy for the Allies!

It came as no surprise that the first request from the Iraqis was not long in coming, "was Mr Bill able to fly to Amman for a meeting". Bill confirmed his willingness to visit Amman and the meeting was arranged to take place in the Marriott Hotel where he would be contacted with the exact meeting arrangements.

Jordan was in a difficult position as it was very dependent on its much larger neighbour for oil and gas supplies but was equally aware that it had to abide by the UN resolution.

The Iraqis had maintained in Amman over the years numerous front companies specifically set up to bypass possible sanctions and it was to one of these offices that Bill was taken for the meeting. As expected the meeting was to see if Bonaventure was able to transfer title of certain shipments that were "stranded" in Turkey and Jordan.

Bill advised that he would "investigate" the possibility of transferring ownership of the cargoes.

Once back in France he reported his findings to Pierre.

The next call he received was from Capt Moussa - his main contact at the Hutteen Establishment - to ask if he could meet with Bill in Zagreb where he was on "holiday". The meeting took place as planned and similar requests on ways and means of breaking the embargo were discussed. This time Bill was able to take detailed notes of the front companies that the Iraqis were using.

At the end of the meeting Moussa suggested that they should take a walk before lunch and much to Bill's surprise asked if it was possible for Bill to assist him and his family to defect to Italy.

Given the amount of detail he had obtained in Zagreb and news of the possible defection Bill was debriefed in Paris and asked to maintain contact with Captain Moussa.

Shortly after the invasion of Kuwait the American defence of Saudi Arabia was put in place, with thousands of troops amassing as part of Operation Desert Storm. In November the UN Security Council passed a resolution authorising the use of force against Iraq if it failed to withdraw from Kuwait by January 15th 1991. Meanwhile Allied forces were taking up positions at strategic points in readiness for the liberation of Kuwait.

Bill was in the UK on his annual shoot in Anglesey when a call came through to attend an urgent meeting in Paris that evening. He was asked to drive immediately to Manchester airport where a private jet was on standby to fly him to Le Bourget.

It seemed that the Iraqis had opened a new back door route for military supplies via Tunis and that DGSE were certain that Bill would be contacted by the Tunisians for an urgent meeting to discuss the supply of "spare parts". Sure enough a call came through from Tunis a few days later and Bill was invited to fly to Tunis for a meeting with the importer who would arrange his hotel and local transportation.

Bill had expected the meeting to take place in the importer's offices in Tunis but instead when he arrived he was met by the importer's representative at the airport who advised that the meeting was to take place that evening in a villa outside of Tunis where they would be staying.

They drove for over an hour finally arriving at a very palatial villa in the countryside. A sumptuous dinner had been arranged and Bill was introduced to a number of people all who described themselves as Directors of the import company but no further details were provided and no visiting cards were exchanged.

After dinner the meeting started with the senior "director" declaring that Bill had been selected to attend because he was "a real friend of Iraq and would never betray them to the UN or foreign governments". It sounded more like a threat than a compliment but Bill realised that he was probably about to hear something that would be important to the Allied plans.

Then - much to Bill's surprise - the Director produced a tape recorder and asked him to listen to the tape which appeared to be an exchange between US Ambassador Glaspie and Tariq Assiz confirming that the United States would not take any action if Iraq took possession of the Northern oilfields of Kuwait.

He went on to say that Bill could be confident that the US Government secretly supported the invasion of Kuwait and he was therefore not obligated to observe the "phony UN Resolution".

They were well informed and knew Bill had visited South Africa some months previously in the Spring together with an Iraqi delegation to discuss the purchase of G5 155m artillery pieces and a new type of anti tank mine which incorporated a powerful shape charge guaranteed to penetrate a tank's hull with very lethal results.

Bill was asked if could arrange for the shipment of G5 units and ammunition from South Africa to Tunisia. He explained that he would have to check with his contacts there and would let them know as soon as possible.

Of course he never made contact again with the Tunisians. The French Government subsequently "warned off" the South African Government not to respond to any approaches which appeared to originate in Tunisia.

As the massive build up of equipment and military personnel continued in Saudi Arabia near the Kuwait border, in preparation for the Allied invasion, the level of Iraqi contact with Bill gradually dwindled and finally ceased by late December 1990.

On January 17th, 1991 coalition forces launched a massive air and sea bombardment on the Iraqi positions in Kuwait. The coalition was made up of NATO troops as well as Egyptian and several other Arab nations and they benefited from the latest military technology including stealth bombers, cruise missiles, smart bombs and infra red night bombing equipment. The Iraqi air force was either destroyed or opted out of combat.

Operation Desert Storm had started, it lasted just six weeks by which time Kuwait had been liberated and the Allies were on the outskirts of Baghdad.

Bill thought that he could discreetly withdraw from any further connection to Iraq other than potential future compensation claims but that was not to be.

Suppliers to Iraqi military industries were under attack from the British left wing press and TV including the Guardian who wrote a lurid story about Bill and his company Bonaventure "making millions in Iraq" and Channel 4 TV produced an hour long documentary in their despatches series giving a decidedly one-sided view of Bonaventure's activities. Neither of those pillars of British media bothered to mention that no laws had been broken or that Bonaventure had stopped all deliveries to Iraq the instant the embargo was announced. Bill repeatedly refused to be interviewed by the TV crew who had camped outside his home in France, his offices in Geneva, his London residence and even his Club in St James's.

The programme, despite an attempted injunction by his lawyers, was broadcast in 1992 unfortunately just around the time his latest project was being launched in the UK.

Channel 4 had discovered Bill's recent involvement with Fonte Sole mineral water so some very quick PR was necessary as several UK supermarket buyers had seen the programme on TV and were concerned about any bad publicity.

Bill felt frustrated that he was unable to respond to the press and TV attacks but he had undertaken not, under any circumstances, to reveal his intelligence work in assisting the Allies prior to Operation Desert Storm.

Ref: NTC 104/359/15

Date: 06 AUG 1994

Foreign & Commonwealth Office

Nationality, Treaty & Claims Department
Clive House
Petty France
London SW1H 9HD

Telephone: 071–270– 4099

Dear Claimant

You are advised that your claim for compensation has been sent to the United Nations Compensation Commission in Geneva, in Her Majesty's Government's consolidated submission of claims by British nationals or residents, pursuant to UN Security Council resolutions 687(1991) and 692(1991).

Whilst H.M. Government can in no way guarantee whether or when compensation will be paid in respect of the claims, it affirms that it has no reason to believe the information stated in the claim is incorrect. The Government is of the view that the claim has been properly submitted on the appropriate claim form and all required affirmations have been given by each claimant.

Yours faithfully

Michael Sullivan

M F Sullivan
Head of Nationality Treaty and Claims Department

OPENED LETTERS OF CREDIT

CUSTOMER	ORIGIN	GOODS	CUR	AMOUNT	DELIVERY	SWISS CORRESP.
SOTI	Austria	Round Steel Bars	DEM	633,786.04	12/10/90	Barclays Bank
NASSR	Italy/UK	Air pressure valves Test rigs for air valves	USD	1,316,337.20	31/11/90	Barclays Bank
NASSR	Italy	Stainless steel cutters and diaphragms	USD	339,179.20	31/10/90	Barclays Bank
QAQAA	UK	Elec. Test Equip.	GBP	229,985.00	31/08/90	Barclays Bank
AL KADESIAH	Italy	Various types of Steel sheets and bars	USD	868,791.00	31/12/90	Barclays Bank
AL KADESIAH	Irish	Tracked Robot	GBP	54,750.00	22/10/90	Barclays Bank
SOTI	UK	Environ. Test Equip.	GBP	492,214.22	06/04/91	Barclays Bank
AL FARUK	UK	DC Motors	GBP	485,961.00	10/01/91	Barclays Bank
AL KADESIAH	Swiss	Springs	USD	22,000.00	25/07/90	United Overseas Bank
HUTTEEN	UK	Indus. X-Ray System	USD	1,497,395.00	19/06/91	Barclays Bank

No export licenses were required at time of the conclusion of the businesses.

1 of 6 DOCUMENTS

February 4, 1991

LENGTH: 583 words

HEADLINE: The Gulf War: Saddam deals were 'all above board' - The British businessman who made millions from Iraq's war factories

BYLINE: By ALAN GEORGE

BODY:

'ALL the equipment we supplied there went on a very correct and sensible basis,' said William Pellew-Harvey. 'We never tried to hide that we were doing business in Iraq.'

Talking to him over coffee in his solicitor's office in St James's, London, it is hard to believe that this soft-spoken man has been the subject of intense interest by Western government agencies.

For more than two years, until the invasion of Kuwait and the imposition of UN sanctions, he was the middle-man for European companies' supplies of equipment and machinery to Saddam Hussein's war factories.

As Mr Pellew-Harvey admits, his firm competed with now-notorious Iraqi-linked companies such as Euromac of Italy, whose British associate company of the same name was a target of last year's operation by British and US Customs to foil nuclear trigger supplies to Iraq.

Mr Pellew-Harvey, who is British, is owner and chief executive of Bonaventure Europe, a company registered in the Turks and Caicos Islands, a British territory in the Caribbean. His business base is Geneva and he is a resident of Monaco.

In the two years up to the invasion, Mr Pellew-Harvey won contracts with Baghdad valued at some Dollars 10 million (Pounds 5 million). His biggest customers included the Hutteen State Establishment, Iraq's largest manufacturer of mortar and artillery shells; and the Qadissiya State Establishment, its main small arms producer.

In Italy, some of Bonaventure's contracts were secured through a small import-export firm, Italian Technology and Innovations (ITI), based near Brescia. Mr Pellew-Harvey's key Italian contact, however, was Paulo Maraviglia, a business consultant.

Maho Macchine Butensili Italiane (MMBI), based near Milan, won an estimated Dollars 1.5 million order from Bonaventure in 1989 for the supply and commissioning of five machining centres.

'The exact destination was never mentioned,' said a company official. That it was Iraq emerged when engineers were sent to commission the machines.

In 1988, Bonaventure bought another machining centre from Baltec of Switzerland. Again, the firm discovered the destination Qadissiya only when an engineer was sent to help with installation.

Bonaventure also procured for Iraq testing equipment which, besides having standard industrial applications, can be used in the development and manufacture of ballistic missile components.

From Acutronic of Paris, Bonaventure early last year bought a centrifuge, which was installed at Baghdad University. Acutronic says the machine is 'capable of testing electronic or electro-mechanical devices'.

CHAPTER 19

A New Start - Fonte Sole Italy & California

By Christmas 1990 Bill had come to accept that the Iraqi debacle would continue for many years and it was high time to reassess his financial future.

Shipments destined for Iraq had either been confiscated or held in indefinite storage in multiple warehouses in numerous locations between Europe and the Iraqi border. To make matters worse most of the equipment produced to Iraqi specifications was so specialised that it had only limited commercial value on the open market if it could subsequently be resold.

The company almost always purchased goods from suppliers on an ex factory basis in order to maintain confidentiality so that the supplier was not able to identify the specific destination in Iraq. This enabled suppliers to present their documents to Barclays for payment even though the goods had not physically been shipped to the client with the result that the goods had to be put in warehouses in bond with the cost accruing to Bonaventure.

Barclays Bank in Geneva were in panic as letters of credit to suppliers issued on behalf of Bonaventure were in most cases still valid and the bank had to disburse funds to each supplier provided the documents presented were correct despite the on-going UN embargo. By early 1991 the sums owing to Barclays by Bonaventure were running into many millions with an ever decreasing chance of repayment.

Bill's personal financial resources were becoming stretched with four children in expensive private schools and a large mortgage to be paid on his London apartment in Kensington Gardens which he had purchased the previous year. Urgent steps were required to maintain his income and the family's life style.

A year earlier Barbara had been in discussion with the Bodei family - owners of an Italian mineral water plant near Lake Garda - for her and Bill to acquire a 50% stake in the business. The Plant owned the source known as Fonte Sole - a leading local brand of mineral water but otherwise virtually unknown outside the provinces of Brescia and Verona.

With everything that had been going on in Iraq, this was before the invasion of Kuwait and the UN embargo, Bill had initially taken little interest in the acquisition negotiations which he regarded at the time as a sort of "hobby investment" for Barbara who had designed an outstandingly beautiful emerald green multifaceted bottle to be used for the launch of Fonte Sole as the flagship of the brand. This was at a time when most mineral water bottles were decidedly dull to say the least and the "designer water" concept was unheard of.

The Agreement to purchase the shares in Fonte Sole had already been signed and with promissory notes becoming due later in the year it was time to find a co-investor with deep pockets to ensure that the acquisition could proceed!

Bill and Barbara were close friends with an American couple based near Geneva who owned a successful business designing and selling desalination and water purification plants produced for them under license in Scandinavia. The husband - Tom Bove - was an entrepreneur and risk taker very similar to Bill. A deal was soon agreed - Tom became a co-shareholder and the acquisition in Fonte Sole was concluded. In the aftermath of the financial disaster of Iraq Bill and Barbara devoted themselves full time to the new business.

In many ways it was a return to his original career in the food industry for Bill given that the main potential customers would be supermarkets and the restaurant sector. The plan was to develop Fonte Sole into an international brand focused on the new emerging demand for mineral water lead by the likes of Perrier and San Pellegrino.

The challenges and investment required to make this happen soon became apparent!

Fonte Sole up to this point had in reality just been a local family owned bottler of mineral water licensed as an Alpine mineral water source. They were licensed to extract mineral water from this source similar in most ways to countless other small family owned regional mineral water plants - 120 at the last count - dotted throughout Italy.

Very few national brands existed in Italy with the exception of San Pellegrino who had been trading since 1899 and had recently been acquired by Nestle. Almost all mineral water in Italy at that time was being produced in refillable glass bottles while plastic bottles were being introduced for the cheaper end of the retail market. Bottles had standard "flip tops" and their sizes were standard throughout Italy at 1 litre or 50cl.

Mineral water plants, including Sole, relied on wholesalers to supply restaurants, bars and retail outlets and to return the collected bottles for reuse by the Plants and in exchange to pick up fresh loads of water.

Old fashioned it may have been but the system worked very well because of the bottle standardisation which meant that each bottle could be reused many times over irrespective of the labels which were removed during the washing process in the plants prior to being filled with fresh mineral water and simply relabelled. No plastics and no "screw tops" were involved!

That's a great system when you only ship your product within a 50 mile radius, a little more challenging if your aim is to become a national and international brand.

Barbara's concept at that time was revolutionary - she had designed a beautiful octagonal single use emerald green glass screw top bottle targeted primarily at the restaurant trade and upmarket retailers. The water was to be bottled in 75, 50 and 20 cl sizes.

The big question was to establish if there was a real market for a premium mineral water primarily aimed at the American and British markets.

Inevitably the Bodei family were very dubious about the concept at the start but were finally persuaded to proceed by their new foreign partners. The existing production lines had been designed solely for the standard reusable Italian glass bottles. A new modern production line would be needed capable of filling, screw capping and labelling the new bottles coupled with export strength cartons instead of the plastic crates currently in use for the traditional returnable bottles.

The next problem was to find a glass manufacturer able to produce the new octagonal sided bottles. Finally a glass plant in Italy and another plant in Croatia were selected and the first bottle contracts were placed. By the end of the year trial runs had been completed and the "new look" Sole mineral water was launched in early 1992.

Bill had spent much of 1991 based in Brescia near the plant and spent frustrating months persuading the Bodei family to accept modern production and accounting methods. For example the production lines had always stopped for a 2 hour lunch break, night shifts were unheard of and accounting was done by hand. Gradually, as sales increased, 2 then 3 shift production was introduced and modern accounting procedures put in place.

Export marketing became the top priority. Bill set up a UK subsidiary to act as the import and marketing arm of Sole appointing the former

Perrier Marketing Director as head of the UK operation.

A major fine wine distributor was selected to service high end restaurants and hotels in the greater London area and container loads of Sole were delivered directly to the warehouses of Waitrose, Tesco and Sainsburys who had agreed to stock this new "fancy Italian mineral water".

Supermarket sales were disappointing but the restaurant trade loved Sole and the bottles were soon to be seen on the tables of many leading London hotels and restaurants.

Barbara organised sales training courses for the distributor's staff and personally visited many leading restaurants to promote Sole. Mineral water sales were suddenly becoming a real profit centre for the catering trade who could purchase Sole at £1 per bottle but charge their clients £5!!

At the same time the couple turned their focus towards the USA which had a far greater potential than the UK. A friend of Barbara's called Luins had contacted her to say that he was working for a Californian based importer who would be interested to be appointed as Sole's importer in California. A big attraction was that the company was ready to purchase Sole as principals and to warehouse inventory for sale to fine wine and liquor distributors on a state wide basis.

Bill flew to San Francisco and a contract was signed for the first 20 x 40' containers representing about 600,000 bottles. Production was ramped up at the plant and shipping commenced. However it soon became apparent that all was not well with the Importer who had warehoused the inventory but had failed to meet the agreed payment terms. Bill returned to San Francisco, engaged the services of a leading lawyer and was able to obtain a lien on the entire warehouse inventory of Sole.

It was obvious that if Sole was to be a success in the USA the company would have to set up its own sales organisation which in turn could only mean one thing, the family would have to move to California.

Barbara and the children were thrilled at the prospect. Barbara had maintained her American citizenship while the children were dual nationals holding both British and American passports. Bill had substantial reservations not the least of which were potential US tax problems and his residence status but he kept his thoughts to himself.

A new company was registered in Nevada called Sole Inc which would act as both importer of record and sales vehicle for the entire USA.

In the meantime the couple went house hunting in the San Francisco area. Barbara knew the surrounding area well as she had been brought up in San Francisco and had graduated from the prestigious Convent of the Sacred Heart Girls High School before attending the University of California Berkeley where she read Modern languages.

They found an ideal property located in the town of Mill Valley in Marin County just a few miles North of San Francisco.

Bill and children in the house at Mill Valley

The 5 bedroom house was located in the redwoods, adjacent to the town centre, had a swimming pool and most importantly a large garage for storing mineral water samples and publicity material coupled with an adjoining apartment which they were able to equip as an office.

Returning to France they arranged to move all their furniture, Bill's guns, his powerboat and classic Lincoln Continental. Soon the move was complete and the family, including their housekeeper, driver and four dogs, flew to San Francisco to settle into their new life in California.

It was straight to work - there was a huge inventory of Sole to be put into distribution and the plant back in Italy was desperate to start shipping new product and cash flow became paramount.

Barbara concentrated on brand promotion and training of each Distributor's sales team while Bill concentrated on visiting and appointing suitable distributors in each State to ensure national coverage of all the major potential markets.

The strategy was very simple as they intended Sole to become the premium mineral water of choice in all fine restaurants and hotels and who better to appoint than fine wine distributors who already served this precise target market? To make matters even better US liquor regulations restricted each liquor distributor to each individual State with no sales permitted beyond State borders thus ensuring that each Distributor had no option but to restrict their activities to their own State and could not compete with each other for clients.

Whilst they had already appointed a leading Californian fine wine distributor other major markets would be essential in order to establish a national presence in particular New York, Boston, Miami and Chicago. A target list of fine wine distributors in each State was drawn up and examined for their potential. The objective was to equal or preferably surpass San Pellegrino as the leading Italian Mineral Water of choice!

The few States that lacked any potential due to small populations, poor tourist potential and low incomes were removed from the list including Alaska, Alabama, the Dakotas, Mississippi, Montana and Wyoming. The chances of a pickup driving farmer in the mid west spending more on a bottle of water than he spent on his meal was slim.

Bill then proceeded to visit every State of the Union other than those excluded from the list to talk to potential distributors. Once the State distributor had been appointed Barbara would fly in to address their sales staff and to arrange promotional activities tailor made for each specific market.

Together they made a good team!

Barbara soon commenced publication of the Sole Newsletter which featured all the main exhibitions or social events featuring Sole. These included Hollywood award ceremonies, the opening of major new restaurants and hotels and top California winery events attended by movie stars and business moguls including Donald Trump at Mar a Lago!

The brand took off and within two years the Sole plant was shipping in excess of a million plus bottles per month to the USA alone!

However matters were not going well amongst the Sole shareholders - too many alpha males involved Barbara would joke! Tom Bove had persuaded Bill and Barbara, against their better judgement, to allow a certain Elwood Sprenger to join Sole as an advisor on the grounds that Elwood was a water promotional expert having previously sold his own mineral water company called Silver Springs to Nestle.

Tom was convinced that Elwood would take Sole to ever greater heights while Bill and Barbara become convinced that he was a conman trying to take control of Sole!

Elwood by this time had moved himself from Santa Rosa to Newport Beach and proceeded to set up a second Sole office to "oversee global sales", prepare Sole USA for a "public offering" of its shares and even more suspiciously to "monitor Sole's cash flow".

This led to a confrontation and matters came to a head when he attempted to take control of Sole's bank accounts. Tom appeared incapable of controlling Elwood. Fed up with the infighting and bored by the whole business Bill and Barbara presented Tom with an ultimatum - either back the Pellew-Harveys and remove Elwood Sprenger or else "buy us out". Tom decided to back Elwood and offered to buy out their shareholding.

Bill immediately accepted the offer and felt a huge burden was being lifted from his shoulders. Barbara was very upset to see her beloved Sole being "taken over" by a crook - she had done so much to make Sole a national brand! It was time for the couple to sit back, take stock of their situation and to decide what to do.

The couple's warning to Tom Bove sadly proved correct when, some months later, Elwood Sprenger absconded with all of Sole's bank deposits - well over a million dollars - leaving all the Sole USA staff unpaid and the company in chaos.

There is much evidence available to suggest that Mr. Sprenger is continuing his criminal activities to con unsuspecting victims and employees out of large sums of money. An easy reference is to go to www.complaintsboard.com and type in the man's name!

In the midst of this turmoil Bill received the devastating news that Adrian, his only child by his first wife Maria, had tragically died from a drug overdose.

Following the funeral in Richmond Bill had asked his old friend Michael Pascal - a leading private detective - to investigate Adrian's death and to track down the dealer who had supplied the lethal drug which had been identified as a badly "cut" mixture of heroin and cocaine which the young man had "sniffed".

Several weeks later the dealer was tracked down to a motel in San Diego and "detained" by Pascal and experienced what it was like to be in Mike's hands. Mike had then rung to ask for further instructions.

After a long discussion with Michael - Maria's husband - it was agreed that no punishment or retribution would bring Adrian back to life so the dealer was released with dire warnings of what would happen if he ever was found to be pushing drugs again!

Not surprisingly with all that happened with Adrian followed by the machinations of Sprenger, Bill and Barbara felt emotionally exhausted.

They decided to take some time off with Hawaii as their first destination.

Adverts for Sole

SOLÉ™

olé is a natural spring water bottled at source at the Fonte Sole Spring in the foothills of the Italian Alps.

- Designed to enhance any table setting. Available in 750 ml, 500 ml, 330 ml and 200 ml stylish green fluted bottles made with environmentally-friendly recycled glass.

- Guaranteed purity and natural low mineral content make Solé suitable for all the family. Accepted as a water of exceptional quality by virtue of its status as an "oligo mineral water" licensed by the Italian government – a complete analysis is on each label.

- Try lightly sparkling Solé Gold or refreshingly still Solé Blue. Both sodium free.

SOLÉ™

THE ELEGANT COMPLEMENT TO FINE DINING.

SOLE™
ACQUA MINERALE NATURALE

APRIL, 1995

Future Dining Trends

Sal Falcone—Florida-based food expert and frequent speaker on radio and television—casts some light on Solé's place in today's culinary scene. **Sal sez...**

I t is clear that the educated diner today is looking for food with good taste, low fat, low calories and low sodium. To achieve this goal, the young club of today are reincarnating their grandmothers' old world country cooking. Simple peasant style cooking features all types of pastas, fresh vegetables, beans and leaner meats. Brick wood-burning ovens have become the *chic*-est pieces of equipment in the most modern restaurants. Today's young consumers search out small unique mom and pop home style restaurants where they can receive personal attention from the proprietors.

The chefs that I interview show an increasing interest in the wines and waters that are served with their delicate creations. Solé more than any other water, fits that description. Sodium free, lightly carbonated, wonderful taste with a great balance for both the body and the palate. One chef said, "Solé is like that proverbial glass slipper that is the finishing touch to my beautiful creations." To your health!

Solé Chairman Barbara Pellea-Harvey shown at left with Sal Falcone and Donald Trump, and above with Marla Maples at the gala Club Mar-a-Lago Fête.

FLORIDA

Donald Trump opens *Club Mar-a-Lago* at his sumptuous *Palm Beach* estate. The glorious waterfront manse built for Marjorie Merriweather Post and more recently owned by real estate magnate Donald Trump will be opened as a private club with memberships available by private invitation only for $50,000. *Ocean Drive Magazine* threw a fabulous preview party at the club for all the beautiful folks and Solé was the chosen water. Donald and Marla Maples were on hand to greet guests who danced poolside and sampled the splendid feast on the mile-long buffet tables.

Philanthropist Mrs. Sheila Shulevitz (center) with daughters Julie Scheckvitz (left) and Linda Osur (right) at the Tiffany event

The Who's Who of *Miami* turned out to celebrate the 20th Anniversary of designer Elsa Peretti's association with *Tiffany's*, the legendary fine jewelry house. Held in Tiffany's prestigious Bal Harbour store, Solé's elegant fluted bottle was right at home among the ultra-chic Tiffany's crowd.

NEW YORK

The Big Apple has really jumped onto the Solé bandwagon and some of the city's most prestigious restaurants now serve Solé. *Harry Cipriani*, tucked up next to the *Sherry-Netherlands*, is an outpost of the legendary Venice-based Cipriani family empire. Solé is now the official bottled water in the house. Ask for Solé to accompany the divine grilled selections at *China Grill*. The emerald green bottle looks spectacular in the elegant and spacious dining room. High atop *Rockefeller Center* you'll find Solé at home in the world famous *Rainbow Room*. For those who like the Rock and Roll scene, you can enjoy a frosty Solé at the famous *Hard Rock Cafe*.

In New York Solé is also offered at *Kiss, Dish, Flowers, Metronome, Le Sorelle, Chiam, Du Valentino, Arcadia, Walkers* and *Maruzella* to name but a few!

CONNECTICUT

Solé has been making itself very much at home in Connecticut. In the Stamford/Greenwich area you'll get a chance to try Solé when you check in to the *Hyatt Regency, Mariott* or *Sheraton* hotels. Say Bon *Apétito!* with Solé at the *Tuscan Oven, Centro, Arturos, Pasta Nostra* and the *Red Lion*.

Picture top left Barbara with Sal Falcone and Donald Trump

CHAPTER 20

Back to Business - Turkey

Spring of 1995 was not the best of times.

Bill's involvement in Sole was at an end and time to look to the future. There was the prospect of income from shares in Sole and the previous year the UN Iraq Compensation Fund had been established which opened the door to possible compensation to Bill personally and to Bonaventure albeit the Company was not trading and its only assets potentially were possible compensation payments.

The couple were both mentally and physically exhausted as a result of the Iraqi dramas followed by the infighting trauma of Sole so decided to take a round the world trip to enable Bill to decide on a new career path. The trip was arranged to start in Hawaii followed by a stay with friends in Australia and then on to Bali followed by a luxury camp on a private game reserve in South Africa before returning home via London.

Two days after their arrival in Maui Bill received out of the blue a totally unexpected phone call from his old Turkish friend Emin Sirin. Emin had moved from Geneva in 1992 following the Gulf War to emerge like a Phoenix in his native Turkey where he had maintained close contact with his friend and former employer Mehmet Karamehmet, the owner of one of Turkey's largest banking and industrial conglomerates - The Cukurova Group.

Never one to miss an opportunity the twice married Emin had scored his hat trick the previous year when he married an attractive wealthy widow called Nasli Llicak. Nasli was a renowned journalist and political commentator in Turkey who often appeared on TV, had served as a member of parliament and was very well connected to many influential politicians including the then Mayor of Istanbul Recep Erdogan!

Mr.Erdogan was to become the Prime Minister and later the President of Turkey in 2014.

Nasli, ever the voice for democracy, was arrested in 2016 following an attempted coup against the Erdogan regime and sentenced to 8 years and 9 months in prison on trumped up charges of spreading anti regime propaganda. In February 2019 her sentence was increased to life imprisonment but she was released on probation in November 2019.

Her son Mehmet had, with family backing, acquired a small national newspaper called Aksam previously owned by his deceased father and created a new media Group called Aksam Holdings.

Mehmet, backed by his mother Nasli and assisted by Emin, had come up with an original and, as it turned out, ingenious way to dramatically increase the sales of Aksam. At that time Aksam was struggling to increase its daily sales from a meagre base of 100,000 circulation. Aksam's target readership was strictly working class - a sort of Turkish "Daily Mirror" with lots of photos and virtually no serious content.

It is also worth noting that at that time the majority of working class Turks had no access to bank accounts or savings accounts - they mostly lived on a day by day "cash" basis.

Mehmet had the idea to offer a free 14" colour TV to every reader who purchased Aksam on a continuous daily basis for 12 months. This was based on the concept of increasing the price of Aksam from the equivalent of 15 US cents to around 85 US cents thus providing an additional annual revenue of USD $255.00 per would be TV owner.

A colour 14" TV at that time in Turkey could be distributed at a cost of no more than $120.00 thus yielding a potential additional revenue of $135.00 per annum for each newspaper sold. In order to qualify for a TV the reader had to cut out and retain a daily coupon which was then exchanged at their local newsagent at the end of each month for a monthly calendar based coupon.

With 12 consecutive monthly coupons in hand the reader was guaranteed to receive their TV.

This was conditional upon the reader having to purchase the newspaper every single day of the year without fail. One day missed meant that the reader had to forego the opportunity to receive their TV. Readers were free if they so wished to purchase any number of Aksam's daily newspaper in order to receive more than one TV set. The promotion was launched early in the New Year of 1995. The result was astonishing and the promotion became a national success virtually overnight with daily sales of Aksam rising by mid 1995 to 1.2 million copies to finally reach over 2 million copies per day by early 1996.

As a result newspaper revenues jumped to $1.7million per day producing annual revenues of over $620 million. The established newspapers in Turkey were astonished and then outraged that Mehmet Llicak, this 25 year old upstart, had virtually overnight become a major competitor!

Initial results and analysis of readers purchasing patterns soon established that over 700,000 TV sets would need to be delivered at the end of the 12 month period.

Emin was now in charge of this huge procurement programme. He had travelled to South Korea ahead of the promotion's launch and had reached an agreement with Daiwoo to deliver the TV sets for around $120 - at that time estimating that no more than 50,000 sets would be required initially.

Suddenly Emin was faced with having to purchase 700,000 + sets! He had expected to be able to negotiate a lower price for these huge additional quantities but instead, to his consternation, the reverse happened and the Koreans upped the price to around $180 per set.

This was the point that had been reached when Emin decided to call Bill for help, could he urgently fly to meet in Hong Kong on a very urgent "business matter".

Bill was less than excited, he explained to Emin that an immediate meeting was impossible as he was in Hawaii at the start of his "sabbatical" but finally, after a long discussion, he was persuaded to fly to Hong Kong the following day. The fact that Emin had said it was "the deal of a lifetime and Bill could name his own price" had sparked his interest.

Barbara stayed on in Maui while Bill made a quick dash to Hong Kong via Tokyo to meet up with Emin.

In Hong Kong Emin gave Bill the overview of the situation and stressed the urgency of the matter given that the countdown to the delivery of the TV sets had already started. He wanted Bill to take over immediately the entire procurement and logistics of the operation. Every day mattered as the 12 month countdown of the delivery of the TV sets had already started.

He appealed to his vanity by stating that the Aksam board had already been briefed on Bill's "years of experience in arranging major procurement and logistical projects and meeting timing deadlines". He also confirmed that Aksam would pay him a fee of $20,000 per month plus all expenses including first class travel worldwide.

Bill agreed to proceed immediately providing the fee was increased to $25,000 per month and that Aksam would bear the cancellation cost of his current "sabbatical" which he would now have to postpone for a few months. He returned to Hawaii to explain the situation to Barbara. She agreed with his decision and the couple returned to San Francisco.

Two days later Bill was in Istanbul for a series of meetings with the Aksam board and then returned to Hong Kong as his temporary base to start negotiations with potential TV manufacturers in Hong Kong and China.

There were substantial hurdles to overcome as Chinese TV exports to Turkey, unlike Korea, were subject not only to import quotas but also to import duties on fully finished TV sets in order to protect local manufacturers in Turkey.

The second problem was one of quality. Chinese brands were considered inferior to those produced in Japan and Korea and the Aksam readers had been promised their TVs would be a "leading international brand".

Bill worked on the basis that at least three manufacturers would be required to produce the sets within the time scale.

To get around the question of the quotas and duties he arranged that the sets be export packed as "knock down Kits" and then be shipped by sea container from China and Hong Kong directly to a company in Korea whom Bill had persuaded to act as the importer of record.

Upon arrival in Korea the containers were kept in a duty free zone as temporary imports, the cartons relabelled and then loaded into Korean sea containers for shipment to Turkey.

The shipping documents were reissued by the Koreans now showing the goods as being exported from Korea.

The next problem was how to re-assemble the kits into fully operational and quality tested TV sets in Turkey? As luck would have it Emin had located in Turkey an ideal assembly plant owned by Akai of Japan which had originally been set up to produce Akai radios for the local market. Akai had decided not to proceed with their project so the plant was available for rent.

Bill flew to Tokyo for meetings with Akai and a royalty agreement was reached whereby Aksam would rent the Turkish facility and the TV sets would be re-assembled in the Turkish plant under the Akai brand. In addition Akai would also provide several supervisory technicians from Japan to oversee the local assembly and testing process to ensure each set met their quality standards.

Timing was critical and to ensure all went smoothly Bill arranged for the container bookings and oversight with the Geneva office of the leading Swiss logistics company Danzas under the direction of its local

Manager Christian Wyss[1]. Christian's father was a Director of Danzas and the pair were to play an unforeseen role as later events unfolded.

Bill supervised the Chinese producers, the shipping programmes to and re-exporting of the kits from Korea up to the delivery to the Turkish ports of Istanbul or Izmir.

Aksam thereafter accepted the goods as the importer of record, transported the containers inland for re-assembly under the Akai label. The completed Akai TV sets were then warehoused in various locations throughout Turkey ready for delivery to those readers of Aksam who had qualified or were due to become qualified to receive their promised TV set.

The massive operation was successful and the first TV sets were available on time as the programme unfurled.

Meanwhile Bill's life had become even more frenetic. Buoyed up by the success of the TV promotion Mehmet had decided to increase the size and scope of the Aksam promotions. Other newspapers also joined the fray and the Turkish public were soon to be offered an extraordinary array of goods based on similar loyalty coupons.

Local TV sales had started to collapse as customers awaited their "Aksam TV's" resulting in local manufacturers led by Beko and Vestel lodging complaints with the Government and lobbying for stricter import controls on foreign produced TV sets.

The next two Aksam promotions to be run in parallel with the TV promotion was targeted at readers who only wished to purchase Aksam for a more modest 90 day period. Even this shorter period would result potentially in an additional potential profit for Aksam of $63 per copy.

It was decided to feature for this 90 day redemption period a set of Italian cutlery and/or a set of crockery for six persons.

Circulation had continued to rise and following a review of the potential redemption figures Bill, with possibly the world's largest shopping list in hand, was instructed to purchase over 5 million pieces of crockery and over 5 million pieces of cutlery. All had to be produced and

---

1 Christian Wyss was arrested by the Swiss police in 1998 and charged with committing fraud in respect of the containers supplied by Danzas to Aksam for their worldwide shipments of sea containers relating to the newspaper promotions - see Chapter 20.

Unknown to Bill it turned out Christian had secretly been raising fictitious invoices in Bill's name to Danzas showing commission payments relating to the supply of containers.

The invoices had unwittingly been paid by Danzas to a Swiss bank account controlled by Christian. He was subsequently sentenced to a year in prison and ordered to return the funds to Danzas.

delivered within 180 days, a logistics nightmare.

He located three crockery plants in Brazil, China and Italy that would be able to produce and ship the required quantities within the time frame. Crockery imports were not subject to import quotas so the origin did not matter - all that mattered was speed of production and price. Bill arranged with Angelo to supervise the Italian production near Naples and for a friend of his brother called John Ward to move on a temporary basis to Tsingtao to supervise the Chinese production while Bill flew to Brazil to meet the Brazilian factory owners.

The trip was a real eye opener for him as the factory was located in a small town in the German speaking part of South East Brazil. Not only were the factory owners 5th generation Germans from Pomerania but the entire town was German in every way. Every street sign, every shop, even the newspapers and TV stations were in German. No wonder the area was reputed to be a haven for Nazis suspected of war crimes who had fled Germany towards the end of the second world war!

Cutlery posed a much more difficult problem as it had to come from Italy. At that time Italy was the world's leading producer of cutlery with virtually all production concentrated in or around the Val Trompia valley in the Province of Brescia.

The solution was obvious - to contract the entire order to his old friend and major supplier for Bill's former Iraqi business - Angelo Prati - who would be on the spot in Brescia and could be entrusted to oversee the cutlery production. Angelo got to work and within days at least 10 local plants had started to produce the cutlery.

Throughout this time Bill was crisscrossing the globe supervising the multiple production of TV sets, cutlery and crockery while having to attend meetings in Istanbul every couple of weeks.

His monthly travel bills often exceeded $20,000.

The Aksam media empire was growing to include a TV and radio station and multiple leisure magazines. Mehmet was becoming a celebrity so steps were taken by Emin to protect him as various threats were being received at the Aksam offices. Just moving him around Istanbul's crowded streets was becoming a logistics nightmare. A minimum of 4 vehicles were needed - firstly a large black SUV with bodyguards followed by Mehmet's newly acquired armoured limousine with a further two SUVs bringing up the rear.

When in Istanbul Bill was usually invited to join Mehmet and Emin for dinner which meant a tour of the city's leading restaurants and night clubs or dinner at the family's beautiful villa situated on sloping gardens on the Asian side of Istanbul overlooking the Bosporus. He was regularly invited to stay at the villa as a guest of the family.

Emin also invited Barbara and the children over that summer with all expenses paid arranging their stay at the luxurious Cirigan Palace situated on the western bank of the Bosporus.

Life for Bill became almost surreal to say the least.

New promotions in the newspapers were starting to be featured to include washing machines and similar white goods causing even more dismay amongst the local manufacturers who saw their local sales plummeting. More and more newspapers joined the fray and the promotions became ever more frenzied.

The situation could not last!

The 1995 elections saw major gains by the Islamist Welfare party which was headed by the Islamist, Necmettin Erbakan who took over power in 1996 as head of a coalition government.

Like much of the press Aksam was careful to reflect the views of this governing coalition.

In the run-up to the election Erkaban had advocated leaving NATO and developing closer ties with Syria and Iran. Once in office there was growing concern that he was trying to Islamise the country. In February 1997 the military issued a series of "recommendations" which the Government had to accept. Erkaban agreed to impose a headscarf ban at universities and other measures dictated by the military including the decision to stop newspaper coupon promotions on the grounds that they were immoral.

Despite this co-operation the military forced Erkaban to resign a few months later in early 1998, the Welfare Party was banned entirely with Erbakan prohibited from political action for five years.

The outlawing of newspaper coupons was a mortal blow to Aksam's ambitions and to make matters worse Mehmet was suddenly put under investigation by the military for failing to perform his compulsory national service. The family quickly sold Aksam to Emin's old employer - the Cukorova Group - which continues to own the newspaper to this day.

Ironically the circulation of Aksam soon fell back to its original level of 100,000 copies per day. Mehmet Ilicak decided that a military career was not for him fearing an "accident" might happen on live fire exercises and fled to Miami. He continues to live in Miami working as a journalist.

During his time with Aksam Bill was approached by a French banker who worked for Credit Agricole, his name was Jean Bui and they were to become firm friends.

Jean accompanied Bill several times on his visits to Hong Kong, where his contacts proved invaluable, and also introduced him to leading Vietnamese businessmen in Paris. Jean had a most interesting background. His father was the last Emperor of Vietnam, Bao Dai, and his mother Bui Mong Diep was the emperor's third wife. Born in 1944 Jean had moved with his family and their entourage to France in 1956 when the family went into exile and settled comfortably into a large villa near Cannes. The Empress had subsequently moved to Paris after her divorce from Bao Dai who, much to the disapproval of the Royal Family, had married a French woman called Monique Baudot.

When in Paris Bill would invariably meet up with Jean at Les Deux Margots in Saint-Germain for drinks and often accompanied him to visit his mother who was a great raconteur of the history and intrigues of the royal court and the family's last years in Vietnam.

As for Bill after a manic 18 months he suddenly found himself back in California facing the prospect of establishing yet another new career but at least starting out with a quarter of a million dollars in his Swiss bank account!

Things were looking up in other directions as well. Tom Bove had still not paid for his Sole shares so Bill had initiated court proceedings in California against him for non payment of the Sole share sale.

The case was subsequently moved by mutual consent to the US Consulate in Nice. Bill flew down from Italy and Barbara from San Francisco to attend the hearing.

Tom settled his debt.

In addition the UN Iraqi claims commission was starting to put in place the mechanisms for compensation so there were potentially income streams ahead.

However the family overheads were high and Barbara had come up with a new product idea which would need financing so Bill realised he had to look for pastures new with no time to waste!

AKŞAM NEWSPAPER

Economy Department

Editorial Board

Foreign news department

Printing Press

General view from printing press

CHAPTER 21

Back to Europe & the Russian connection

While Bill started to look at possible new projects Barbara was busy on a project of her own, She was very involved in the increasing popular area of fitness and yoga classes, health spas and the like and had become aware of the importance of measuring body fat to establish an ideal body fat to weight ratio. She had designed a simple but effective measuring tool which she called the "Body Caliper".

She was convinced that a large market could be quickly established for such a product providing it could be well presented in good packaging and sold for under $20.

Bill was persuaded to back her idea and proceeded to register a Nevada corporation called the Caliper Company Inc and in June 1997 the patent for the Body Caliper was formally lodged with the US Patent and Trade Mark Office.

Meanwhile he had travelled to Italy to visit his old friend in Brescia - Angelo Prati - to order to arrange for the manufacture of the device and a suitable carrying container to protect the caliper from damage.

As always Italy was the answer and Angelo Prati could be relied on to find a suitable local plant specialising in the production of high strength plastics and a suitable manufacturer of the high pressure moulds that would be required for the product and its case.

Bill placed an order with Angelo for 20,000 units at a cost of just under $5 per set.

All in all a substantial investment but essential to have sufficient inventory in hand if the product was to be launched successfully.

The first 10,000 sets were shipped to Nevada and warehoused in Reno. Barbara was convinced that a national launch was essential so a full page advertisement was taken out in the New York Times at a cost of $50,000! Bill arranged with an established telemarketing company in Reno for the order taking and shipping process.

All was set to go!

Launch day arrived with the telemarketing office on standby prepared for a "flood of orders" which never arrived! The first days' sales were less than 30 units and the following days showed no improvement.

A costly disaster to put it mildly and a timely lesson to Bill to focus on projects where his expertise could be put to good use. A lot of money was down the drain and it became even more imperative for him to seek potential projects overseas - not in the USA where he had now been "twice burned" - firstly with Sole and then with the Body Caliper saga.

During his visits to Italy Bill had discreetly started to lay the groundwork for a possible move back to Europe. The truth of the matter was that he was homesick and could not envisage living in California for much longer.

In November 1998 during a visit to Italy Bill had been contacted by Christian Wyss who by now had been accepted back into the Danzas organisation having served his jail time relating to the shipping matters for the Aksam operations. Christian had just returned from a visit to Central Asia on behalf of Mercedes to investigate the potential logistics market in the region as Chinese exports continued to expand. Basically, he was looking for a suitable transport hub along the route of the old Silk Road.

Christian had focused on Kyrgyzstan and its capital Bishkek as the most interesting potential location due to a number of factors. The country, formerly known as the Kirghiz Socialist Soviet Republic, had declared its intention to become the "Switzerland" of Central Asia by welcoming foreign investors, offering low tax rates and most importantly the setting up of free economic zones.

The Capital, Bishkek, had retained a substantial population of educated ethnic white Russians some of whom traced their roots back to early Russian settlements in the 1860s.

It also had a potentially world class airport at Manas which had the potential to be a major regional air logistics centre for the entire region.

Christian offered to accompany Bill on a trip to Bishkek to "scout out" potential projects and most importantly to introduce him to the Tolstunov family who had strong connections to the President - Askar Akayev.

Akayev had been elected as the first President of the newly independent Republic back in 1991 and had consolidated his power base with strong support from Moscow who had retained an important military base just outside Bishkek with its own extensive airfield and barracks.

Leonid Tolstunov was a former Minister of Education under the Soviet Regime. His elder son Sergei held a PhD in Engineering and had risen to the rank of First Deputy Secretary of the Communist Party by 1990 - just prior to the breakup of the Soviet Union. Sergei and his team were in a position to strongly influence the appointment of the President to the fledgling regime.

The question was who should be appointed?

The first two candidates had been disqualified so a compromise candidate was essential.

It had to be someone who was Kyrgyz, well educated, pliable, economically liberal and known to be strongly supportive of Russia.

In October 1990 Akayev, who had recently been appointed President of the Kyrgyz Academy of Sciences had also been elected as a Deputy in the Supreme Soviet of the USSR.

While on a visit to Moscow for a meeting with Russian President Gorbachev, he was contacted by Sergei who asked him to agree to be nominated as the new President.

Initially he refused the position but was finally persuaded by his wife Maycam, who was a friend of the Tolstunovs, to accept. He returned to Bishkek where he was voted in unanimously as the new President by the Supreme Soviet of the Kyrgyz Republic.

Following the installation of the new President Sergei was appointed as Director of International Relations in the Presidential Office - a highly influential position as anyone who wished to communicate with the President had to make the appointment via Sergei.

Gold had been discovered in the Kyrgyz Republic as far back as 1978 but was considered too costly to mine as the potential mine location was at an altitude of over 4,000 metres on the mountains overlooking lake Issykul. During 1992 Sergei was in touch with Cameco, the Canadian mining giant and largest producer of uranium in the world who agreed to undertake a major geological study to ascertain the viability of the open cast mine to access the gold.

The results were positive and an agreement, overseen by Sergei, was signed with the Government granting Cameco exclusive rights and responsibility for 100% of the production with the Kyrgyz State owning 26% of the shares of the newly formed Kumtor Operating Company.

The Kumtor mine, the second highest gold mine in the world, finally opened in 1997 with the processing capacity of 16.000 tonnes of ore per day. Gold extracted from the treated ore was then poured into Dore bars containing 80% gold which were then purchased from Kumtur by the Kyrgyz Government owned company called Kyrgyzaltyn. The purchase price was established on a pre-agreed formula based on LME pricing. The bars were then transferred for processing to the Kara-Balta Refinery near Bishkek for transformation into pure 99.9% ingots.

By 2017 after 20 years of operation the mine had yielded over 11.5 million ounces of gold and had accounted for over 10% of the national GNP.

Kara-Balta, the city and the similarly named refinery, have an interesting history. The city itself dates back to 1825 with the refinery having been set up in Soviet times as the largest Uranium refinery in Central Asia with the raw uranium ore being transported by rail from the mines in neighbouring Kazakhstan.

By 2005 uranium production had ceased due to a lack of raw material although gold and molybdenum refining continue to this day.

The city of Kara-Balta when Bill first visited it in 1998 was still at that time almost 100% inhabited by ethnic Volga Germans who had been exiled to the area by Stalin in 1941 after the onset of the second world war.

It was strange to see such a large group of fair haired Europeans living and working in a country that was now reverting to its strong Mongol roots. Germany had recently opened its doors to its countrymen by offering the right of return with free passage and housing which resulted in most of the German population emigrating to Germany around the end of the 20th century.

Kyrgyzaltyn it should be noted enjoyed the exclusive right to sell refined gold and silver both within and outside the Kyrgyz Republic.

Enter the Tolstunovs who had meanwhile, back in December 1995, set up an Austrian Company called MTFC under their ownership but ostensibly under Austrian shareholding and management. MTFC purported to be an expert shipper and seller of precious metals - in particular gold.

Negotiations were conducted via the President's office with Kyrgyzaltyn and MTFC was duly appointed the exclusive shipper and marketing arm of refined Kyrgyzaltyn gold.

Sergei Tolstunov had by then resigned from the President's administration on good terms and settled in Vienna with his wife Luba and their son Vasily, to supervise the smooth running of MTFC leaving his younger brother also named Vasily in Bishkek to watch over the local situation and to ensure the local relationship between Kyrgyzaltyn and MTFC was maintained "in good order".

The good relationship with the Presidents administration was undoubtedly helped by the fact that Vasily Tolstunov's mistress just happened to be the Minister of Justice!

The Tolstonovs' owned a major office and showroom in the centre of Bishkek and it was in this location that Bill was introduced to Vasily by Christian Wyss. It was to be the start of a long and successful relationship between Bill and the Tolstunov family.

Security was tight with CCTV and bodyguards aplenty outside Vasily's office which was rather like a prison cell with no windows - just an exhaust fan. Vasily was a short barrel chested man in his mid thirties of classic Slavic appearance with a mischievous smile. Bill took to him immediately and it marked the start of a long friendship.

Vasily, encouraged by Christian Wyss, had developed an interest in the logistics of a new silk road with Bishkek and its nearby airport at Manas as a potential hub. The airport, owned by the State Property Fund of the Kyrgyz Republic, had also been highlighted as potentially being of significant value to the development of the newly independent state by the World Bank and European Bank for Re-development (EBRD).

Vasily advised Christian and Bill that the first contract for the airport terminal renovation had already been granted but the Airport Authority was very keen to find a foreign investor to develop the next two important development phases relating to a new state of the art air cargo centre and an air catering facility.

A meeting was arranged the following day for Bill, accompanied by Christian, to meet the President of the Airports Authority and to have a guided tour of the Airport and its current facilities. The new passenger check in area had been modernised but the remainder of the facilities were dreadful - in particular the so-called air catering kitchen and as for cargo handling facilities they were non-existent. In other words the airports facilities were ripe for development.

Bill rapidly concluded that here was his next project in a new and challenging environment.

CHAPTER 22

Bishkek

Bishkek was to become Bill's main residence for the next two years of 1999/2001.

The first Russian settlement started as early as 1868 and it became the capital of the newly named Kirghiz Soviet Socialist Republic in 1926 and in 1936 was re-named Frunze after the famous Russian General. Only after independence did the city revert to its original name of Bishkek.

The capital became an important military industrial centre and was built virtually from scratch by the Soviet Army Engineers.

It became the centre for the manufacture of torpedoes and sea mines which were tested in Lake Issykul well away from the prying eyes of NATO.

Lake Issykul was unique being the second largest saltwater lake in the world after the Caspian Sea despite being located at an altitude of over 5,000 ft.

Surrounded by high mountains the lake covers an area of over 6,000 square kilometres with an average depth of 1,000 feet and in excess of 2,000 feet in some parts. It was ideal for testing torpedoes!

Prior to independence in 1991 the population of Bishkek was mainly ethnic Russians but by 2004 the Russian population had reduced to 20% and by 2011 had dropped to 7%.

South of the city a fantastic backdrop was provided by the Tian Shan mountains which rise to over 25,000 feet. The climate was typical of central Asia with cold winters down to -34C and hot summers rising to +40C but spring and autumn temperatures being very pleasant.

Even today much of the Bishkek city centre has grand Soviet style public buildings, dreary apartment blocks and grand parks but no longer any major industrial base. Wealthy locals have built luxurious villas in the suburbs south of the city and a number of high class hotels have opened but the vast majority of the population remain poor.

In the late 90's the city was still at first sight rather austere but in fact the first signs of entrepreneurship were sprouting and, for those in the know, there were numerous small, good restaurants, bars and night clubs. Vasily was well known about town and could usually be found in one the city's night spots with ladies in tow.

Following his initial airport visit the next step for this new project was for Bill to gain, via Vasily, the political support of the Chairman of the State Property Fund who owned the Airport Authority, the Director of the Civil Aviation Authority and the Minister of Justice. The latter's support was guaranteed as she was not only Vasily's mistress but also rumoured to be "very close" to President Akayev.

All concerned in the president's administration welcomed the new airport project and Bill was promised their full co-operation and support.

It was agreed to incorporate a new Kyrgyz company which was to be called the Manas Management Company.

The Company was to be owned 50/50 by ITI in Italy, the Brescia based company owned by Bill's friend Angelo Prati as the umbrella company representing the "foreign investors" and the State Property Fund of the Kyrgyz Republic representing the Government.

Bill was to be the Chairman of the Board with a casting vote.

The Manas Airport Authority agreed to allocate a prime site on the airport periphery adjacent to the Terminal Buildings with direct access to the main terminal aircraft parking area. The next and most important matter was to arrange the financing of the project.

Bill flew back to Rome where Angelo had arranged for them to meet with MedioCredito Centrale: the Italian bank owned by the Ministry of Economy. The role of the Bank was to support Italian exports of capital goods by granting long term loans to overseas projects utilising Italian manufactured capital equipment. A Torino based company was engaged to design the project buildings, the internal layouts and the required equipment specifications for both the air cargo centre and the flight kitchens.

Following a major business plan presentation the Bank agreed to fund the project with a loan of USD 10 million repayable over a 10 year period starting in Year 2 following the completion of the construction and equipping phase. However there was still one major hurdle to overcome as the Bank insisted that political risk insurance cover be arranged to protect their loan.

Bill had been in touch with Lloyds underwriters in London and the World Bank in Washington to explore the availability of political risk insurance. He was referred to a specialist division of the World Bank referred to as MIGA which stood for Multilateral Investment Guarantee Agency.

The Agency had been set up by the World Bank specifically to provide project insurance cover against confiscation or nationalisation without due compensation primarily in developing countries such as the Kyrgyz Republic. Bill flew to Washington to present the Project business plan which was duly approved by MIGA's board and the insurance cover put in place in favour of MedioCreditoCentrale.

The Project corporation, by now registered as The Manas Management Company, was finally ready to start discussions with potential suppliers and to engage staff. This required the appointment of an experienced project engineer based in Italy and a suitable General Manager to be based in Bishkek to oversee the construction of the buildings and equipment installation.

Bill was able to persuade the chief design engineer from the Torino consultants - Dario Bonacino - to join ITI as the project chief engineer. For Bishkek he appointed a British friend of his brother Steve, called John Ward, as the General Manager. To assist John he recruited Jason Hammon - the son of his old friend Ron Hammon from South Africa, as assistant to John Ward. The expat team was now complete.

While all the equipment had to be of Italian origin in order to comply with the terms stipulated by MedioCredito the building contractor was not subject to any nationality restrictions. At that time most major building contractors in Bishkek, who worked to international standards, were Turkish firms. Unfortunately Kyrgyz firms were considered incapable of meeting the required standards and could not be trusted to complete the project on time.

The entire financial control of the operation and drawdown signatory rights with MediCredito was placed in Bill's hands to avoid any possible unauthorised use of funds.

By coincidence one of Vasily's senior team was a former KGB Major called Anatoly Kalashnikov who it turned out had been in Afghanistan, based in Helmand the very same year that Bill, as mentioned in chapter 15, had been engaged in sourcing and shipping military hardware via Egypt and Pakistan to the American backed Mujahedeen forces in Helmand. Anatoly 's role was to intercept these shipments.

It was agreed that he would join the Manas Management team as Director of Operations for the cargo centre. The two men became firm friends and it turned out that Anatoly was to play an important role in Bill's private life.

Bill was living in an apartment belonging to Sergey. It was conveniently located near the city centre and, as most of the other residents were senior Kyrgyz government officials, the security was good.

Construction work started at the airport site in the summer of 1999 and the foundation prepared for the official opening by President Akayev accompanied by Bill and his senior team. The ceremony also included the President and Bill laying a time capsule to be opened in a thousand years time!

Construction of the buildings continued apace and by early 2000 the first shipments of equipment from Italy commenced their long and rather tortuous journey by truck and rail to Bishkek. There were only two practical transportation methods with the most expensive but quickest involving trucking by road from Italy - a distance of 6,500 kilometres which took about 10 days depending on the weather. This involved a route via Austria, Hungary, Ukraine, Russia, Almaty in Kazakhstan and finally across the border to Bishkek.

The alternative but cheaper method was via rail but this could take at least 30 days and sometimes longer as not only was the routing over 7,000 kilometres but cargoes could spend days stuck in Russia or Kazakhstan. There was also the additional problem of potential theft en route.

It was finally decided that road transport was the best solution with the exception of a huge German built self propelled high loader for air cargo capable of reaching the cargo decks of B 747 aircraft. In order to minimise the height and width of the unit to comply with Russian rail standards the machine was partially disassembled prior to shipment.

In any event it arrived safely many weeks later at the Bishkek railhead, driven by road to the Manas airport site where it was successfully re-assembled by the German engineers flown out to commission it.

During the construction stage Bill found himself, between visits to Italy and to Istanbul for meetings with the Turkish contractors, with time on his hands and started to look at additional potential projects in Bishkek.

By now he had established excellent connections within the "White House" - the pseudonym for the President's Headquarters. He was also introduced to the Mayor of Bishkek to evaluate potential capital projects for the city. This was soon followed by a Presidential Decree appointing him as the official Advisor on Aviation to the President of the Republic.

He also had become a close friend of the President's son - Aidar Akayev. They had first met earlier the previous year in Vienna during a visit by Bill to update Sergey Tolstunov on progress with the Manas

Airport Project. Aidar had returned to Bishkek in 1998 from America having obtained a degree in business studies and in 1999 had married Aliya Nazarbayeva the daughter of the neighbouring President of Kazakhstan, Nursultan Nazarbayev.

It was hoped that the marriage would cement relations between the two countries and form some sort of Central Asian dynasty but the marriage did not last long and they separated in 2001 which was not surprising as Aidar had become notorious for his heavy drinking, womanising and the rough company he was known to cultivate.

In February 2001 he was appointed Chief Advisor to the Ministry of Finance which provided him with ample opportunity to poke his nose into everyone's business!

Unfortunately he died of a heart attack on 5th February 2020 in Moscow, aged just 43.

Italy in the late 1990s was starting to instigate a total ban on utilising waste landfills. Brescia was ahead of the game and had built one of the world's most advanced waste to energy plants producing heating for the city of Brescia and electricity for the national power grid with virtually no pollutant emissions.

Engineers from around the world were despatching delegations to Brescia to study the plant's operation and technology. The cost of these huge plants at that time was in excess of $500 million but the higher rates that could be charged for the power generated provided a 100% capital return over a 10 year period. In the case of Italy at that time the price per kilowatt hour for oil or gas generated power was 5 cents per kilowatt hour whereas waste to energy plants were entitled to charge 15 cents per kilowatt hour.

Bishkek had a horrible problem with its garbage disposal with all waste being collected and then simply dumped into or on top of a giant landfill located just outside the city. Whole families actually lived and worked on the landfill digging out any discarded item which potentially had some value. Some would actually tunnel into the waste with a total disregard for their safety or health.

Soon after Bill had visited the site with the Mayor a major cave-in occurred resulting in the death of fourteen people. There was a national outcry and the Mayor was forced into action. The Deputy Mayor was instructed to form a task force and several weeks later Bill accompanied a delegation to Brescia where his partner Angelo had arranged for a visit to the Brescia waste to energy Plant followed by a full technical presentation.

Following the signing of a MOU the delegation were taken to a lakeside hotel on Lake Como to celebrate. This visit to Italy also proved indirectly to be the final nail in the coffin for Bill's now tenuous relationship with Barbara.

The couple had de facto been separated for many months as Bill had by now moved semi permanently to Bishkek with side visits to Italy where he had taken up residence in a Brescia Hotel. Accompanying the Kyrgyz delegation to Italy was a pretty Russian redhead who Bill had asked to act as their translator. In reality they had been dating in Bishkek months previously but had kept their affair well under the radar. Unfortunately, during the Brescia visit, the lady in question answered the bedside telephone in the middle of the night not knowing that it was a call from America by Bill's daughter Alix.

The cat was out of the bag!

The affair soon ended after their return to Bishkek and Bill resigned himself to the prospect of being a bachelor again with the pretence of his marriage to Barbara irretrievably broken. With his four children still at school or about to enter college his overheads were substantial so he had to focus on generating income and recouping his capital base.

By early 2000 both the air cargo centre and the air catering facility construction had been completed and all the operational equipment was in place so that training courses for local staff could commence.

Bill had negotiated a management contract for both facilities with a well established London based firm called Abela & Co who specialised in air catering with operations in London and the Middle East. The Abela family were well regarded by their bankers and being of Lebanese origin, were confident that their staff would be more than capable to operate in an ex Soviet Republic.

The contract called for Abela to not only manage the facilities but to guarantee loan repayments to MedioCredito with surplus revenues to be shared between Abela and the Manas Management Company.

Bill had retained the services of his expat team in Bishkek in order to monitor the Abela management and to keep an eagle eye on the financial supervision of the project. The operation had got off to a rocky start as the local Russian and Kyrgyz staff objected to taking orders from "Arabs" albeit that Abela's staff were all Lebanese Christians.

Rumours of financial mismanagement soon began to emerge and the Airport Authority asked Bill to intervene.

The only option that he could envisage was to take direct physical control of the operation and to unilaterally terminate the Abela contract on the grounds of fiscal mismanagement. The physical takeover would not be easy as Bill's team pointed out that Abela's staff were in full physical control of the site with their own security contingent.

The only solution was to use a paramilitary force to enter the site, round up the Abela staff and declare a lock out. Luckily it was much easier to take this course of action at that time in the former Soviet Republics where armed "takeovers" were not unusual to settle disputes.

Anatoly was put in charge of the operation and he was able to arrange with the Chief of Police to "rent" a 50 strong contingent of heavily armed police. Early one Monday morning lookouts were in place outside the site with radio communication back to Anatoly who was with his police contingent discretely parked several kilometres away in a nearby village.

As soon as all the local Abela people had arrived on site at the airport the signal was given to move in. The Police convoy drove up to the gates and with Anatoly in the lead demanded entry to the site. The security guards put up no resistance and all the Abela staff were quickly rounded up at gunpoint then locked out of the site.

In preparation for the "takeover" Bill had decided to promote Jason Hammon as the new General Manager of the Project with Anatoly as the Director of Operations. The new management took immediate control and by the end of that day details of the financial mismanagement started to come to light. Over the next few days it became obvious that large sums of money were either missing or could not be properly accounted for.

Bill flew to London to meet with Albert Abela to explain face to face the reasons for their contract termination.

Jason and Anatoly made a good team - Jason was strong on financial controls and Anatoly was an excellent Operations Director. Soon the operations were cash flow positive and the first repayments started to flow to MedioCredito.

A disastrous start had been reversed! Bill and his team could relax - at least for the time being.

In September 2000 Anatoly introduced him to a beautiful woman. Her name was Irina Kacheiva and she was to become his wife.

Bill (left) with President Akayev (2nd right with sunglasses)

Bill unveiling plans for the waste to energy plant with the Mayor of Bishkek

Aidar Akayev

Manas Airport Cargo Hub

КОМПАНИЯ МАНАС МЕНЕДЖМЕНТ
THE MANAS MANAGEMENT COMPANY

Компания Манас Менеджмент является владельцем и эксплуатантом Комплекса грузового терминала и цеха бортового питания в международном аэропорту «Манас». Компания Манас Менеджмент была образована в 1998 году. Цель проекта Компании, стоимостью 10,5 миллионов долларов США, создание условий для узлового стыковочного аэропорта, связующего страны СНГ с рынками Центральной Азии, Тихоокеанского региона, Дальнего Востока и Европы.

Компания Манас Менеджмент имеет тесные и профессиональные связи с руководством аэропорта «Манас», Авиаперевозчиками и пользуется полной поддержкой указанных организаций как единственная лицензированная Компания, оказывающая услуги по обработке грузов и предоставлению бортового питания в аэропорту.

Наше совместное предприятие имеет необходимую инфраструктуру, достаточный объем знаний и опыт для определения будущих стратегий и требований к грузовому терминалу и цеху бортового питания в аэропорту «Манас».

The Manas Management Company is the owner and operator of the Air Cargo and In-flight Catering complex at Manas International Airport. The Manas Management Company was established as a Joint Venture in 1998, at a cost of USD 10.5 million, with the intention of creating conditions for a Hub linking the CIS countries and the markets of Central Asia, the Pacific Rim, the Far East and Europe.

The Manas Management Company has a very close and professional association with both Manas Airport authorities and Kyrgyzstan Airlines and have their full support as the sole licensed service provider at the airport.

In this light we feel that as a Joint Venture we have all the necessary infrastructure, breadth and depth of knowledge and experience to assist you in formulating your future strategic, Cargo and In-flight Catering, requirements here at Manas Airport.

CHAPTER 23

Perestroika

With the Manas operations now running smoothly and finally generating some income Bill was free to turn his attention to other business ventures in several other former Soviet States.

He had made throughout the year a number of trips to Sergey's discreet and well furnished offices located right in the heart of Vienna's business district, where many of the private banks for which Vienna was renowned were located., The discussions related to his future business relationship with Sergey and Vasily who were pushing him hard to join their Austrian holding corporation known as Finrep, as its Executive President and offering him a 25% share ownership.

The Company had been founded as the flagship entity of the Tolstonuv brothers to invest their profits arising from the Kumtor Mine gold sales on special projects within the former Soviet Republics. The brothers also had very high level connections not just in Moscow and Kyrgyzstan but also in some of the former Soviet Republics - in particular Moldova, Georgia and Kazakhstan.

Sergey invited Bill to accompany him on high level visits to these Republics in order to present Finrep as an organisation capable of arranging the construction of major capital projects relating to the aviation, logistics and energy industries. The company's capabilities were enhanced by Finrep's relationships with several leading banks in Austria together with Bill's connections in Italy with MediocreditoCentrale and with the World Bank in Washington for political insurance.

The first of such visits were to Moscow followed by Moldova in September 1999.

Bill in fact had visited Moldova some years previously back in 1991 to negotiate the purchase of some military equipment for Algeria and his memory of the trip was not a positive one.

It had been a very harrowing trip as Moldova had only recently declared independence from the Soviet Union with its territory East of the border, populated mainly by ethnic Russians and Ukrainians, refusing to join the new Republic declaring itself to be the Republic of Transnistria with its own capital called Tiraspol!

Communications were difficult at that time and the best way to reach the Moldavian capital of Chisinau was by car from Romania. Romania too was in a state of chaos trying to recover from the armed uprising against its former President - Nicolae Ceausescu - and poverty was widespread. Bill had flown into Bucharest and then rented a car and driver to take him to Chisinau some 500 kilometres away.

The journey took over 12 hours as much of the road was in a bad state of repair and there were numerous stops at police check points on both sides of the border.

The trip with Sergey and two Finrep Directors some nine years later was to be very different and much more pleasant despite a difficult start.

Bill's brother Steve had flown in to Vienna to join the Finrep team for the trip. It had started off badly in Vienna when, having boarded their flight to Chisinau, they discovered prior to take off that no luggage had been loaded on board the ancient AN-12 of Air Moldova.

The captain announced to the passengers that the aircraft was overloaded so no passenger luggage could be put on board and that it would be sent on the next flight which turned out to be several days later. Bill led a passenger revolt by persuading everyone to disembark from the aircraft and to be allowed back in to the Terminal building. Once inside he demanded a cash refund for their tickets which the booking agent refused to do.

He was able to establish from a nearby friendly Austrian ticket agent the name, address and telephone number of the Moldovan Agent who by this time had left the airport for her apartment in Vienna. Accompanied by Sergey and Steve he took a taxi to the agents' home and threatened to call debt collectors unless their ticket money was refunded in cash on the spot! The cash was reluctantly handed over - problem partially resolved!

By now it was late evening so the only solution was to try to reorganise the trip the following day. It turned out that no suitable flights were available so Sergey decided to charter a private jet. Several hours later they were on their way with a packed lunch and several bottles of champagne.

There was insufficient space for all the team so Steve decided to head back home.

Sergey had arranged for the delegation to meet with the President of Moldova, Petru Lucinschi and his son Chiril. During Soviet times Petru was the first secretary of the Communist Party of Moldova - a similar position held by Sergey in Kyrgyzstan - and they had become friends during party conferences held in Moscow.

Chiril, who had had been asked by his father to look after the "Finrep Team", was on the tarmac waiting to greet the visitors as they disembarked from the aircraft.

Bill had brought along as a gift for the President a beautiful handmade .45 pistol manufactured in Brescia by the Valtro Plant - a part of the ITI Group. They were whisked off, without any immigration or customs checks much to Bill's relief as he had the pistol in his brief case. They were taken to a magnificent Government guest house situated within extensive gardens which had formerly been the private estate of the Romanian Royal family.

Chiril had arranged an amazing welcome dinner for his guests which, after the speeches and toasts, was followed by a special "after dinner" treat. Heralded by a small string orchestra Chiril led a procession of at least a dozen beautiful girls who one by one climbed on to the dining room table to better show off their attributes. Each person made their choice of companion for the night and then discretely retired to bed.

The next day it was all business and meetings were held with various ministers in order to establish which infrastructure projects might be best suited for potential promotion by Finrep. It was agreed that priority should be given to financing a waste to energy plant for Chisinau and a toll highway running North East from the Romanian border to Chisinau then to Ukraine (bypassing Transnistria) to link up with the Kiev - Odessa highway.

The party flew back to Vienna without incident and from there Bill returned to Italy for discussions in Brescia with ITI and MedioCredito and Rome on the possibility of financing the projects both of which reflected Italy's leading edge engineering capabilities.

Mediocredito Centrale expressed an interest in arranging the finance but once again it would be subject to the World Bank being ready to provide political insurance cover. His next stop was Washington for meetings with MIGA.

Trips to Washington were always a pleasure for Bill and October was always a splendid time to visit with summer's heat long dissipated and the Capital's trees turning to their autumn colours. He invariably stayed at The Army and Navy Club or the Georgetown Inn - both located within easy walking distance of the World Bank.

MIGA advised that they would certainly consider approving the necessary insurance cover provided full feasibility studies were carried out on both projects.

Bill returned to Italy for discussions with Dario Bonacina - the head of the ITI civil engineering team - to start the feasibility studies before travelling back to Bishkek.

The most popular meeting place in Bishkek at that time for expats was the American Bar and Bill and his team were to be found there most evenings. Jason's girlfriend - soon to be his wife - worked there and Anatoly Kalashnikov was another regular visitor with his close companion Maria Kachaeva.

One late October evening Bill had arrived there to join Anatoly for a drink but found him accompanied by Maria and a tall attractive woman who was introduced as Irina, Maria's elder sister. Irina had just returned to Bishkek after finishing a two month tour of China with a ballet company and was currently teaching ballet and dance on a voluntary basis at the Bishkek Opera and Ballet Theatre.

Following the dissolution of the Soviet Union funding for the arts had all but vanished and the so called independent states, including Kyrgyzstan, were unable to fund the arts as previously. This in turn meant that all the arts had become very reliant on volunteers to keep alive what had been one of the leading ballet companies in the USSR.

Irina had been enrolled in the ballet school since the age of eight and had been trained in the discipline of Russian Classical Ballet created and perfected by Agrippina Vaganova.

In addition to their ballet training students were expected to complete all their normal school work, to be active members of the Young Pioneers and subsequently to join the Komsomol. Irina being very athletic was a keen member of the Young Pioneers and like many of them had been trained to strip, clean and fire automatic weapons.

Drinks were followed by dinner and soon Bill and Irina started seeing each other most evenings and the weekends would see them trekking high up in the National Park at the base of the Ala Too mountains always accompanied by Irina's beloved dog Argo.

In late November Sergey asked Bill to join him on a visit to Georgia to meet with the President of the Government of Tbilisi. Firstly they travelled to Paris for briefing meetings with their Georgian interlocutor, Gotcha Tchogovadze the Georgian Ambassador in Paris with co accreditation in Madrid and the Georgian Representative to UNESCO where he was to become the Head of Mission.

Gotcha was the ideal person to "unlock" every door in Georgia being a close friend and appointee of President Eduard Shevardnadze and as a well known and highly respected figure in his own right. He was also a well known professor of Technical sciences and fully understood the necessity for Tblisi to urgently resolve the city's growing waste collection and disposal problems. Sergey and his Georgian friend from university, also named Gotcha, had both studied engineering under the Professor at Moscow State University.

Bill and Sergey arrived in Tblisi on the first of December and spent the first few days visiting the city's huge waste dump and waste collection centres.

On December 3rd - Bill's 59th birthday - the President of Tblisi hosted a dinner party in honour of their visit. Bill had not mentioned it was his birthday but the President had noted the occasion and after dinner presented him with a Georgian dagger and hunting whip and - best of all - put through a call in his name to Irina in Bishkek so that she could wish Bill a happy birthday!

Bill loved Georgia and he and Irina were to return many times in the following years.

Christmas 2000 was fast approaching and Bill was determined to spend the New Year with Irina in Europe and had persuaded her to postpone her return to the touring Ballet Company. He was able to arrange a visa for her and the couple flew to Italy and then drove to Paris returning back via Lake Geneva where they celebrated the arrival of New Year 2001 at the lakeside village of Yvoire.

Following their return to Bishkek they decided that Bill's flat was not really secure despite the fact that they were at all times accompanied, when outside, by an armed bodyguard who accompanied them to the front door of the flat and then inspected the interior before departing. The crime rate in Bishkek was at an all time high with numerous reports of robbery and rape so they moved to a secure and comfortable hotel called the Centrum situated south of the city adjacent to several parks and offering a fine view of the mountains. The food was good and it had the only heated indoor pool in the entire city.

The hotel was within easy reach of Vasily's office and near to Irina's mother's apartment.

It was equally convenient for meetings with Aidar Akayev as the hotel was located very near to the President's private residence. The Director of the Civil Aviation Authority, who was later to become the President of Manas Airport, also lived within several minutes walking distance of the hotel.

He often invited the couple to his house for dinner and they became good friends.

The May of 2001 saw Bill in New York visiting his lawyers who were finalising and collating the back up evidence to his UN claims against Iraq as permitted by various UN resolutions. He had spent the previous weeks visiting Barclays in Geneva and the house in Mill Valley collecting all available backup records.

Why did he utilise American lawyers when so much of his legal work was normally undertaken by his London Lawyers? Back then UK law firms were unable to accept work on a contingency basis so his London firm had recommended him to use the services of a New York based law firm who were not subject to such restrictions.

Following Iraq's invasion of Kuwait in August 1990 the UN sanctions had remained in place with various resolutions and modifications issued from time to time. The UN Compensation Commission known as the UNCC was created in 1991 as a subsidiary of the UN Security Council specifically mandated to process claims and to pay compensation for losses and damage suffered as a direct result of Iraq's invasion of Kuwait. Claimants were divided in to 6 categories with Bill considered a Category C claimant for individual losses above $100,000 and his Company Bonaventure being considered a Category D claimant for compensation for business losses.

Over 2.6 million claims had been lodged in total of which 57% resulted in some sort of award with $42+ billion having been paid out by 2013.Priority was given to smaller category A and B claimants.

In 1995 the Oil for Food Programme permitted Iraq to export specific amounts of oil with the revenues being monitored by the UN for the purchase of food, medicines and related products. Only in 2000, after years of wrangling, UN Resolution 1330 was passed enabling Iraq to export as much oil as possible but with all the proceeds arising there from being paid by the oil purchasers directly to the UNCC. The UNCC then allocated the proceeds based on 72% to humanitarian needs, 25% to the UN Compensation Fund for war reparation, 2.2% to cover UN administration costs and 0.8% to UN weapons inspection.

By this time the numerous smaller Category A and B claims had been settled finally permitting the larger personal and corporate claims to be processed by the Commission. Bill personally as a British citizen and his company Bonaventure, based in the British Virgin Islands, were both considered to be "British" and therefore came under the jurisdiction of the UK Foreign Office who were one of only 5 countries sitting as permanent UN members of the Security Council.

The Foreign Office were delegated to dispense all UN compensation funds which were to be awarded to all relevant British citizens or Companies. The individual claims were considered and then awarded, amended or rejected on a case by case basis by special panels of legal experts - a long and time consuming process to say the least. Many of the claims, including Bill's, were extremely complicated and the back up paperwork finally weighed in at over 50lbs!

It was during this week that Bill received a phone call from Irina and her sister from a clinic in Bishkek to announce that Irina was pregnant with the baby due in November. Bill was thrilled albeit slightly worried about being a father again at 60!

There was also the matter of his divorce from Barbara.

The previous year Bill had visited California for Christmas to see his children and during this visit Barbara had presented him with papers requesting his assent to seek a divorce which he had signed but he had heard nothing further. It seemed at that time that Barbara had decided to put matters on hold.

founded as the Austrian subsidiary of a major international trading and investment group specialising in project finance for developing countries ● MTFC was founded specifically to provide investment finance and marketing to the mining industry ● TRADE & FINANCE was founded to assist E-European and CIS countries in the export of industrial agricultural and lumber based products ● FINREP was

TRADE &
FINANCE

GROUP COMPANY PROFILES

FINREP HANDELS Ges.m.b.H.

Finance & Investment Advisory Enterprise

Finrep was founded in 1994 as the Austrian subsidiary of a major International Trading and Investment Group specialising in Project Finance for developing countries.

In 2001 the Company was purchased by a Group of European Private Investors to provide investment and project finance to the emerging markets of East Europe and the Commonwealth of Independent States (C.I.S.).

The share capital of the Company is EUR 1,000,000.00.

MINING TECHNOLOGY & FINANCIAL ADVISORY CORPORATION

MTFC is a West European based holding company founded in 1980.

The operational Company MTFC Investitionsprojekt-entwicklungs Ges.m.b.H. (formerly MTAC) was founded in 1996 specifically to provide investment project finance and marketing to the mining Industry.

TRADE & FINANCE Ges.m.b.H.

Finance & Investment Advisory Enterprise

Trade & Finance was founded in 1999 to assist East European and CIS countries in the export of semi-finished or finished industrial and lumber based products to West Europe and North America with its principal trading office in Moscow.

group
company
profiles

GROUP PROJECTS

A HISTORY OF SUCCESS

The group has a significant history of successfully raising investment and project finance coupled with project services and due diligence preparation for financial institutions. Contracts and services and financial advisory contracts successfully concluded amount more than US$ 1,000,000,000.

MTAC provided since its inception in 1996 specialist advisory services to Kara-Balta Mining Combinate (KMC) - one of the leading producer´s of uranium and gold in Central Asia. MTAC negotiated on behalf of KMC long term agreements for the supply of gold ore from the Kumtor Operating Company (KOC) Mine and the major off-takers including Bank Rothschild & Sons Ltd. in London.

Thereafter MTAC acted as financial advisor to KMC and significantly improved upon the original terms agreed with Bank Rothschild resulting in major increases of profit to KMC. The total value of the credit lines amounted to US$ 850,000,000.

MTAC also assisted in the physical and operational management of the project logistic services. The major success of the KMC - MTAC cooperation was the listing of Kara-Balta Mining Combinate on the London Bullion Market Association (LBMA) in October 1999.

HISTORY

Financial advisory contracts successfully concluded amount more than US$ 1,000,000,000. ♦ MTAC

- Ministry of Energy Georgia -
  Hydro Electric Rehabilitation Programme
  CIS

- Sunflower Seed Oil Production Plant
  CIS

- Waste to Energy Plant
  CIS

- Gas Condensate Plant Modernisation
  Russia

- Fruit Concentrate & Fruit Puree Plant
  CIS

- Medical/Pharmaceutical Production
  Russia

- Tomato Paste Plant
  CIS

- Mineral Water Bottling Plant
  CIS

- Baby Food Plant
  CIS

- Claas Combine Harvester Fleet
  Russia

- Air Cargo Terminal & Air Catering Complex
  CIS

- Ocean Airlines (International Air Cargo)
  Italy

- Georgian Airlines - Aircraft Procurement
  CIS

- Air Cargo Terminal Project
  Slovakia

- Kyrgyz Air (International Airline & Air Charter)
  Kyrgyz Republic

- Waste to Energy Plant
  Poland

- Telecom Georgia - Financial Advising
  CIS

group
projects
history

GROUP SERVICES

The Group specializes in arranging direct investment, structural finance, loans and joint venture arrangements for turn key infrastructure projects from conception to start up including:

- Feasibility studies

- Business Plans including sensitivity studies

- Engineering studies

- Negotiations with Banks and Investors

- Negotiations with equipment suppliers

- Civil works and construction

- Operational and maintenance training

In particular the team of Group specialists have extensive Project Structural Finance experience in the following fields:

- Turnkey Infrastructure Projects

- Parts production plants for the engineering and automotive industries

- Food processing plants

- Waste to energy and Hydro electricity

- Gold Mining and sales

- Air Cargo and Air Catering facilities

- Aircraft Procurement & Leasing

The Group works on an exclusive basis with Avon Group of the UK in the sale, dry, semi-dry and wet lease of civil aircraft. Detailed evaluation, startups, route and business planning can be quickly prepared by the Avon team of specialists for passenger, cargo and combi configurations.

group
services

GROUP
PARTNERSHIPS

The group represents a number of leading Companies and Organisations in the CIS including:

- **Malaysian Mining Corporation** - precious metal mining

- **Priargynskoje Industrial Mining Unification** - Chita
  Russian Federation - largest CIS uranium producer
  ranking No. 3 worldwide

- **Jahncke Germany** - joint venture partner with Finrep in
  Geohorti Company Ltd - a new joint venture to build an ultra modern fruit juice concentrate and
  fruit puree plant in Gori - Georgia

- **ITI Group Italy** - High precision engineering plants and components

- **Aster - ITI Group Italy** - Waste to Energy Plants for both urban and hospital waste and
  rehabilitation of hydroelectric plants

- Official Advisor to **Ministry of Nuclear Energy of Russian Federation** infrastructure
  project developments in Tomsk Region in joint venture with Aventis and in co-operation with
  Eli Lilly, Vienna

- Financial advisor to National Telecom privatisation projects in the CIS and East Europe in
  conjunction with **Global Telecommunications & Investment Group of San Francisco**

- **European Aviation Group** - exclusive mandate for Russian Federation and CIS territories for
  aircraft fleet Boeing 747, Airbus A-300, Boeing 737 and BAC 111

- **Avon Group** - UK´s leading Independent
  Group of Aviation advisors in both the
  passenger and air cargo industries -
  exclusive mandate for Russian Federation
  and CIS territories

- **Skyway Technologies Italy** - Turbo
  separators for cereal classification of
  milling flour

group
partnerships

189

CHARITIES/

Since 1996 Finrep has made contributions to the Municipal Hospital located in the Chuiskaya region of the Kyrgyz Republic. Financial h

- Since 1996 Finrep has made contributions to the Municipal Hospital located in the Chuiskaya region of the Kyrgyz Republic. Financial help was provided to the surgery department of the hospital including the purchasing of medical equipment, medicines, reconstruction of the surgery department interior.

- In 1997 Finrep financed a documentary film about life and work of the well known surgeon, Ernest Akramov.

- Between 1997 and 1998 Finrep contributed to the construction of the Orthodox Church in Bishkek, the capital of Kyrgyzstan.

- In 2001 Finrep was a sponsor of the Moscow Theatre of Satire, headed by Alexander Shirvindt.

- Between 1999 and 2001 Finrep organized and provided financial support for the publishing of two books, both devoted to famous scientists and personalities.

  These books were published in six languages (English, Turkish, German, Macedonian, Kyrgyz and Russian) and are intended for children and young adults.

- In 2002 Finrep supervised the project of publishing a biography of the Patriarch of Moscow and all Russia His Holiness Alexii II, named "The Creator of the Unified Russian Church". The book is devoted to his 40 years of service to the Orthodox Church.

The first part of the book is written in the form of an interview with His Holiness, contains the biography of the Patriarch, his views on different social, political and moral problems of modern Russian society. The second half of the book contains interviews with bishops and leading state officials, including the first President of the Russian Federation Boris Yelzin, the current President of Russia Vladimir Putin and Prime Minister Mihail Kasianov.

Together with the book, Finrep initiated a project to produce a film about the childhood of the Patriarch during the Second World War.

SPONSORSHIP

In 2002 Finrep, through Vasily Tolstunov, participated in publishing the book by Paola Volkova "Arseniy Tarkovskiy. Life of the family and history of the clan".

The book is about the life of Arseniy Tarkovskiy, father of the famous producer Andrei Tarkovskiy and his friendship with a number of great literary figures, among whom were poets Anna Ahmatova and Marina Tzvetaeva. The history of the Tarkovskiy clan is inseparably linked to the history of Russia.

In May 2002 a fund was created in Moscow, in honour of Artem Borovik, the famous journalist, who tragically died in a March 2002 aircrash. The initiators of the fund were Artem´s father, Genrikh Borovik, a modern writer, publicist, journalist, and Artem´s wife Veronika Borovik-Khilchevskaya. Finrep plays an active role in the work of the Fund. Vasily Tolstunov, who is in charge of sponsorship activities at Finrep, is also vice president of Artem Borovik fund.

The Fund assists journalists who work in high risk areas and provides support to the families of perished journalists. In addition the fund pays scholarships to the most gifted students of journalism faculties and yearly holds a contest for the best investigative journalist. The Fund exists entirely on donations from businessmen and private companies such as Finrep.

The president of the Fund Genrikh Borovik was invited to Vienna by Finrep to visit his son´s favorite places in the city. He also met Simon Wiesenthal and with the help of Finrep plans to shoot a film about his life.

Together with mediaholding "Sovershenno secretno" Finrep participates in the project "Books for blind children", a part of the UNO and UNESCO program "World decade for cultural development".

Finrep pays great attention to charity and sponsorship and aims to combine business with philanthropic activities.

charities/
sponsorship

CHAPTER 24

The Move to Italy

Irina had applied for an Italian visa with sponsorship from Angelo Prati and in July 2001 the couple flew to Italy. It was to be the last time that Irina would see Kyrgyzstan! To establish permanent residency in Italy it was essential for her to stay until after the baby was born.

Up until this point Bill had spent the previous few years living as a hotel dwelling nomad but with a new baby en route it was time to settle into a more permanent home. Angelo and his partner had recently completed the construction of a new apartment building in Gardone Val Trompia not far from the headquarters of the Beretta premises.

A supermarket was located in the lower level which was ideal for Irina - all she needed to do was to descend by the lift outside the front door directly to the store! Bill, as part of his "package deal" with Angelo, leased one of the penthouse apartments - rent free and fully furnished. The apartment had a wonderful panoramic view of Val Trompia facing north to the Alps and south down the Trompia valley in the direction of Brescia.

He was keen to introduce Irina to his sister Tassie so in August the couple set off by car on a long tour of South West Europe to visit her. They drove through France to Biarritz staying in several magnificent chateau hotels en route and then crossed the border into Spain staying in the Basque countryside for a few days before moving on to Northern Portugal and then down to Faro on the Algarve coast.

Tassie and fiancé George had recently purchased a very dilapidated old farmhouse together with sufficient acreage for her horses near Tavira. Extensive conversion was underway in what would eventually become a beautiful villa complex. While the work was underway Tassie and George were living at another of their existing rental properties.

Following a very enjoyable visit the couple started their journey back visiting Seville, Granada, Carcassonne and Monte Carlo.

The following month in September Maria and Michael visited them in Italy. It proved to be the start of a close friendship between Maria and Irina with Maria being invited to be Godmother to the forthcoming baby.

On the morning of the 26th of November Irina went into labour but 24 hours later the baby's heart rate was dropping and Irina was exhausted so the doctors decided to opt for an immediate Caesarean section.

Justine entered the world weighing in at a healthy 3.6kgs. Maternity hospitals in Italy prefer mothers to remain for at least 4/5 days before returning home so Irina was well rested by the time she and the baby left.

Irina, like many Russians, took her faith seriously and was very keen to have her children baptised into the Russian Orthodox faith so the following spring Justine was baptised in the Russian Orthodox Cathedral of Saint Nicholas in Vienna. The Tolstunovs had made all the arrangements and hosted a dinner party that evening. Maria and Michael had flown in from America and Anatoly Kalashnikov and his wife Clara flew in from Bishkek. Maria, Sergey's wife Luba and Anatoly became Justine's God parents.

During this period of 2000 - 2002 Bill was working with both his Russian Partners in Vienna and Angelo in Brescia to develop a number of new projects and travelling a great deal but always making sure he was home for the weekend. He commuted between his Finrep office in Vienna and his ITI office in Brescia with side trips to Moscow, Moldova, Poland, Bishkek and Georgia.

Sergey was pushing Bill and Irina to make a permanent move to Vienna so that the Finrep partners could be in one location and take advantage of Vienna's superior access to Eastern Europe.

However Irina was adamant that they should stay in Italy as she was not keen to become part of the Russian expat community in Vienna nor to be too involved with the "Tolstunov Clan" who she could see had an increasing hold over Bill.

Russia, and in particular Moscow, was booming. Putin was about to become President, oil and gas revenues were growing and an ever increasing number of wealthy "New Russians" as they were called were looking to invest their money in the West. The Tolstunovs were ideally placed to tap into these new contacts in Moscow many of whom were friends from their University and Communist Party days.

It was odd how these former communist party members were now the greatest exponents of free enterprise and were happy to show off their new found wealth and high level contacts within the new Russian administration. Moscow remained an exciting but dangerous business environment and an easy commute for Bill from Bishkek or Vienna on his multi entry Russian visa.

Following introductions by the Tolstunovs he became friends with Artyom Borovik, son of the well known Soviet writer media diplomat Genrikh Borovik, who provided the "Finrep team" with access to some of Russia's newly emerging and powerful elite.

Meetings were arranged with Moscow's Mayor Yuri Luzhkov to discuss possible waste to energy projects for the capital, with the head of the Atomic Energy Authority to discuss possible uranium supplies from Kyrgyzstan and with Oleg Deripaska the owner of Rusal - the country's leading Aluminium producer.

Artyom and Sergey had been friends since their student days in Moscow. Artyom graduated from the Moscow State Institute for International Relations after which he was posted to the Soviet embassy in Peru. He had soon forsaken diplomacy for journalism specialising on the Soviet invasion of Afghanistan which had made him famous. His frank and open journalism brought home to the Soviet public the futility of overseas war. He covered the withdrawal of Soviet troops in 1989, some 5 years after Bill's involvement with arms supplies to Egypt for the Afghan Muhadeen and his book - The Hidden War - was published in English in 1990.

By 1991 he had his own TV programme on Russian State Television specialising in stories relating to crime, corruption and about business friends of President Yeltsin and the political elite. Political protection was essential for journalists so his friendship with Yuri Luzhkov the powerful Mayor of Moscow, who was in favour with the Kremlin at that time, became very important. Inevitably his TV programme was eventually dropped after the Government accused the producers of smearing politicians.

Not one to be "put off" Artyom's next step was to create his own TV station and to produce his own weekly newspaper called Top Secret - an expose of political and business illegalities. At the same time he had begun investigating the mysterious bomb explosions in Moscow during September 1999 killing over 300 people which was blamed on Chechen terrorists. It was used as the pretext to launch a new military campaign against Chechnya by Putin who had just been appointed as Acting President by Boris Yeltsin. In fact no conclusive evidence was produced implicating Chechens, no arrests made and many believe the bombs were placed by the FSB - Russia's successor to the KGB.

In early March 2000 Sergey had proposed that Artyom should join Finrep as a 25% shareholder and the partners met up in Tblisi for a special dinner to celebrate the appointment. Bill and Irina flew in from Italy. Little did they know that this would be the last time they would ever see Artyom alive!

On March 9th, 2000 he was due to take a scheduled flight to Kiev from Moscow's Sheremetyevo Airport. When his flight was delayed he was offered a seat on his private plane by Ziya Batheyev, a Chechen oil industry executive. The Yak-40 jet which was taking them from Moscow to Kiev crashed immediately after takeoff from Sheremetyevo airport killing all on board.

The official version was that the aircraft had not been properly de-iced but the opinion of many was that the aircraft had been deliberately sprayed with water containing no de-icing fluid with the resultant ice build up causing the aircraft to stall just after takeoff.

His friends are certain that it was an "arranged" accident as his article about Putin's childhood and early years was about to be released only days before the March 26th Presidential election which confirmed Putin as President. However it is just as likely that the Chechen oil magnate was the planned target and Artyom was an unfortunate additional victim. It is safe to say however, given Artyom's criticism of Yeltsin and his successor Vladimir Putin, that there were few tears shed in the Kremlin after his death. Bill and the Tolstunovs attended his funeral and his burial in Moscow's beautiful and prestigious Novodevichy Cemetery. His grave is very near that of Nikita Khrushchev and Boris Yeltsin.

Artyem's widow Veronika inherited her husband's recent stake of 25% in Finrep and joined the partnership. Vasily was sure that Putin would expand the power base of the Church in Russia and that it was to become an integral part of and force behind the new political elite. He considered it essential to ensure that Finrep was to be seen as a strong supporter of the Church. He was rapidly building Finrep's status as a friend and sponsor of the Russian Orthodox Church both in Vienna and Moscow. He had long cultivated the Bishop of Bishkek and on several occasions had taken Bill with him for after dinner visits, cognac in hand, to the Bishop who loved a fine tipple. On one occasion the Bishop accompanied them to Issykul to visit the Holy Trinity church which had reputedly been the base for a last stand in 1918 by the white Russian forces against the Red Army.

Vasily also arranged for Finrep to make donations to the fund for the rebuilding of the Cathedral of Christ the Saviour in Moscow headed by Patriarch Alexey II of Moscow and all Russia and in 2002, on behalf of

Finrep and had arranged for the publication of the biography of Alexey II.

The first edition of the book was presented to the Patriarch by Vasily accompanied by Sergey and Bill during a private audience held at the Cathedral attended by President Putin.

That same year Finrep sponsored the creation of the Artoym Borovik Fund to provide scholarships for Investigative Journalists.

In 2006 a scholarship was awarded to Anna Politkovskaya, a journalist and human rights activist who reported on political events in Russia and who was becoming increasingly critical of the Kremlin and its actions in Chechnya.

She was assassinated in October of that year - gunned down in the lift of her Moscow apartment. The case remains unsolved to this day.

Irina

Anatoly and Clara Kalashnikov at Justine's baptism in Vienna

CHAPTER 25

Kyrgyz Air

In early 2002 Bill was back in Bishkek to meet with President Akayev, his son Aidar and the Head of the CAA, Timur Muratov. Timur had invited Bill in his capacity as Aviation Advisor to the President.

Timur and Bill were old friends. When Bill first visited Bishkek Timur was President of Kyrgyzstan Airlines and had been instrumental in pushing the Airport Authority to back the air cargo and air catering project.

The State owned national carrier - Kyrgyzstan Airlines - had been in decline for years.

Formerly a part of the Soviet State airline Aeroflot it had become an independent entity following perestroika and the breakup of the Soviet Union. Aeroflot aircraft, based in Bishkek, were acquired or nationalised to form the fleet of the new entity. The aircraft were a somewhat motley collection of ageing IL-76 military aircraft, Tupulov 134 / 154 and Yak-40s many of them grounded for lack of spare parts. In 1998 the airline had dry leased its only modern aircraft, an Airbus A 320, from a Dutch based Lessor, which it used mainly on its Moscow rotations. It also doubled up as the Presidential aircraft.

In late 2001 the airline's A 320 had been flown to Germany for a heavy maintenance check to be undertaken by Lufthansa at a cost of around $750,000. Unfortunately the airline did not have the sufficient foreign exchange to pay as its income was heavily dependent on the Kyrgyz Som. Timur had asked Bill and Sergey to join him in Amsterdam to assist in negotiating a lease extension with the Lessor and a spread payment plan with Lufthansa to enable Kyrgyzstan Airlines to bring the aircraft back into service. Unfortunately no agreement was reached so the airline was back to operating its elderly Russian TU-154's on the Moscow route just at the time that Aeroflot was introducing new Boeing and Airbus aircraft into its fleet!

President Akayev was under no illusions about the state of his country's national airline. He had called the meeting with Bill to ask if Finrep was willing to start a new private airline using modern Western manufactured jets. He was ready to offer full Government support to establish it as the new flagship airline of the country. Timur was instructed to assist in every way, in particular to ensure the new airline would be awarded route permits into the Russian Federation and elsewhere under existing international route bi-lateral agreements.

Aidar Akayev also advised Bill that he was in the process of acquiring or planning to open a number of "travel shops" who would be ready to promote the airline within the local travel market and that he would personally ensure that all Government agencies would be "encouraged" to use the new carrier.

Bill agreed to discuss the proposal with his Finrep colleagues.

The Finrep Partners were keen to proceed as the airline's creation could be an obvious "fit" with their current joint venture ownership of the Manas Management Company - the holding company for their existing air cargo and air catering operations at Manas Airport in Bishkek.

Vasily's office premises in Bishkek were located in the city centre so it was decided that this would be an ideal headquarters and main ticket office for the new airline. The Turkish contractor who had successfully built the Manas Airport facilities would be invited to carry out the conversion work.

Back in Vienna Bill and Sergey met with the European Sales Director of a major US leasing firm who owned a fleet of modern MD-82 jets available for wet lease. A wet lease is where the lessor provides not only the aircraft but also the crew, maintenance and insurance. Luckily they had an aircraft just coming out of heavy maintenance in Bucharest so Bill flew there to inspect the aircraft, signed the lease on behalf of Finrep with an option for two additional aircraft and handed over the design for the aircraft painting.

The aircraft had a range of 3,800 kms with 14 business class and 128 economy class seating.

In the interim he had engaged an experienced CEO for the airline called Linton Bell.

Linton had decades of start-up airline management, was the former Managing Director of Air Zambia and most importantly was happy to reside in Bishkek. A team of local flight attendants were trained to British CAA standards by Linton's ex wife and were pre-qualified prior to the aircraft's arrival in Bishkek.

Catering was arranged "in house" with the Manas Management Company - the Finrep/ Airport joint venture air catering operation located at the airport. Tickets had been printed according to IATA regulations and were distributed to all the appointed travel agencies, including a Moscow agent, who had been vetted and appointed by the airline management. Advance bookings and ticket sales commenced in July with a September start-up for the new airline concentrating initially on the Bishkek- Moscow route with a daily round trip flight of 4 hours each way.

In September as planned the aircraft arrived in Bishkek with the full complement of cockpit crew, maintenance engineers and operational spares. Bill meanwhile following advice from Vasily had warned the leasing company to alert the crew not to declare upon arrival their emergency dollar funds for security reasons. However the senior Captain ignored the advice and signed a customs declaration upon arrival in Bishkek stating that he had around $20,000 in cash!

Sure enough - trouble was brewing!

Vasily had arranged a crew bus and hotel accommodation in a comfortable out of town hotel. He accompanied them to the hotel and ensured they were safely checked in. He warned them not to open their doors to strangers or to accept the usual telephone calls offering the services of young women. The advice fell on deaf ears and sure enough the next morning the captain woke up to an empty bed and the dollars were nowhere to be found!

Despite this the airline got off to a good start with virtually all flights fully booked. For most of the passengers it was their first experience of decent airline service unlike the take it or leave it attitude of Aeroflot and the local airline that prevailed at that time. Meanwhile Aidar Akayev was taking a great interest in the airline and true to his word his travel agencies were selling a lot of tickets but by the year end Linton was reporting an ominous slow down in monies being forwarded to the airline from Aidar's travel agencies.

Early in the new year of 2003 Bill flew to Bishkek to meet with Aidar who blamed "administrative problems" within his organisation but promised to speed up the transfer of funds. At the same time he asked if Finrep would like him to become a "shareholder" in the airline. Bill responded that it was too early for the airline to consider additional shareholders. He returned back to Europe feeling somewhat uneasy with good reason as it turned out.

Aidar's influence in the President's administration was becoming ever more pervasive and his reputation for bullying his way into lucrative sectors of the economy was growing. The promised forwarding of ticket sales monies did not materialise and rumours spread that tickets were being sold for cash on the black market.

In addition questions were suddenly being raised that the MD-82 aircraft had not been type rated by the Russian Federation CAA. A complete nonsense of course as MD aircraft operated by Western airlines had been flying for years in to and out of Russia and the MD series of aircraft were the successors of the famous DC-9 aircraft which had long received type rating approval from the Russian CAA.

The writing was on the wall so in April 2003 just 6 months after the maiden flight of Kyrgyz Air the Finrep partners decided to close the airline and to fly the aircraft back to Europe without prior notice to the Kyrgyz authorities. Needless to say it was not a popular move with the Kyrgyz CAA!

Meanwhile Bill continued his weekly commutes between Brescia and Vienna finding more and more of his time devoted to Finrep matters. The commuting was in fact very easy involving an hour's drive to Verona Airport early in the morning to catch the 0800 daily one hour flight to Vienna followed by a 20 minute taxi ride downtown to be at his desk by 09.30!

He always stayed at the Hilton Plaza which was just a 5 minute walk from the office with an excellent restaurant to boot! He normally flew home to Italy on Thursday or Friday evening.

Sergey continued to push Bill to move the family to Vienna. Bill went so far as to view a number of apartments in the residential areas of Vienna and the nearby town of Baden - a 30 minute commute from the city centre.

Irina, who by now was pregnant again, was adamant that she wanted to stay in Italy. Their daughter Catherine - always known as Katy - was born on June 17th, 2003.

The couple loved their apartment in Val Trompia with its wonderful views, convenience and it was an easy drive to the ITI building where Bill continued to have his office but with their new addition to the family additional space was becoming essential so it was time to start looking for their own home.

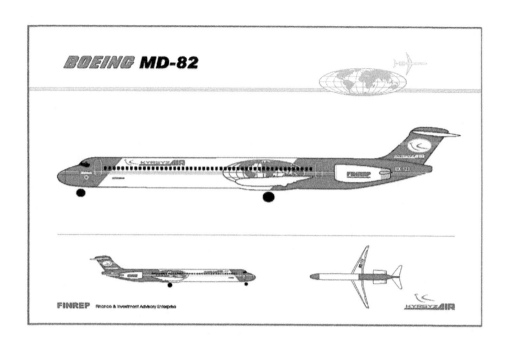

CHAPTER 26

2000-2004

The first part of the 21st century can only be described as the period of multiple projects for Bill.

Prior to the closure of the airline in 2003, together with the Tolstunov brothers, he had been looking closely at other potentially lucrative projects in the Kyrgyz Republic together with backing from Aidar Akayev.

An area of particular interest was the mobile telephone market.

In 2000 a local firm had been the first to introduce a mobile service in the Bishkek area but there was no national coverage. Aidar promised to arrange government support for a second foreign owned operator to obtain the applicable licences if Finrep could find a suitable "partner".

Bill immediately thought about making contact with his old friend from his Geneva days - Mehmet Karamehmet - the owner of Cukurova Group who happened to be the major shareholder of Turkcell - the largest mobile operator in Turkey. He flew to Istanbul to start negotiations with Turkcell who were quick to realise the potential of the project.

A meeting was arranged with President Akayev and Aidar to receive a delegation from Turkcell to encourage them to invest with the promise of a long term operating license. Mehmet and his team flew in to Manas on their private jet and Bill and Vasily accompanied them to the meeting at the White House with the President. That evening Vasily hosted a dinner for the delegation and the following morning they flew back to Istanbul to start preparing a feasibility study.

However a few months later the second mobile licence was awarded to another local company owned by none other than Aidar Akayev!

Another project encouraged by the President was to ask the Finrep partners to look into the setting up of a National Lottery whose proceeds would be split between the Government and the shareholders.

Unofficial lotteries and other forms of gambling had been in existence in the country for many years controlled by several local mafia clans. Vasily had connections with all the gang leaders who also owned many of Bishkek's bars, restaurants and massage parlours. It was considered essential to seek their co-operation and to make use of their existing outlets if a national lottery was to be successful. The initial survey looked positive so Finrep was asked to find a suitable well established foreign lottery operator as a possible joint venture partner.

The Malaysians were very active investors in Bishkek at that time with particular focus on hotels and tourism. One of these companies, called Magnum Holdings, was the largest lottery operator in Malaysia. Vasily and Bill accompanied by Vasily's assistant were invited to Kuala Lumpur as guests of Magnum to be shown their operating procedures and to be present for that months "National Draw".

Soon afterwards Magnum despatched a team of senior managers to Bishkek in order to evaluate the Kyrgyz market potential. Meetings were held with the President's team and the Ministry of Finance. The Malaysians agreed to recommend the investment to their board and a MOU was signed by the joint venture parties with a view to starting in 2003.

However events elsewhere, including the deterioration of the relationship with Aidar Akayev connected with Kyrgyz Air, were to preclude the establishment of the lottery business.

In late 2001, soon after the September 11th attacks, the US Government signed an agreement with the Kyrgyz Government to establish a base at Manas Airport for US troops in transit primarily en route to the Bagram Air Base in Afghanistan.

The Russians and Chinese were very upset and did their best to oppose the opening of the base but President Akayev pressed ahead with the agreement as the lease payments of $60m per quarter were to be paid directly to the State Treasury.

In addition the US Air Force undertook to provide substantial improvements at the airport - in particular the airport access roads and aircraft parking areas. By early 2002 the usually sleepy airport was an extraordinary sight with aircraft of every type to be seen parked near the terminal. Manas was suddenly not just an American air base but a NATO base with fighter aircraft, in flight refuelling tankers and huge US Air Force transport aircraft.

In addition to the Americans one time or another aircraft from almost all NATO countries used the base including the British, French, Australians, Canadians, Danish, Italians, New Zealand, Norwegians, South Koreans, Spanish, Dutch, Polish and Romanians.

US troops heading for Afghanistan would arrive on civilian aircraft, transit at Manas and then travel on military transports to the Bagram Air

Base in Afghanistan.

Troops returning back to the USA would be rotated back in reverse with the result that the airport suddenly saw a huge rise in passenger numbers rising to several thousand troops passing through the airport on a daily basis.

A canvas town had sprung up in the heavily protected US Zone of the airport complete with accommodation, medical facilities, dining halls, sports facilities etc. US Military personnel were forbidden to visit Bishkek and had to remain at all times within the base.

The opening of the base was a "gift from heaven" for the Finrep partners with all the US forces chartered civilian aircraft requiring the catering services of the Manas Management Air Catering Centre. American troops have hearty appetites and "double portion size" business class meals were the standard requirements of the USAF.

Profits at the Manas Management Company increased dramatically and by 2003 - just around the time when Bill and the Finrep partners were deciding to close the Kyrgyz Air operation - Aidar Akayev started to enquire if he could become a "shareholder" in the Manas Management Company. The Government had installed a new President of Manas Airport who indirectly reported back to Aidar.

There was little doubt that Aidar was going to try to take control of the Manas Management Company via this appointee who suddenly tried to withdraw the exclusive cargo handling rights that had been previously awarded to the Company.

At the annual general meeting of 2003 the Airport representatives refused to sign off the accounts. Bill realised that the only way to stop this power grab was to involve the World Bank in the dispute on the grounds that the Kyrgyz Authorities were trying to indirectly nationalise the Company with little prospect of adequate compensation being paid to Finrep as the 50% owners of the operation.

Under the terms of the political risk insurance policy with the MIGA division of the World Bank, MIGA were obligated to compensate both Finrep and MedioCreditoCentrale in the event of nationalisation or political interference.

The original investment agreement signed by the shareholders - Finrep and the Kyrgyz State Property Fund - called for international arbitration in London in the event of any disputes.

Bill flew to Washington to seek support from the World Bank who were very co-operative and arranged for a senior MIGA Director to accompany him back to Bishkek for meetings with the State Property Fund. Despite MIGA's intervention and the possible threat by the World Bank to withhold further funding the Kyrgyz maintained their uncooperative stance leaving the foreign investors with no alternative but to call for arbitration in London.

The arbitration proceeded with Sir Charles Haddon-Cave being appointed as the sole arbitrator on behalf of the International Chamber of Commerce.

A distinguished QC, Sir Charles had spent most of his time as a barrister specialising in shipping, aviation and commercial law. He represented victims of the Herald of Free Enterprise Ferry disaster, the Marchioness collision disaster between two vessels in the Thames, and the Kegworth Air Crash.

No one could have been more qualified to hear the case!

Finrep won the case and much to the dismay of the Kyrgyz Government were awarded an additional 30% of the shares of the Manas Management Company thus increasing their shareholding to 80%.

The relationship between the Finrep partners and Aidar was deteriorating rapidly and political rumblings had already started as early as 2003 with calls for a change of President due to corruption within the Government and in particular the greed of the first family. Aidar seemed to have his hand in every major business in the country which would eventually bring down the First Family.

Finally in March 2005 the President was overthrown in a popular coup known as the Tulip Revolution and the family including Aidar fled to Moscow. Aidar died suddenly in Moscow in early 2020 of an unexplained heart attack, he was 44 years old. By 2004 Moscow was becoming increasingly the focus of attention of the Finrep Partners and was to see the start of their most ambitious project to date.

CHAPTER 27

Ocean Airlines

Katy's birth in June 2003 convinced Irina and Bill that their Gardone apartment was too small for their growing family and it was time to buy a family home. Despite pressure from Vienna they had definitely decided to settle in Lombardy so they started to house hunt in the area west of Brescia - preferably near Lake Iseo - with good access to the main A4 autostrada running east to west between Venice and Milan and within easy distance of the airports of Verona and Milan.

They purchased a beautiful old villa that had originally formed part of a convent in the old part of the village of Erbusco. The villa had just been renovated by the owners who were in the process of moving into a smaller house they had recently inherited. It was to be a perfect family home with sufficient space for a live-in couple to take care of the children when Irina accompanied Bill on some of his business travels.

The couple loved Georgia and had started a small collection of icons. During several of these trips they also purchased icons for Maria who was creating her own icon collection in Richmond.

It was in the spring of 2004 that Irina felt the first lumps in her right breast. The couple headed to Geneva for an appointment with a leading cancer specialist who confirmed it was cancer and that an immediate procedure would be required necessitating the removal of her left breast.

Devastating news but Irina was heartened to hear that her chances of a full recovery were good. The operation was followed by chemo and radiation. All appeared to have been successful and Irina was cleared to have six monthly check ups.

Meanwhile in Moscow Veronika Borovik had been very busy promoting the Finrep name and introducing the Tolstonov's and Bill to several major potential project investors who were looking to invest their surplus dollar and euro funds in Western Europe.

One such investor was Rashid Sardarov. Born in Dagestan in 1955 Rashid had studied Geophysics at the State University and rose to become the Head of the All Soviet Geophysics Rescarch Institute.

In 1991 following the collapse of the Soviet Union and the creation of the Russian Federation Rashid had acquired ownership of the South Urals Industrial Holdings known as SUIC. Situated in Orenburg near the Kazakhstan border SUIC was a producer of gas condensates, LPG and natural gas which was processed by the adjacent Gazprom facility.

By 2003 Rashid had built his own refinery and SUIC was now able to sell its production directly to its customers such as BP. Products were shipped by rail to the Baltic ports thence loaded onto condensate tankers. Rashid had become one of Russia's richest men but wisely had kept and continued to maintain a low political profile. Today his net worth is estimated by Forbes to exceed $5 billion. In addition to his Moscow home he also maintains large estates in France, Austria and a 28,000 hectare ranch in Namibia whose ownership only came to light following the release of the Panama Papers in 2016.

Veronika arranged for Sergey and Bill to meet him in the autumn of 2003 at his Moscow office and this was soon followed by an invitation to dinner at his dacha just outside the city.

Dacha was hardly the correct word to describe the enormous compound and residence to which they were driven in a darkened Mercedes with two bodyguards. The compound was situated in the middle of a forest surrounded by 20ft high walls built entirely of giant logs in the style of an old American fort of the 18th century. The floodlit entrance had two huge gates, also built of logs, with watch towers on either side and several heavily armed guards in paramilitary uniforms.

The newly completed residence itself was extraordinary being built in the style reminiscent of an 19th century Austrian country house but with a modern interior décor. No expense had been spared with paintings by Chagall and other Modernists on the walls. All the windows were constructed of armoured glass. There was a swimming pool and movie theatre in the basement.

Rashid's study was an enormous room fitted out with numerous glass cabinets containing antique Japanese swords and daggers of every size. On his desk for use as a paper weight was a one kilo solid gold ingot - a birthday present from his wife!

Also present at the dinner was Rashid's elder son - Timur - who was currently attending university in Moscow but who clearly was not too enthralled with university life! Rashid asked Bill to look out for a suitable project in Italy or elsewhere in Europe in which he could invest with a view to Bill "teaching" Timur on how to manage a business as a possible alternative to him remaining at university in Moscow.

Around this time Bill's old friend Angelo Prati had introduced him to a Rome based business promoter and his associate who had the idea - but not the funding - to start Italy's first all cargo airline to be called Ocean Airlines. The Ocean Airlines promoter Fabio Console and his colleague Michelle Useli had heard that Bill had close Russian connections so asked for a meeting with him and Angelo at the ITI offices in Valtrompia. They had registered Ocean Airlines, prepared an initial business plan and were now looking for potential investors.

Bill was intrigued with their concept as Italy lacked air cargo capacity with the majority of air cargo being flown into major EU airports such as Paris, Frankfurt and Luxembourg and then trucked to and from Italy - an expensive and time consuming operation to say the least. Brescia airport was to be the proposed base for the airline due to its central position in Lombardy at the heart of Italy's excellent highway network.

The airport was in fact owned by Verona Airport but its President was Dr Hugo Beretta, whose family owned the famous Beretta Company and who Bill had come across in his Iraqi days when the Italian pistols were manufactured there under licence. To add to the coincidence, the Beretta Headquarters were just a few hundred metres up the road from Bill's previous Gardone apartment, Dr Beretta was a household name in Brescia with strong regional contacts and was actively promoting the concept of opening up Brescia airport as an alternative hub located mid way between Verona and Milan.

Bill met with Dr Beretta who promised that Brescia Airport would provide maximum co-operation with any new airline and were ready to invest immediately in expanding the existing air cargo facilities.

The next step was to find a major investor with deep pockets capable of joining Finrep as equal partners in the new airline. The obvious candidate was Rashid Sardarov who agreed to invest $8 million in exchange for 40% of the shares providing Finrep also acquired 40% thus ensuring total control of the new airline leaving the two Italian founders with 20%. In fact it was to be a very good deal for the Italians as they had no hope themselves of raising the required start up capital of $16 million.

Another condition agreed with Rashid was that Bill was to be President of the Airline with Rashid's son Timur to be appointed as the Vice President to be trained by Bill as his "understudy".

The major issue for starting the airline was to be the acquisition of two suitable nose loading B747 cargo aircraft. Nose loading was a key factor as it enabled very long dimensional loads to be carried in addition to normal palletised loads. The concept was to establish the first and only B 747 all cargo scheduled flight operations between Brescia, Hong Kong and Shanghai.

Locating suitable aircraft was no easy task as demand exceeded availability at that time and high prices were being paid for used aircraft of this type. Bill was finally able to secure two good used aircraft from Lufthansa who were gradually phasing out their B 747-200 cargo aircraft fleet to be replaced by MD-11 units.

It was agreed that Finrep would purchase the aircraft and subsequently sell them to the Airline at a later date while retaining title to the aircraft in the interim thus enabling the Finrep partners to fully control the assets of the airline during the start up phase.

Delivery was scheduled for March 2005 but was continuously delayed while Lufthansa awaited the delivery of their own new replacement cargo aircraft from Boeing. This was an extremely frustrating and expensive time as all facilities and personnel were ready at Brescia airport and Ocean Airlines had also set up a full office and team in Hong Kong. The airline had been audited by both the Italian and Hong Kong civil aviation authorities and bi-lateral route licenses issued.

Plans were put in place to wet lease an aircraft on a temporary basis while awaiting the Lufthansa freighters but this did not work out.

Finally the first newly painted and refurbished jumbo with its Ocean livery was delivered by Lufthansa in September almost 6 months late followed by a second unit in November.

Ocean Airlines was finally in business!

Bill and Irina had also decided to set up an alternate residency in Hong Kong and had leased and furnished an ocean view apartment on Lantai Island within easy reach of the airport. By this time it was also fast becoming obvious that looking after and "training" Rashid's son Timur was to be no easy task and would require a great deal of tact. Bill liked the young man personally and, as his move to Italy was his first real taste of freedom away from his family in Moscow, did his utmost to help him settle down. However there were numerous difficulties finding and retaining apartments for him with irate landladies complaining to the airline about noise and the upkeep of the apartments.

New cars had to be provided to him and his friend from university who was to be a sort of chaperone. In addition Rashid expected all his son's costs were to be borne by the airline as a perk for his investment despite the fact that none of these costs were in the airline's budget nor could they be treated as legitimate company expenses by the tax authorities. The Italian office staff also found it difficult to deal with continuous requests for information from the two young men who often failed to channel their requests through Michael Meager the General Manager of the airline.

Around this time Bill had been approached by a boutique Milan based Investment Company to consider engaging them as advisors with a view to floating the airline in 2007 on the London AIM market or the Milan market, that being their third year of trading.

The Italian air cargo market was booming and by mid 2006 it was obvious that a third B 747 would be required for the "fall season" period from September to December. A wet lease was arranged with Atlas Air for this third unit to fly principally on the Brescia - Shanghai rotation.

Unfortunately matters with Timur were becoming increasingly difficult to the point where they were affecting the Finrep relationship with Rashid - it was time to part company!

The Tolstunov brothers had found another Russian investor who was willing to purchase Rashid's 40% in the airline for $20 million on the understanding that the airline would endeavour to list on the London Aim market during 2007.

Rashid, who was spending that September in his villa near Cannes invited Sergey and Bill to visit him in order to try to find a solution to the ongoing problems.

After a long discussion it was agreed that Finrep would purchase Rashid's 40% equity for $18 million payable when the airline was listed on the AIM market the following year. Timur was to resign as a Director and soon thereafter an agreement was reached with the two Italian founding shareholders for Finrep to acquire their 20% in Ocean Airlines and for them to resign from the Board.

Finally Finrep had 100% ownership of the airline but in order to expand the fleet from two to eight B747 freighters over the coming two years, with purchase arrangements and delivery agreements in hand, it was vital that Finrep should proceed to raise additional funds by locating a new investor to buy the 40% of shares recently acquired from Rashid together with 10% from the Italians' holding.

The Tolstunov brothers had for some time been cultivating a relationship with Ivan Savidis the owner of Donskoy Tabac which was the largest manufacturer of cigarettes in Russia. Ivan, of Russian Georgian origin, was also one of Russia's richest men, an MP and head of several committees in the Duma and a close friend of Vladimir Putin.

Sergey reached an agreement with Ivan to purchase 50% of the Ocean shares for $20 million and to appoint two of his Geneva based accountants as his representatives on the Ocean Board.

Meanwhile Bill had negotiated on behalf of Finrep to purchase an additional six B 747 freighters from Air France for delivery to Ocean Airlines over an eighteen month period starting in June 2007. Finrep had agreed to pay Air France an initial deposit of $12million (representing $2million per aircraft) with the balance payable at delivery. The total contract purchase price of the six aircraft was around $100 million to be funded from proceeds of the London flotation. Throughout this period preparations were under way for a listing on the London AIM market with the flotation expected to take place in May 2007.

Nominated advisors, lawyers and accountants were appointed to manage the flotation and Bill brought on to the Ocean Board as Finance Director an experienced American accountant - Jeffery Portanova. Jeff had extensive knowledge of B 747 freighter operational costs and was crucial in overseeing the work of the Italian and London accountants.

Ocean Airlines had ended 2006 with strong results in line with its forecasted revenues of $100 million for the year - the future looked promising.

The house in Erbusco, Italy

Rashid Sardarov

Ivan Savvidi (right) pictured with Vladimir Putin

CHAPTER 28

2007 & Early 2008

2006 had ended on a high note for Bill personally and his new "baby" - Ocean Airlines.

On the personal front Irina, following her first diagnosis of breast cancer in 2004, remained in good health and their daughters were both attending the convent run kindergarten in Erbusco.

The airline had achieved its targets operating its three freighters at near full capacity for the high season period of September - December and was on track for a successful 2007.

Bill and his team were focused on preparations for the stock market launch in May.

The timing was essential to ensure the flotation would take place before the "summer break" period when many City hedge fund managers take their annual vacations.

The lawyers were well on time with their due diligence reports as were the Italian auditors but a problem had arisen at the UK auditors when the designated lead accountant at Baker Tilly fell seriously ill. The launch had to be put back to June with the possibility of extending into July.

This was a cause for considerable concern not only because it put the launch closer to the holiday season than they would have liked but also because the stock markets had started to show signs of volatility when on June 20th Bear Stearns was forced to bail out two of its major hedge funds at a cost of $20 billion.

The London stock brokers had done a good job in lining up many major institutions some of whom had been visited by the Ocean team for a preliminary presentation early in June to "test the water" ahead of the official road show. The feedback was 100% positive.

It was mid July before the flotation accounts and forecasts were signed off by Baker Tilly enabling Bill and the Ocean team to finally start their road show to potential investors in the city! However the stock markets had by this time become very nervous resulting in many hedge funds, led by Bear Stearns, starting to liquidate their positions and holding back on new investments.

On August 6th American Home Mortgage filed for bankruptcy and BNP Paribas blocked withdrawals from three hedge funds. Stock markets worldwide started to reflect the potential stress on the banks who were holding massive investments in US mortgage placings.

Hopes for a successful flotation were suddenly beginning to fade and the company's stockbrokers were concluding that the flotation should be postponed until later in the year in the expectation that the markets would be calmer.

The postponement resulted in the airline suddenly and unexpectedly facing a cash flow crisis as the first of the new 747 freighters purchased from Air France was ready for delivery to be followed by a second aircraft in October 2007. The deliveries had been based on completion of the flotation by July at the latest.

Bill asked the stockbrokers to assist in arranging bridge finance for the airline and they were able to negotiate a medium term loan of $32 million to pay for the first two incoming aircraft from Air France. The loan to the airline was granted by their stockbroker's parent company - Landsbanki - Iceland's largest bank who, out of almost nowhere, had become a major "player" in the City of London.

However bad luck was to follow.

On August 10th whilst Irina and Bill who were having dinner in Bergamo Alto with their accountants. Bill suddenly collapsed and was rushed by ambulance to Bergamo hospital. He thought that he had suffered some sort of stroke! Following a barrage of tests it turned out that three of his upper neck vertebrae had developed arthritic growths which were applying pressure to his spinal column thus creating the paralytic effect of a stroke.

Unfortunately all the hospital's neurological specialists were on their August vacations so Bill contacted his surgeon in Geneva who was a specialist in spinal injuries. Luckily he spoke Italian and was able to issue telephonic instructions to the hospital staff and arranged for him to be moved from Bergamo to Geneva by ambulance for an emergency operation.

His stay in hospital was to last a month at a very critical time for the business. A special implanted brace had to be inserted into his neck which involved two complicated operations. Irina stayed with him the entire time! The results were spectacular and he soon regained the full use of his limbs and, much to his relief, his bladder.

While in hospital he continued to supervise the important issues affecting the airline and in particular the critical issue of the airline's cash flow which remained the number one priority. At the same time Sergey was urging their Russian partner Ivan Savidis to play his part by providing the balance of his funding to the airline, which was by then overdue. Meanwhile everyone awaited for the expected flotation to take place in October as the stock market had by then started to make a recovery.

Finally by mid September Bill was released from hospital and Irina drove him back home to Italy.

An urgent shareholders meeting was arranged with Savidis and his team to discuss the funding of the airline. This was in fact the first time that Bill had met him face to face as all previous shareholder meetings had been with his two Swiss based nominees who had joined the Ocean board. Savidis became rude and aggressive during the meeting and tried to insist that his Russian P.A. also be appointed to the Board in addition to his Swiss representatives. This from a man who had repeatedly promised to pay the balances he owed, promises that he had repeatedly failed to keep.

The Finrep partners found his new demands unreasonable and were becoming concerned that he had still, despite repeated promises, failed to pay the balance of his funds leaving the Finrep partners to continue funding the airline. The chances of the airline's flotation proceeding were fading by the day as the bursting of the American housing bubble was revealed and banks scrambled to increase their cash balances.

The Finrep partners realised that immediate steps were required to try to save the airline. Continuous meetings took place with a number of potential investors in Italy and Kazakhstan but with no finite results. The airlines local bankers continued their support but by early 2008 were becoming increasingly concerned and demanded that Finrep issue a full corporate guarantee to secure the lines of credit in place for the airline.

The second of the Air France aircraft, funded by the loan from Landsbanki, had been delivered in December bringing the Ocean Airlines fleet to four aircraft. Ocean Airlines was now asset rich but without sufficient working capital to operate so the decision was reluctantly taken to ground the fleet pending re-capitalisation of the airline.

Under such circumstances Bill and his Finrep partners decided that they were not willing to issue such a guarantee to the Italian bank as they had paid cash deposits to Air France of $7 million for the additional incoming aircraft and were due to pay a further $1 million deposit in

January 2008.

The financial crisis deepened in early 2008 when the Bank of America agreed to buy Countrywide Financial - the largest mortgage lender in the USA. By March Bear Stearns itself was bankrupt and finally purchased by J P Morgan Chase which itself had sustained billions of dollars in losses and was only saved by the intervention of the US Federal Reserve who facilitated the sale of $30 billion of the firm's high risk assets. The global financial crisis had arrived.

With no white knight to be found the Ocean shareholders had no option but to put the airline into administration. A very sad day for the shareholders and its over 100 employees!

CHAPTER 29

Post Ocean

The closure of Ocean Airlines was a major blow to Bill and his colleagues.

The international financial news continued to worsen during the following months culminating in the collapse of Lehman Brothers in September 2008 with worldwide repercussions for the aviation industry and the demand for cargo aircraft virtually ground to a halt.

Bill and his partners were hoping to recoup their $8 million of deposits already paid to Air France by re-selling the aircraft at least at cost price but this was not to be. Aircraft prices continued to tumble and it was obvious that the chance of recovering their deposits was fast slipping away. The buyout obligation by Finrep to Rashid Sardarov for his Ocean share holding also needed to be covered and was ultimately settled by transferring to him the Finrep's ownership of the Manas Management Company in Bishkek.

It was the end of an era and Bill realised that he was going to have to create yet another career just at a time when most of his contemporaries were contemplating retirement. The big question was what to do?

His connections within the aviation community were strong but the industry was in freefall.

Bill had lost most of his capital along with his partners in the airline coupled with the Air France deposits and had limited savings. Luckily the house was fully paid up and he had no other debts but Irina's breast cancer was starting to return and was being held at bay by a new and extremely expensive drug costing around $3,000 per month which was only available in Switzerland. Each month meant a long drive to a pharmacy in Como to purchase the vital medication.

Luckily the girls were leading a happy and normal carefree Italian life being at school locally with a big circle of friends. They also had an English tutor who gave them a good grounding in their written English which was to prove so important several years later. Justine was already showing early signs of her preference for heavy duty sports while Katy preferred a more relaxed life style!

Finrep was still operational in Vienna but the worldwide recession was in full swing. Most if not all capital projects upon which Finrep depended were on hold as the banks scrambled to hoard cash in order to rebuild their capital structures.

In the autumn of 2008, all of Iceland's banks including Landsbanki declared bankruptcy. The two ex Air France B747 aircraft which they had financed for Ocean Airlines were now the subject of litigation between the Ocean Administrator and Landsbanki. Meanwhile the aircraft remained parked in Paris and Hong Kong.

By Christmas 2009 Bill decided to branch out again on his own. He resigned from Finrep, sold his shares to Sergey and Vasily and flew to Hong Kong to meet up with an acquaintance - Stephen Wong - who was pushing him to start his own air cargo charter brokerage firm.

Bill continued to maintain his friendship with Sergey over the years but not with Vasily who had taken the unusual step of becoming a priest of the Russian Orthodox Church and entered holy orders at the Russian Orthodox Cathedral in Vienna.

Certainly a complete change from his hedonistic life style in Bishkek but perhaps not so surprising in view of his many years of intimate contact and promotion of the church coupled with his determination that Finrep should be seen as a staunch supporter of the faith and charities in general.

In May of the following year Bill incorporated Trans Asia Charters and brought in Stephen Wong as his partner with registered and secretarial office of the new company at the Fortune Centre in Causeway Bay.

He loved the name!

At the same time, he maintained an operational office with Stephen and his staff nearby.

It was back to commuting again between Italy and Hong Kong.

His first charter was a full load of Apple computers from Hong Kong to Los Angeles and the sale of a B737 passenger aircraft to Nova Airlines in the Sudan. He travelled extensively, together with Stephen, throughout the Chinese mainland visiting freight forwarders from Shanghai to Urumqi which was just an hour's flight from his old stamping grounds in Bishkek. Excitement was returning to his life.

Irina remained very supportive and was probably pleased no doubt to have Bill out from under her feet from time to time. She was very busy not only looking after the children but also freelancing as a translator for a local estate agency who had numerous Russian clients.

Stephen Wong was turning out to be a rather damp squib - all talk and not much action. To make matters worse it turned out that he was paying personal expenses from the company's funds. Bill would be invited out to dinner little knowing that he was footing the bill for the entire Wong Family. This only emerged when the first year's company audit was undertaken.

Confronted with the auditor's findings Stephen Wong agreed to hand back his shares to Bill who meanwhile had reached an agreement with an old friend from his Ocean days to acquire the shares along with a working capital injection. The Company was now a joint venture between Bill and his new partner.

The two men trusted each other completely and it was to prove an excellent partnership with Bill expected to locate business with the financial muscle of the new partner on hand as and when necessary to provide working capital.

By 2012 Bill and Irina felt it was perhaps time to consider whether to stay on in Italy or think about a move so that the girls could have a more international education. It was a hard decision as they loved Italy and their beautiful villa but one they felt had to made sooner rather than later so they put the villa up for sale and started to think about where they might wish to live.

It was not an easy choice - they considered Hong Kong, the UK, Malta and Cyprus.

Irina's knowledge of the UK was limited to visits to London and a holiday in the Outer Hebrides!

They both loved Hong Kong but felt it was rather remote so perhaps Cyprus or Malta might be a good choice?

By 2013 they had sold the villa with completion due only in July the following year of 2014 which gave them plenty of time to consider where to live.

In April of 2013 Bill had a terrible shock when his younger brother Stephen died.

It was almost unimaginable as the brothers were very close and Bill had just spoken with him only several days earlier. It was to be the start of a terrible year for the family.

In June, after the girls had broken up from the long Italian summer holidays, the family set off by car to explore possible locations in England that might suit them. Bill had in mind Norfolk - his county of birth and Lincolnshire where he had set up his frozen food plant or Cornwall his county of heritage. His grandfather William was born in Truro and his grandmother Elizabeth in the nearby village of Chacewater.

However soon after their return to Italy Irina began to have a series of severe headaches and her general condition deteriorated. Bill was devastated and prepared for the worst while the girls luckily enough were too young to realise the severity of their mother's condition. By early October Irina was admitted to hospital for a series of tests and was found to have a brain tumour - the cancer had spread.

The doctors moved her to a specialised neurological unit in Brescia in order to have the tumour removed which by now was affecting her speech. On the night of October 22nd - the day prior to the scheduled operation - she fell into a coma. The doctors decided to proceed with the tumour removal anyway as they had planned to keep her in an enforced coma for several days feeling sure she would recover.

Bill was permitted to stay by her side in the intensive care unit following the operation. It was obvious though that despite the best efforts of the doctors that she was failing. He could only watch her heart rate getting slower and slower on the monitor.

Irina died peacefully without regaining consciousness on the evening October 24th and was laid to rest in Erbusco cemetery on October 31st following a moving ceremony in the local church. The girls' school classmates became the choir and the Priest had prepared a sermon in both Italian and English. Almost the entire village turned out for the funeral, all of their Italian friends, Irina's sister Maria from Istanbul, Bill's former Russian Partner Sergey flew in from Vienna and sister Ann and husband David Gore from London.

Life of course had to move on - the girls returned to school and Bill to his business but at the same time he became increasingly unsettled and started to make final preparations for a move the following summer although he still didn't know where to.

Bill's first wife Maria and husband Michael - the girls' trustees in the event of Bill's death - were wonderfully supportive and arranged to fly the family to Florida for a stay in Disneyland.

His daughter Grace was also determined to play her part by inviting the family to spend Christmas with her boyfriend's family in Colorado to be followed by a visit to daughters Alix and Jordan in Phoenix.

It had been a very painful year but Bill felt able to face the New Year of 2014 with some feeling of hope for the future.

He was now a single parent aged 72 with two young daughters to bring up - quite a challenge at any age but he was determined to be the best parent he could for them.

For the February half term he decided to take the girls on a trip to visit his sister Tassie in Portugal to discuss ideas with her. It was to be a great adventure for the girls to herald the start of the new year.

They flew to Portugal spending a few days with Tassie before taking the train to Lisbon where they embarked on a cruise ship and headed south to Casablanca then on to the Mediterranean to visit Barcelona and finally disembarked in Genoa where daughter-in-law Eunice met them and drove them to Erbusco for a visit to their great friends Simona, Alberto and their three girls all of whom were "best friends" with Justine and Katy.

The villa sale was scheduled to close towards the end of June so an urgent decision was necessary as to where the family would live. Was it to stay in their beloved Italy, move to Hong Kong, or was it to be a move elsewhere for a private English education for the girls?

On the business front Bill maintained his base in Hong Kong but reduced his activities on aircraft chartering to focus on more specific military projects where he could use his expertise built up over years of military supplies to foreign governments.

The first of these military projects to reach a successful conclusion was the sale of a modified ATR aircraft to the Pakistan Navy for maritime patrol. It was to provide an opportunity to visit Pakistan again for the first time since the eighties at the time of the Russian occupation of Afghanistan.

He was to build up a close relationship with his local agent and friend Rizwan.

Another area of focus for him was to develop close relationships with Government owned military plants in Ukraine. Kiev beckoned!

His chosen route was taken, the wheel had gone full circle. A new chapter had started - the Trader was back in action

TAC

- Home Page
- About Us
- Our Partners
- About MercFuel
- Cargo Aircraft
- Passenger Aircraft
- Aircraft & Engine Procurement & Sales
- Contract Negotiations
- Aircraft & Engine Inspection Services
- Security Courses
- Loadmaster
- Pilot Training Aircraft
- Contact Us

2

The Children

Adrian

Warren

Alix

Jordan and family

Grace

Justine at Everest Base Camp 2019

Justine

Katy

Bill 2020

Maria

Barbara

THE END

ACKNOWLEDGEMENTS

A very special thanks to my editor Kevin Wilkinson who has worked tirelessly throughout the entire editorial process and devoted his time to checking all the historical facts.

Many thanks to Joe and all the team at Spiffing Covers for designing the cover and the website, arranging the printing and guiding me through the complexities of the publishing world.

Thank you to my brother-in-law Col. David Gore for inspiring me to write this book and thanks to my panel of test readers - my sister Tassie, nieces Chania and Alison and close friends Janine Mumford, Judy Boylan and Christopher Vulliamy for devoting their time reading through the manuscript.

ABOUT THE AUTHOR

Bill Pellew-Harvey was born in Norfolk and moved with his parents to Kenya at the outbreak of the Mau Mau Rebellion.

Aged 21 he moved to London to join a well known City trading house and four years later was to set up his own trading company. A series of events saw his business base take in many parts of the world including Thailand, Libya, Egypt, Iraq, California, Kyrgyzstan, Ukraine, Turkey, Italy and Hong Kong.

His trading activities included food, armaments and security equipment, televisions, large infrastructures, airlines and much important work for various government agencies. This is a story like no other and also reveals his work as an intelligence agent.

Wrongly vilified by the media at the time of the Iraq war this is the story behind those headlines and many others.

Domiciled in Hong Kong, Bill continues his aircraft trading activities with his focus on Asia.

Printed in Great Britain
by Amazon

39589131R00137